DATE DUE

JUL 3 1 1996	
DEC 0 9 1996	
AUG 2 1 1997	

The Strength of a People

The Strength of a People 🌿 *The Idea of an Informed Citizenry in America, 1650–1870*

🌿 Richard D. Brown

THE UNIVERSITY OF NORTH CAROLINA PRESS

Chapel Hill & London

Material from chapters 1–4 of the present
work appeared in a slightly different form
in "The Idea of an Informed Citizenry in
the Early Republic," in *Devising Liberty:
Preserving and Creating Freedom in the
New American Republic,* ed. David T.
Konig (Stanford: Stanford University
Press, 1995), © 1995 by the Board of
Trustees of the Leland Stanford Junior
University, all rights reserved, and
"Bulwark of Revolutionary Liberty:
Thomas Jefferson's and John Adams's
Programs for an Informed Citizenry,"
in *Thomas Jefferson and the Education
of Citizens,* ed. James Gilreath et al.
(Washington, D.C.: U.S. Department
of Education and the Center for the
Book in the Library of Congress, 1995).
Published by permission of the publishers.

Library of Congress
Cataloging-in-Publication Data
Brown, Richard D.
The strength of a people : the idea of an
informed citizenry in America, 1650–1870 /
by Richard D. Brown.
    p.   cm.
Includes bibliographical references and
index.
ISBN 0-8078-2261-2 (cloth : alk. paper)
1. Political science—United States—
History. 2. Political socialization—
United States—History. 3. Freedom of
information—United States—History.
4. Civics—Study and teaching—United
States—History.   I. Title.
JA84.U5B74   1996
306.2'0973'0903—dc20   95-35013
                                        CIP

00   99   98   97   96   5   4   3   2   1

FOR I. Q. B.

Contents

Illustrations

Acknowledgments

Thanks are due to a number of people and institutions who contributed significantly to this work. In 1990 the Center for the History of Freedom at Washington University in St. Louis, directed by Professor Richard W. Davis, invited me to write a chapter on the idea of an informed citizenry in the early American republic. As a nonresident fellow of the center in 1990–91, I was the beneficiary of material and intellectual support, particularly from David Thomas Konig, editor of *Devising Liberty* (1995), in which my essay appeared; Lance Banning; Paul A. Gilje; Jan Lewis; Peter S. Onuf; and Alan Taylor. Two of the center's invited critics, Robert A. Gross and Linda K. Kerber, also provided constructive suggestions. In the early stages of the project, J. A. W. Gunn, Isaac Kramnick, and Gordon J. Schochet all supplied valuable advice. In 1992–93 an American Antiquarian Society–National Endowment for the Humanities Fellowship enabled me to do extensive research in nineteenth-century printed sources and to benefit from the community of scholars that gathers around the remarkable library of the American Antiquarian Society. Among those whose conversation and specific suggestions helped my project were Mary H. Blewett, Steven C. Bullock, William J. Gilmore-Lehne, Bruce Laurie, Lillian B. Miller, Kenneth J. Moynihan, Jane R. Pomeroy, Marcus Wood, Mary S. Zboray, and Ronald J. Zboray. I would also like to thank AAS staff members Georgia B. Barnhill, Joanne D. Chaison, and John B. Hench for their generous contributions to the study.

Support from the University of Connecticut has taken several forms, including two small grants from the University of Connecticut Research Foundation, one with provision for research assistance by John C. Davenport and W. Guthrie Sayen; an RTD award to supplement the 1992–93 AAS-NEH Fellowship; and secretarial help from Doris B. Bassett and Debra L. Crary. The entire text was written in a study carrel in the university's Homer Babbidge Library, where the staff provided expert assistance, particularly Robert W. Vrecenak and the staff of the interlibrary loan department. I would also like to thank History Department colleagues Susan Porter Benson, Christopher Collier, Karen Ordahl Kupperman, R. Kent Newmyer, Donald Spivey, and Bruce M. Stave, as well as Professor Gerald N. Tirozzi of the School of Education, who helped in various ways. Mary Kupiec Cayton and Richard R. John made valuable suggestions on an early conference paper, and several other scholars generously shared their unpublished papers with me: Nancy F. Cott, William J. Gilmore-Lehne, Marc W. Kruman, Lorraine Smith Pangle, and Thomas L. Pangle. At the University of North Carolina Press, Paula Wald contributed her editorial skills to preparing the final text. For any substantial errors and omissions that remain, I am responsible.

March 1995
Storrs, Connecticut

Introduction

For at least two centuries, Americans have believed in the idea that citizens should be informed in order to be able to exercise their civic responsibilities wisely. At the birth of the republic, the necessity of an informed citizenry was proclaimed loudly and often by such notables as Samuel Adams, John Adams, George Washington, Thomas Jefferson, and James Madison, in addition to a host of less well known leaders. Indeed, one of the legacies of the early republic was an ideology of an informed citizenry that would become a central theme in American public life, encouraging a wide array of voluntary associations such as political parties as well as promoting the printing industry, the post office, and the development of public education from primary schools through technical colleges and universities. Among Jefferson's most prized and enduring historical contributions was state-supported public education in Virginia, especially the university; Abraham Lincoln, who as a lad had trudged barefoot to a frontier schoolhouse, sponsored and signed the 1862 law that gave federal lands to the states to endow agricultural and technical colleges. By the Civil War era, the idea of an informed citizenry had grown into an article of national faith.

Moreover, the ideology of an informed citizenry, which continues to sustain the principle of free speech and press, has been a cornerstone of democratic politics. In our own time, a whole panoply of educational institutions —from Head Start classes to graduate schools—supports the popular presumption that the citizenry is informed sufficiently to choose public officials and policies at the ballot box. Educational institutions are thought to provide the necessary basic skills and knowledge, while a free press and political campaigns supply the specific information consumers require to make particular decisions. No one supposes that this system guarantees that the citizenry is fully informed, but when American democracy is assessed in a global context and its huge size and exceptional heterogeneity are figured in, it is widely agreed that the idea of an informed citizenry has been a crucial ingredient in the United States' success.

The idea of an informed citizenry has been so familiar since the late nineteenth century, and so interwoven with the rhetoric of democracy and education, that we have been tempted to take it for granted. From the era of John Dewey and the Progressives, Americans have debated segregation and integration, evolution and creationism, school prayer, public funding of private and parochial schools, parental choice of schools, and even home schooling; but the principle that America should have an informed citizenry has been above controversy—a fixed star in the rhetorical universe.[1] Perhaps it is for this reason that the history of this bright, familiar star has not been examined.

The more closely we approach the idea of an informed citizenry, however, the more evident it is that the meaning of this idea is not fixed but fluid and imprecise. Being informed has changed its meaning across the generations, as has the common and legal understanding of who can be a citizen and the rights and responsibilities of citizenship. Consequently, in order to understand what Americans have meant when they have asserted and invoked the idea of an informed citizenry, we must trace the idea back to its origins and analyze the ways in which it has changed over time. Only then can we comprehend both how this idea has shaped American society and how intellectual and cultural movements as well as social and political forces have in turn reshaped it.

As with many of the United States' fundamental institutions, the idea of an informed citizenry began in Tudor and Stuart England, where in the sixteenth and seventeenth centuries gentlemen first defined and asserted quasi-republican principles of citizenship. Not surprisingly, these ideas crossed the Atlantic and became embedded in the political culture of the Anglo-American colonies. But as long as the seat of empire lay in Britain and ruled by a monarchy, the American colonists felt no particular urgency to engage in public discussion of notions of an informed citizenry. Only occasionally, when issues of a free press or public education were being considered, did the idea of an informed citizenry command more than passing attention in the American colonies.

The opposition to imperial policy and the independence movement it spawned changed the situation decisively in the 1760s and 1770s, propelling the idea of an informed citizenry onto the center stage of public discourse. Now, suddenly, it mattered greatly whether colonists knew their political rights and understood the ways in which Parliament and the king were infringing on them. When the Continental Congress declared independence in 1776, and thus transformed the thirteen colonies into functioning, de jure republics, the idea of an informed citizenry took on new meanings and added significance. Defining citizenship and its rights and responsibilities posed urgent questions that had immediate importance as well as fundamental, long-term consequences. In the early republic, the effort to elaborate the meaning of an informed citizenry involved legislators, governors, presidents, and the intelligentsia of gentlemen, clergymen, and journalists.

To many of these men, the idea that an informed citizenry was critical to the success of the republic served as a guiding principle when they designed American institutions. The press, the post office, and public education were the leading candidates for government subsidies and encouragement but not the only ones. In the old Puritan colonies, now states, of Connecticut and Massachusetts, churches, too, were subsidized to help assure an informed and virtuous citizenry; and everywhere voluntary associations promoted their own versions of an informed citizenry. As all sorts of people and organizations took up the call for promoting an informed citizenry, the original political objectives of the idea became increasingly blurred with each passing decade, and a variety of other purposes were extolled as contributing to moral, cultural, social, and economic improvement, both individual and collective.

During the same era when the meanings of being informed were multiplied—that is, the first half of the nineteenth century—the boundaries of the right to full citizenship were being contested. The freeholder citizenry of white, property-holding men established by the Revolution was directly challenged by workingmen, African Americans, and women. By the 1830s and 1840s, spokespersons for these people were contending that since they could be just as informed as most freeholders, there was no logical reason to continue to exclude them from full political participation. They turned the old notion that a citizen's *participation* should be informed on its head. In essence they asserted that if *people* were informed and otherwise qualified to be citizens, they should enjoy the right to participate as voters and officeholders, even if they were poor, or black, or female.

As a result of these claims, a major contest over the boundaries of citizenship developed. Ultimately property was deleted from the qualifications for full-fledged citizenship, and race was officially excluded from consideration by the Fifteenth Amendment. Still, notwithstanding the logic of the idea of an informed citizenry, the men who ruled the United States reinforced sex as a barrier to political participation. No matter how well-informed women might be, in 1870 they were excluded implicitly from enfranchisement by the Fifteenth Amendment, and five years later, they were expressly denied the right to vote by the Supreme Court of the United States. By this judgment, as well as by the wholesale enfranchisement of African American men and, still earlier, of white men whose only qualifications were residence, race, and sex—not literacy or learning—the idea of being informed was practically and symbolically severed from considerations of active citizenship. The idea of an informed citizenry that had been formulated during the Revolution and early republic lived on in rhetoric and could still be pressed into political service, but it no longer operated as a guiding principle.

Parts of this history have long been known to scholars, but the emergence and development of the idea of an informed citizenry, and its various permutations, have never before been explored systematically. By telling the story of the evolution of this idea across more than two centuries, this study makes a beginning. The effort is useful, I think, because it enables us to understand better the dynamic secular and religious forces that were responsible for shaping some of American society's key institutions, particularly in the fields of communication and education. An uncensored, competitive press, a nationally subsidized postal service and transportation networks, and a wide spectrum of public and private educational agencies, particularly schools, colleges, libraries, lecture series, and museums, are all founded on the belief that America must have an informed citizenry. By studying the history of this idea, we can gain insight into the shifting character of the fundamental social, cultural, and political values that have been shaping this society since its formation.

This history is important for more than academic reasons. In contemporary public life, it is vital to be reminded that central articles of political faith like belief in an informed citizenry are not platonic ideals embodying fixed meanings that stand outside of time and place. The history of this idea demonstrates conclusively that it was formulated and shaped across many generations according to the beliefs and objectives of particular people and movements in the context of specific events. By tracing the historical record, this study enables those who wish to invoke the ideal of an informed citizenry and apply it to contemporary policy making to do so in ways that are consistent with past realities and are not merely rhetorically convenient.

This study will not, however, be of much use to those who are trying to determine whether Americans were in fact informed or ignorant at any time in the past. Although I have touched on past economic, social, and political realities in order to understand the context in which the idea of an informed citizenry developed, I have avoided any attempt to assess the extent to which the peoples of the colonies and the United States were actually informed because the task is impossibly subjective. Even though scholars have assembled data on literacy and schooling for some places and periods in the eighteenth and nineteenth centuries, this information can supply no substantive knowledge as to whether people were informed. To address such a question, one would have to specify the subject of knowledge: informed about what? Then, as now, the range of possibilities is endless. People can be informed in a multitude of specialized subjects—personal, local, occupational, recreational.

Even if one were to specify a subject such as public affairs, it would be difficult to set that subject's boundaries in a present-day context. Establishing such a category or trying to measure with reliability or precision whether people were informed in a past setting would be impossible since only anecdotal evidence survives. Over the past century and a half, many admonitions have been issued about how uninformed the younger generations are. Some or all of these warnings may have been accurate; but this study cannot address those questions. Instead, the work that follows explores the emergence and changing meanings of the idea that gave rise to those cries of alarm, that is, the belief that America's political, economic, and social prosperity requires an informed citizenry.

The Strength of a People

Chapter 1 🜨 English Subjects and Citizens from the Reformation through the Glorious Revolution

Political liberty has long been the pride of England. But if one reaches back to the reign of Henry VIII in the sixteenth century, or to the rule of his Stuart successors, one finds the same kinds of autocracy, repression, and arbitrary government that were then characteristic of Continental monarchies. The political liberty for which England became famous during the Enlightenment resulted from generations of struggle. Indeed, the "rights of Englishmen" were more the fruits of expedient compromises than the products of any deliberate constitutional scheme. Certainly political ideals mattered, and English political theory was not just retroactive rationalization for accomplished facts. But the influence of ideas was subtle, an influence exerted over decades of power struggles among the king, nobles, gentry, merchants, and lawyers who ruled England.

Achieving legitimacy was always an issue for monarchs and their challengers, and it was invariably based upon abstract principles that were more fiction than fact.[1] The hereditary principle was the political legacy of the Middle Ages, a seemingly simple idea that lineage conferred legitimacy. But in reality, as the Wars of the Roses had recently demonstrated, victory on the battlefield and the alliances of magnates were at least as important as lineage in the Tudor era. Still, governance was more than the brute force of the mighty over the weak because it required acquiescence, if not a measure of consent. The divine authority of kings—which should ideally pass from the monarch to his eldest son—supplied a reason to justify the concept of political superiority and inferiority that was replicated throughout the social hierarchy, from the nobility, gentry, and commonalty down to the family of the humblest laboring patriarch.[2]

According to the most basic monarchical theory, only two categories of people existed: a king and his subjects. The king possessed dominion over all who dwelled in his realm, and the subjects owed allegiance to the monarch and his government. Every subject was bound by the laws of the kingdom, laws that also supplied every subject with protection. In this restricted sense, all subjects were equal. Yet at the same time, the principle of hierarchy, which divided the king from his subjects, extended throughout society, dividing and ranking the king's subjects according to lineage, property, and privilege as well as age and sex. Some subjects ruled over others and enjoyed powers and immunities known as rights and liberties. In the House of Lords and the House of Commons, the greatest and most privileged of the king's subjects collaborated with the monarch's own appointees to rule over the realm. Because the principle of heredity lay at the foundation of all legitimacy, those who enjoyed such liberties, immunities, and privileges tended to view them as rights, as being their permanent possessions until such time as they should either forfeit them voluntarily or according to due process of law.

The idea of rights and guaranteed privileges modified the status of a subject powerfully, diminishing the subordinate and submissive character of being a subject. By the Renaissance, it was common to speak of some subjects as citizens, a term that implied the possession of civil and political rights and privileges. In medieval times, the term "citizen" had been applied to townsmen particularly, but during the Tudor era, a more enlarged view of "citizen" came to prevail. This larger view was rooted in the ideas of classical authorities like Aristotle, who recognized the nobility and gentry as citizens, even preferring them as citizens to the merchants and master craftsmen of the towns. According to Aristotle, citizens with landed wealth possessed the leisure needed to fulfill their public roles.[3]

The public role of these neoclassical Renaissance citizens contrasted with the narrow, self-interested, medieval citizenship of the freemen of a town, who were concerned primarily with the preservation of their own particular chartered privileges. The nobility and gentry as well as merchants and lawyers were corulers of the English state—not merely the king's subjects. It was their duty to promote the general public interest, beyond their personal concerns. This public citizenship role was in many respects no more than new language for old political roles. As subjects of the king, the nobility and gentry had always been responsible for taking arms to defend the realm and for ruling it, whether they used the new Renaissance language of citizens or the feudal language of liege lords and subjects. But until the Renaissance, their preparation for these responsibilities was the mostly practical method of learning by observation and apprenticeship in great men's houses. Not much book-learning was needed to perform with a sword or even to render judgments in county courts, where oral traditions sustained local customs. Churchmen needed to master Latin, but otherwise literacy was not a crucial requisite for nobles and their vassals.

It was Renaissance culture and the advent of printing that produced such works as Baldassare Castiglione's *Book of the Courtier* and created new expectations for learning among the English laity in the sixteenth century. Mastery of classical languages—Latin at least—became an emblem of gentility, culture, civilization. The ruling classes joined learning to military prowess in defining the new concept of citizenship as they deliberately and emphatically made themselves the educated classes.[4] Almost simultaneously, the Protestant Reformation gave a further impetus to the growth of literacy and learning.

Because England was one of the first Protestant kingdoms, it might be assumed that the English church and state were generally committed to popular as well as elite learning so as to promote Bible reading, piety, and salvation. But the division between elite "citizen" subjects and "mere" subjects remained powerful in Tudor England. The uniform church and autocratic state that Henry VIII tried to establish rejected popular engagement in religious and public discussion and was hostile to all dissent, popular or elite. Faced with a Catholic insurrection, Henry's 1537 Parliament passed a law for "abolishing diversity in opinions."[5] In the following decade, when various Protestants posed different challenges to the Henrician establishment, the king signed a statute "for the Advancement of true Religion and for the Abolishment of the Contrary." Now king and Parliament prohibited the reading of the Bible in English in every church in the realm. Further, "mere" subjects, including most commoners—according to the law, all artificers, apprentices, journeymen, yeomen, lesser serving men, laborers, husbandmen, and women—were explicitly forbidden to read the New Testament in English, the only language in which they might be literate.[6]

Maintaining order among the "citizen" subjects who composed England's ruling elites was the regime's first challenge, and it would not tolerate any disagreement from its "mere" subjects. In his *Remedy for Sedition* ([1536]), a government spokesman declared "it is no part of the people's play to discuss acts made in parliament." Drawing the line as firmly as he could, he pronounced: "It far passeth the Cobbler's craft to discuss, what lords, what bishops, what councilors, what acts and statutes and laws are most meet for a commonwealth, and whose judgement should be best or worst concerning matters of religion."[7] Such public matters were exclusively the province of rulers, not ordinary subjects. This was the established political orthodoxy.

But if this view had been universally accepted, the ruling elite would not have needed to assert it so vigorously in statutes and declamations. In fact, some commoners were reading the Bible and discussing the tumultuous politics of Henry's reign. After Henry's death in 1547, when Lord Somerset governed under the authority of young Edward VI, the "Act of Words" was abolished and pamphlet controversy flourished.[8] Now one anonymous writer articulated a belief that had long been repressed and that pointed to the Anglo-American future. In the *Discourse of the Commonweal of this Realm of England* ([1549]), every man was invited to express his views, not only "learned men (whose judgments I would wish to be chiefly esteemed) herein, but also merchant men, husbandmen, and artificers." In the body of this *Discourse,* members of these groups spoke their minds, in addition to a knight, a physician, and an artisan.[9]

The radicalism of this viewpoint is underlined by the contemporary words of John Cheke, who in *The Hurt of Sedition* (1549) denounced the idea that "every subject should busily intermeddle with" public matters.[10] Still, the terms of the debate were shifting away from the uniformity of Henry VIII's act for "abolishing diversity in opinions." While it was still generally believed that the first responsibility of ordinary subjects (variously defined) was obedience, not political expression, the idea that a class of "citizen" subjects should be allowed to voice their ideas, even if they disagreed, was accepted. In 1548, for example, the preacher and printer Robert Crowley published a pamphlet called *An Information and Petition against the Oppressors of the Poor Commons of this Realm,* in which he argued that because good government depends on information, men who were literate and learned should speak out publicly. It was all very well, he said, for members of Parliament and the Privy Council to supply information to the king, but other subjects should do so as well. Some Tudor clergymen even saw themselves as social and moral critics, duty-bound to "speak against the faults of all degrees without exception."[11] The elite of educated, experienced, and virtuous men recognized by Plato and Aristotle ought to be allowed, even encouraged, to engage in the discussion of public affairs. Indeed, one authoritative historian maintains that, like Enlightenment theorists two centuries later, the midcentury Tudor pamphlet writers generally believed "in the educability of men for the duties of active citizenship, and in the efficacy of reason."[12]

During Queen Elizabeth's reign, such ideas gained a foothold in England as a clandestine printing trade developed. In politics, both civil and religious, the expectation of absolute conformity was modified by a more flexible, pragmatic acceptance of disagreement. Elizabeth secured civil peace by pursuing a de facto policy of toleration toward Catholics and Protestant sectarians. Moreover, in contrast to her older half sister, Queen Mary, Elizabeth sought the counsel of a variety of learned "citizen" subjects in her Privy

Council, and she listened carefully to the elite citizens who spoke both in Parliament and outside its chambers. Indeed, one could argue that the anti-Spanish policy of the last twenty years of Elizabeth's reign was influenced powerfully by this elite Protestant opinion. Such royal attention, conciliation, and pragmatism brought a new luster to the monarchy after the ruinously divisive reign of Queen Mary. By the time that the first Stuart, James I, peacefully ascended the throne after Elizabeth's death in 1603, the idea that the educated, informed, and sometimes conflicting voices of gentlemen, merchants, lawyers, and clergymen should be expressed had been sanctioned by decades of experience.

Although James VI of Scotland, who became James I of England, was even more learned than his predecessor Elizabeth, by temperament and experience he was less inclined to accept discordant voices. Indeed, when in 1604 James told Puritans, after they had requested his assistance at Hampton Court, that they must "conforme" or he would "harrie them out of the land, or else doe worse," he set the direction for the Stuart dynasty.[13] Coming to power during an era when monarchs throughout Europe were basing their claims to authority over their subjects on a theory of absolute and divine royal right, the Stuarts were much more comfortable with dispensing privileges, monopolies, and indulgences to favored subjects than they were with recognizing their subjects' claims to rights. The ideal of uniformity in both the state and the church appealed powerfully to seventeenth-century rulers in aesthetic and ideological terms while also serving as a justification for raw political dominion. In the Europe of the Reformation and the Counter Reformation, where religious warfare was protracted, the doctrine that the religion of the monarch must also be the religion of his subjects and of the state ("Cujus est regio, illius est religio") generally prevailed, notwithstanding its enormous cost in blood and misery.[14] It was in this unfriendly setting, in which James I himself repeated the motto "No Bishop, no King," that Puritans pressed their claims to exercise their particular forms of religious expression as part of a larger effort to reform the Church of England.[15]

Within the Puritan movement, whose members ranged from Baptists and Brownists to Presbyterians and Quakers, many strands of religious and political opinion existed. The largest and, from the perspective of the Stuart kings, most dangerous group were Puritans who sought not to reject and repudiate the Church of England but to remodel it by taking over its parishes, its colleges, and its hierarchy. Viewing the existing Anglican Church as corrupt but redeemable, these Puritans worked within the system to reform it.

Between the coronation of James I and the advent of civil war nearly forty years later, they worked incessantly to undermine orthodox churchmen and their teachings.

In place of the established centralized, hierarchical, ceremonial religion that focused on sacramental rituals and prescribed prayers, Puritans developed a critical stance in which the Bible—interpreted line-by-line in the sermons of learned divines—became the foundation of religious observance instead of the *Book of Common Prayer.* Believers, they asserted, must not be docile, formalistic captives of ritual; they must examine their own behavior rigorously and search their own souls in order to prepare for the gift of God's grace. Although this religious agenda was always most important to Puritans, it was more than coincidental that the informed, Bible-reading, sermon-going, disputatious, activist laity they encouraged also provided an impetus for the development of an informed citizenry in secular politics. The secular implications of Puritanism were so generally understood in court circles that King James remarked that a presbytery "as wel agreeth with a Monarchy, as God and the Devill." In the king's view, an informed citizenry meant unruly subjects. If Puritans gained power, he warned, "then *Jack & Tom, Will, & Dick,* shall meete, and at their pleasures censure me and my Councell and all our proceedinges: Then *Will* shall stand up and say, it must be thus; and *Dick* shall reply and say nay, mary [to be sure], but we will have it thus."[16] Monarchs had no use for uninvited advice.

During the reigns of James I and his son Charles I, criticism of royal administration mounted inside Parliament and in the manor houses and guildhalls throughout the country as Puritan reformers found allies among the secular critics of the regime. Citizen subjects were becoming alienated from Charles I and his archbishop, William Laud, and therefore the urgency of being informed and being able to inform others mounted. Since 1557 the Stationers' guild of London had provided a substantial measure of censorship through its monopoly on printing, but illicit and imported imprints circumvented this control. Charles I understood that clandestine publications were nourishing his opposition, so in 1637 his royal Court of Star Chamber decreed that all publications must be licensed and registered before being printed. All imported books must also be approved before they could be offered for sale, and all printed matter was required to carry the names of the author, printer, and publisher. Every printing press in England must now be registered with Crown authorities and a bond of £300 given as surety that it would only be used to publish officially approved texts.[17] In seeking to control the flow of information and opinion, Charles I's government reasserted censorship with a vigor and comprehensiveness that had not been seen before in England. No public call for free speech and press had yet been made, but educated, propertied subjects displayed a growing restiveness toward government restraints. Men whose rank and property entitled them to extensive rights and privileges were profoundly interested in public policy, both secular and religious, and they were often resentful of these restrictions.

For a few years, the Star Chamber policy and the outlook that supported it held; but once the civil war began, censorship became unenforceable and the dam burst, releasing a flood of diverse opinions, printed in tracts and broadsides as well as books. The idea of censorship did not die—it was still widely accepted—but now no agency existed to implement it. Moreover, with the whole idea of monarchy under siege and the nature of the king-subject relationship in flux, the notion of censorship itself was problematic. No one could say authoritatively who should act as censor, under what law, and for what purposes. Censorship, after all, was paternalistic, and the locus for such authority was now disputed. It was in this chaotic setting that John Milton published his tract, *Areopagitica; A Speech of Mr. John Milton for the Liberty of Unlicensed Printing, to the Parliament of England,* in November 1644.[18]

This remarkable work, which became a stunning clarion call for liberty of speech and press to nineteenth- and twentieth-century readers, was an extreme, latter-day statement of the ideals of Renaissance humanism regarding the pursuit of knowledge through human reason. Voicing a passionate English nationalism, Milton fused his libertarian beliefs with English identity. The fourteenth-century English reformer John Wyckliffe, not Martin Luther, he asserted, was the real author of the Protestant Reformation.[19] "Our English," Milton proclaimed, was "the language of men ever famous and foremost in the achievements of liberty."[20] England's capital, London, was also the capital, fortress, and arsenal of worldwide freedom; it was "a city of refuge, the mansion-house of liberty," where numerous "anvils and hammers . . . to fashion out the plates and instruments of armed Justice in defense of beleaguered Truth" were tirelessly at work.[21] According to Milton, the nurturing of the liberty to use reason freely to seek the truth was England's ordained mission.

It is therefore no wonder that *Areopagitica* struck hard at Stuart rules requiring the licensing of publications, using appeals couched in the idioms of London merchants as well as university faculties. "Truth and understanding," Milton declared, "are not such wares as to be monopolized and traded in. . . . We must not think to make a staple commodity of all the knowledge in the land, to mark and license it like our broad-cloth and our wool-packs."[22] Appealing to the highest aspirations of merchants, Milton argued that licensing of publications "hinders and retards the importation of our richest merchandise, truth."[23] Restricting the distribution of books, he maintained, "will be primely to the discouragement of all learning, and the stop of truth, not only by disexercising and blunting our abilities, in what we know already, but by hindering and cropping the discovery that might be yet further made, both in religious and civil wisdom."[24] Licensing shackled the progress of reason.

To those who did not share his principled objections, Milton pointed out that in actual practice licensing required a multitude of government inspectors and censors and that even their strenuous efforts could not effectively curb criticism since oral expression could not be regulated. To Puritan moral reformers, Milton pointed out that "if we think to regulate printing, thereby to rectify manners, we must regulate all recreations and pastimes," including music, singing, and dancing.[25] Every village, every tavern would need inspectors, and even dress would have to be regulated. Such censorship, he argued, was utterly impractical since no government could "regulate all the mixed conversation of our youth, male and female together."[26]

The very idea of such broad censorship reeked of the Italian and Spanish inquisitions. Historically, Milton pronounced, such policies belonged to "the popes of Rome, [who] engrossing what they pleased of political rule into their own hands, extended their dominion over men's eyes, as they had before over their judgments, burning and prohibiting to be read what they fancied not."[27] The use of licenses for books was an invention of their "most tyrannous inquisition." To seal the connection, Milton appealed to the most notorious case of censorship known to learned contemporaries: "I visited the famous Galileo, grown old, a prisoner to the Inquisition, for thinking in astronomy otherwise than the Franciscan and Dominican licensers thought."[28] In 1642 the astronomer had died, and if the censors could have had their way, his ideas would have accompanied him to the grave.

Here, ultimately, lay the core of Milton's argument. Censorship, even of false and worthless ideas, was an obstacle to the use of reason, which alone should winnow fact from opinion to establish truth: "The knowledge and survey of vice is in this world so necessary to the constituting of human virtue, and the scanning of error to the confirmation of truth, . . . [that we must read] all manner of tractates."[29] Controversy, Milton dared to assert, was a good thing: "Our faith and knowledge thrives by exercise. . . . Truth is compared in scripture to a streaming fountain; if her waters flow not in a perpetual progression, they sicken into a muddy pool of conformity and tradition."[30] Censorship brought intellectual, cultural, and religious stagnation. Appealing once more to national pride, Milton entreated the "Lords and Commons of England, [to] consider what nation . . . whereof ye are the governors: a nation not slow and dull, but of a quick, ingenious, and piercing spirit; acute to invent, subtile and sinewy in discourse, not beneath the reach of any point the highest that human capacity can soar to."[31] Milton's voice expressed the cultural confidence of the society that brought forth Shakespeare and Newton. His own bold utopianism led him to declare "that Truth is strong, next to the Almighty; she needs no policies, no stratagems, nor licensings to make her victorious, those are the shifts that error uses against her power: give her but room, and do not bind her when she sleeps. . . . So Truth be in the field. . . . Let her and Falsehood grapple; whoever knew Truth put to the worse, in a free and open encounter?"[32] Truth could not suffer from freedom; only falsehood needed the shield of censorship to protect it from exposure.

Such reasoning served as the basis for the development of a new idea of an informed citizenry. Since truth would triumph if restraints were removed, it was unnecessary to restrict the public's knowledge, regardless of rank. In England, Milton claimed, it was best to include the common people because the English were peculiarly suited to the process of inquiry and learning. England was, he asserted, "a nation so pliant and so prone to seek after knowledge," its very soil was so "towardly and pregnant," that it needed only "wise and faithful labourers to make a knowing people, a nation of prophets, of sages, and of worthies." Let there be conflict, he said in the midst of civil war: "Where there is much desire to learn, there of necessity will be much arguing, much writing, many opinions; for opinion in good men is but knowledge in the making."[33] He was certain that most Englishmen, even common ones, were good.

To be sure, Milton's argument was aimed primarily at liberating elite citizen subjects like himself who, he said, were adults and should not be treated like boys at school.[34] But by embracing common men as well, Milton's theory laid the foundation for a broadened citizenship ideal. Censorship, he insisted, was "a reproach . . . to the common people; for if we [elite subjects] be so jealous over them, as that we do not trust them with an English pamphlet, what do we but censure them for a giddy, vicious and ungrounded people." Such a policy could never be called benevolent paternalism because, after all, "in those popish places where the laity are most hated and despised the same strictness is used over them."[35] Milton did not argue for the general inclusion of common men in local and parliamentary politics. But he did believe that they should not be mired in a political ignorance and superstition that made them indifferent or irresponsible at best, dangerous at worst.

Amid the clamor of competing voices during the conflict-ridden decade in which *Areopagitica* appeared, its radical libertarian viewpoint was largely overlooked and without influence.[36] Generations would pass before English rulers were ready to abandon censorship, and even then, they would not embrace most of Milton's principles. Milton himself would serve as a censor under Oliver Cromwell's regime. But the problem that Milton addressed in 1644 remained crucial. The circulation of knowledge and the role of an informed citizenry could not be ignored entirely. In the 1650s, the monarchist theoretician Thomas Hobbes, who differed from Milton on most essentials, expounded a rational humanist position when he noted that reason, knowledge, and science were the natural enemies of ignorance, superstition, and magic.[37] Hobbes opposed any scheme to expand the active role of common people in politics, claiming that the history of Greece had shown conclusively "how stupid democracy is and by how much one man is wiser than an assembly."[38] At the same time, Hobbes was convinced that common people's ignorance and superstition were inimical to peace.[39] "The Enemy has been here in the Night of our naturall Ignorance," Hobbes lamented, arguing that in order for the common people to ever be able to identify their self-interest accurately and behave reasonably, they must be enlightened.[40] In this one respect, at least, Hobbes was echoing Milton's assertion in *Areopagitica* that if common people were kept ignorant, they would be "giddy, vicious and ungrounded." Because Hobbes believed eloquence was a false instrument that appealed more to the heart than the head, he argued that making information available to common people was a necessary antidote to demagoguery. Hobbes even helped to endow a free school in his native village.[41] Milton and Hobbes were at opposite poles of the political spectrum in most respects, but both advocated informing common people as a precondition for rational politics.

Information and enlightenment did not, however, mean empowerment. Their contemporary James Harrington, among the most influential republican theorists of his era and of eighteenth-century America, presented a distinctly elite view of citizenship that drew on Aristotle and on the model of the Venetian republic. In Harrington's analysis, landowners alone were properly situated to exercise the duties and responsibilities of citizens. Physicians and lawyers, he claimed, were too narrowly practical and materialistic, and clergymen were not suitable for citizenship because, like lawyers, they sought to do for citizens what citizens could do for themselves. To Harrington, independence of mind was paramount, and this independence, he believed, belonged to freeholders. Those among the freeholders who cultivated their minds deserved the authority and deference granted to political leadership, and all citizens were responsible for bearing arms to defend the state.[42]

Harrington's linkage of citizenship to landownership was appealing to country gentlemen; however, his readiness to exclude wealthy merchants, lawyers, and clergymen from political power did not accord with the realities of public life. The brief existence of England's republican commonwealth, and the reversion to monarchical forms that began under Cromwell and was capped by the Restoration of Charles II in 1660, meant that the whole consideration of citizenship was again placed in the ruler-subject context. But the same questions remained concerning the roles of privileged citizen-subjects and the extent to which they and ordinary subjects ought to be informed about public affairs. Moreover, the burst of republicanism and religious heterodoxy of the interregnum, together with the temporary collapse of censorship, could not be forgotten, and the possibilities they had raised persisted in political discourse. As a result, when the government of Charles II set about rebuilding the structures of monarchical order, it was urgent that a censorship policy be established. The foundation of censorship for the next generation would be the Licensing Act of 1662.

The "Act for preventing the frequent Abuses in printing seditious, treasonable, and unlicensed books and Pamphlets, and for regulating of Printing and printing presses" combined censorship and monopoly provisions. Its first objective was to secure the new monarchy and that bastion of royal support, the Church of England. Thus, just as all secular disloyalty was banned, so too was any publication that was "heretical, seditious, schismatical or offensive . . . to the Christian faith" or to the established church.[43] As had the earlier Star Chamber decrees, the 1662 law provided for official prepublication scrutiny of all imprints. Only members of the Stationers' guild were allowed to seek permission to publish, and outside of London, their print shops were limited to the university towns of Oxford and Cambridge and the northern cathedral town of York. The law provided for three kinds of approval: "Published by Authority" meant that the government itself had ordered the publication; "Licensed" indicated that the censor had granted written permission; and "With Allowance" meant that the censor had conveyed oral approval. Once printed, the works could be sold legally only by members of the Stationers' Company, a handful of existing booksellers, and vendors who obtained licenses from bishops of the church.[44] To a substantial degree, the 1662 law made the Stationers' Company a quasigovernment agency with the Crown-appointed censor at its head.

In 1663 Roger L'Estrange, who had publicly criticized the Stationers' Company's failure to control the press and who recommended the appointment of a government enforcement officer, was named to precisely this position. As Royal Surveyor of the Imprimery, L'Estrange was charged with censoring printed pictures as well as texts. Then, in addition to his censorship office, the well-connected L'Estrange won an exclusive patent to publish the news. As a result, government influence over printed information was comprehensive. In large measure, to be an informed citizen in the Restoration era meant accepting official censorship.[45]

The only legitimate loophole in the censorship net was the circulation of handcopied, subscription newsletters. Although these forerunners of the newspaper were expensive and could have only a highly limited, elite circulation, they challenged the censorship idea effectively.[46] Handwritten newsletters could be found not only in the homes of great men but also in coffeehouses (which were themselves licensed), where they provided an alternative to L'Estrange's monopoly. Even after L'Estrange brought out the *London Gazette* in 1666, which he operated as a monopoly continuously through 1679, the manuscript alternatives continued.

But this was a dangerous time for public dissent. In the year after L'Estrange assumed the office of Royal Surveyor of the Imprimery, a printer, John Twyn, was hanged, drawn, and quartered according to the penalties against treason after being convicted of printing a call to depose and kill Charles II. L'Estrange himself declared in 1663 that "a public Mercury [newspaper] . . . makes the multitude too familiar with the actions and counsels of their superiors, too pragmatical and censorious, and gives them, not only an itch, but a kind of colourable right and license to be meddling with the Government." During this reactionary era, champions of free speech kept their own counsel because printing was widely understood to be a potential threat to political stability. As one Royalist tract asserted in 1664, printing "[is] so Powerful, when it is cunningly handled, that it is the Peoples Deity."[47] Even John Milton was ready to deny access to the press to Catholics and atheists. John Locke, the quasirepublican whose *Two Treatises on Government* would later provide the theoretical justification for the revolt against James II and then George III, could write in 1667 that the suppression of some publications was reasonable and legitimate on occasions when it was "really necessary for the peace, safety or security" of the state.[48] For the present, a secure monarchy took precedence over an informed citizenry.

Even after 1670, when the throne seemed relatively secure, the government continued to maintain close supervision of political discourse. Coffeehouse politics aroused such anxieties that Charles II ordered all coffeehouses to close in 1676. Because his ban proved to be unenforceable, it was quickly lifted. But thereafter, keepers of coffeehouses were sworn to loyalty and to ban all "scandalous Papers, Books or Libells" from their premises; the following year, nearly two dozen coffeehouses lost their licenses. Britons, and especially Londoners, were restive under royal censorship, and illegal underground publications continued to circulate among a population that was increasingly literate.[49] Consequently, when political differences among government leaders and the Stationers' Company allowed the Licensing Act to lapse in 1679, a resurgence of libertarian expression brought the idea of an informed citizenry into prominence once more.

Two works that immediately expressed the principal secular and religious arguments on behalf of a free press came from the pens of Charles Blount, a deist and republican, and William Lawrence, a Dissenting clergyman. Blount's *Just Vindication of Learning and the Liberty of the Press* (1679) drew directly from *Areopagitica,* though without acknowledgment. Licensing, Blount claimed, was un-English, and a censored press obstructed learning, offended reason, and insulted the common people. In the end, Blount argued, it endangered the government. If there was a threat from Roman Catholicism, then a free press supplied the best defense against it. Acknowledging that some publications were, indeed, illegitimate, Blount asserted that postpublication prosecutions for treason, seditious libel, and blasphemy were the appropriate remedy—not an alien form of censorship.[50]

William Lawrence, publishing soon after Blount, presented a different but complementary emphasis. He argued in 1680 that the press must be less restricted than it had been in order to allow the discovery of Christian truth. Censorship, he declared, "stops the truth of all intelligence, which is so invaluable a Treasure, and difficult to be got into the Gates of Princes." Lawrence was not ready for a total end to censorship; he saw no good reason to tolerate disputes over ceremonial and other nonessential topics because they could so divide Protestants that they would be vulnerable to Catholic incursions. But he argued that the old licensing system was too extreme and fostered both secular ignorance and religious error.[51]

Such voices as Blount's and Lawrence's were probably more indicative of ideas that were in circulation than they were influential, although Blount's tract was republished fifteen years later under another title. Of far greater direct impact was the House of Commons' publication for the first time of its proceedings in 1680. According to a leading scholarly authority, it was the appearance of the *Votes of the House of Commons*—which sold thousands of copies weekly—that most influenced the formation of public opinion. Indeed, with between 30 and 45 percent of all Englishmen and nearly 80 percent of London men literate, the regular printing of the *Votes* combined with expanding newspaper and almanac publication to intensify the public's political engagement in the 1680s and beyond. The three-and-a-half-year hiatus in the licensing law (1679–82) had even led to the publication of two Dissenting and one Catholic newspaper in addition to several political papers.[52]

One of the newspapers, Langley Curtis's *Weekly Paquet* of London, echoed Blount's argument that information was necessary to combat the spread of Catholicism. "You have need of knowledge," Curtis proclaimed, "because your Enemy is subtle to deceive." Looking to broaden the ranks of those who must be informed, he argued that newspapers were essential because they were inexpensive and brief, and therefore their contents "more easily fall into the hands and hearts of the middle or meaner Rank; who having not time nor Coin to Buy or peruse chargeable, tedious, and various Books," would otherwise remain dangerously ignorant.[53] Evidently, a growing range of His Majesty's subjects were developing an appetite for public discussion.

Government authorities fumed over the unexpected emergence of this comparatively free discussion and promptly tried to stop it. The *Weekly Paquet,* for example, was suppressed, and Langley Curtis was punished for violating the law of seditious libel.[54] New regulations were devised to limit printers and "hawkers" of books, and the king's courts ruled that the Crown could prohibit the publication of all unlicensed "News Bookes [small-format newspapers] & Pamphletts of News whatsoever."[55] Acting on this judgment, the Privy Council banned all unlicensed newsbooks, and authorities used general search warrants in their efforts to prosecute violators for sedition. When Parliament returned to session in 1682, it reenacted the lapsed licensing law; before the year was out, all newspapers were banned except for two that were published "By Authority" (one belonging to L'Estrange). The climax of this reaction to the licensing hiatus came in the following year when Charles II staged a public conflagration of seditious books during a visit to Oxford.[56]

By this time, even the monarchy recognized and accepted the need for an informed citizenry, but it wanted to be absolutely certain that its subjects were properly informed. Seeking to control public opinion, court-approved newspapers published frequently—indeed, L'Estrange's *Observator* appeared three or four times each week. Following the exposure of a supposed Whig coup conspiracy (the "Rye House Plot"), the royal court even aimed some of its propaganda at common people by publishing lurid attacks on the subversive plotters.[57] For reasons of practical politics and without a shred of theoretical justification on the royal side, the need to "inform" the general public, if only in a primitive way, including people of small means, became an accepted fact of English politics.

After James II came to the throne in 1685, the instability of the monarchy brought the intertwined issues of free speech and press, religious freedom, and an informed citizenry to the center of yet another crisis between England's king and subjects. The resolution of this crisis in the Glorious Revolution and the subsequent political and religious settlement would lay the foundation for the liberty England would come to represent in the eighteenth century. The achievement of this outcome, however, could not have been predicted. It resulted from a difficult and protracted process wherein ideology and practical politics interacted dynamically, often in discordant ways.

The immediate catalyst for the crisis was James II's assertive Catholicism in public affairs. His accession was peaceful enough, and the new and enhanced Licensing Act that Parliament passed in 1685 was given a seven-year term. Had James II simply pursued his brother's repressive policies, he might have enjoyed a long, if not tranquil, reign. But the new king soon challenged one of the monarchy's fundamental supports, the Anglican Church, by seeking to promote Catholic books and by appointing Catholics as official printer to the king and as head of the printing house in Oxford, the center of the Anglican intelligentsia. Not content with these provocative moves, in 1687 he had his own propaganda distributed in coffeehouses and other public houses, and in 1688 he staged a public book-burning in the capital of the book trade, London.[58]

Yet it was James II's Catholicism, not offenses against free expression or an informed citizenry, that was crucial in bringing about his ouster. When the Whig opposition brought William of Orange to England, the insurgents carried the banner of Protestant liberty against a Catholic ruler. The conflict between Anglicans and Catholics was over control of public opinion, not over the liberation of it. Just as James II had spread his propaganda among English subjects, so the friends of William of Orange distributed thousands of copies of their champion's biography and thousands more of the *Declaration of His Highness William Henry, Prince of Orange,* asserting his commitment to a free Parliament and to ending the outrages of James's rule. Along with muskets and artillery pieces, William's forces were armed with a printing press.[59]

For a time in 1688–89, some form of free speech was triumphant, just as it had been forty years earlier during the civil war. Licensing was in abeyance, and more than half a dozen newspapers quickly appeared. But these newspapers were short-lived, and of the roughly 2,000 tracts printed during these months, only one called for repeal of the Licensing Act. No one chose to reprint either Milton's *Areopagitica* or Blount's *Just Vindication of Learning and the Liberty of the Press.*[60] The monopolistic practices of the Stationers' Company were criticized. Hobbes had called it "a great hindrance to the advancement of learning," and Locke argued that the printing monopoly raised the price of scholarly books and reduced their quality. But freedom of political and religious expression was not an issue.[61]

When the revolution settlement was completed and the new rulers of England adopted a Bill of Rights, free speech and press were omitted from the list. Most striking of all, the new king and Parliament enacted a new licensing law in 1692 that was essentially the same as the statutes of the Restoration era. The most obvious lesson of two generations of political instability and conflict was that it was dangerous to leave the information available to the citizenry unsupervised. Public opinion was essential to maintaining authority, but left to itself, it was unreliable. In 1694, six years after James II had gone into exile, the publication of a Jacobite tract was sufficient to obtain the execution of its printer under the law of treason.[62] This was a world in which words were understood to undermine the fragile legitimacy of the state.

But the Glorious Revolution had also led to the realization that it was impossible to achieve uniformity of opinion in religion and politics and that it was destructive even to pursue complete conformity. Freedom of expression in speech and the press as well as freedom of religion were not the guiding principles or notable achievements of the Revolution, but the events of these tumultuous years did lead to a new readiness to accept differences among Britons as a fact of life. Members of an informed citizenry, even a restricted, elite citizenry, would not all think alike, but they need not be at each other's throats.

The 1688 Act of Toleration, which was at the core of the revolution settlement, symbolized this preference for peaceful expedients over bellicose principles. It provided a kind of "code of indulgences" toward all sorts of non-conformists whereby the old, coercive penalties that had been directed against them were erased, although such disabilities as exclusion from Parliament and the universities were maintained. Now the .5 percent of Englishmen who were Catholics would not be actively persecuted. The 4 percent who were Presbyterians, Baptists, Quakers, and other sects would be free to worship and preach as they wished without suffering legal interference. In effect, the rulers of the 95 percent of Englishmen who conformed agreed to disagree with the remainder.[63]

Ultimately it was this same kind of pragmatism that would undermine government censorship of the press. Not *Areopagitica* but a multitude of self-interested complaints, from printers and booksellers as well as authors and bishops, concerning the aggravations, inequities, and corruption of licensing blocked the renewal of the law in 1695. A memorandum prepared at the time for Parliament by John Locke listed some of the reasons the House of Commons would not accept the new Licensing Act the House of Lords had passed. Preserving the Stationers' Company printing monopoly was damaging to private and public interests. Allowing officials to search anyone's house for contraband books was a violation of privacy that could lead to a multitude of abuses. The criteria for licensing were too vague and failed to establish in any useful way the boundary between texts that were and those that were not "offensive." As a result, the proposed law might be even less serviceable than its antecedents. No one in Parliament attacked licensing in principle, but from bishops to book traders, there was no consensus as to what the law should include.[64]

Thus, in 1695, without fanfare, England's monopolistic censorship system finally lapsed, never to be restored. From time to time, proposals to resurrect it were made, but the problem of reconciling conflicting interests remained intractable. Indeed, with every passing year, the task of censorship through licensing became more difficult logistically because of the proliferation of books and newspapers and the extensive trade in printed texts and images. Locke had pointed out in his 1695 parliamentary memorandum that post-publication "censorship" via common law prosecutions for seditious libel and blasphemy was a wiser strategy, and as time passed, this came to be regarded as a more practical and equitable way to address the problem of dangerous publications.[65]

The ideology of free speech was probably more influential than parliamentary discussion suggests. In the debates of the Houses of Lords and Commons, arguments of interest and practicability were heard more often than innovative flights of theory. But an altered version of Blount's *Just Vindication of Learning and the Liberty of the Press* did reappear in 1693–94, and in 1698 Matthew Tindall, a Socinian, published *A Discourse for the Liberty of the Press* in which he, too, called on Miltonic principles. A free press, he said, was one of Protestantism's gifts to the world, and where freedom of the press was absent, ignorance, superstition, and bigotry flourished. Echoing Milton, he asserted that licensing was the method of the "Romish Inquisition," whereas the discovery and preservation of religious truth required the liberty of the press. In a House of Lords where Anglican bishops expressed the dominant voice on the subject, such arguments could only be viewed as subversive; while in the House of Commons, where puritanized moral reformers opposed cursing, profaneness, and debauchery, the distinction between liberty and libertinism could be hard to draw.[66]

But the old barriers restraining free speech ideology had been broken. The government could not prosecute a statement of the principle of free expression as blasphemy, seditious libel, or treason. Licensing had been restrictive, arbitrary, and partisan. Now the licensing bottleneck was gone, and the new self-censorship practiced by authors and printers who sought to avoid common law prosecutions was flexible, pluralistic, and responsive to public taste and opinion. Henceforth the market for printed information would be more open and many-sided than ever before.

Partly for that reason, but also because the Glorious Revolution increased the power of Parliament and the importance of public opinion, the meaning of being an informed citizen became a renewed subject of interest and concern. Until now, the education of princes had been of primary public importance because it was their knowledge and information that was crucial. Theoretically, the information that citizens possessed had been valued chiefly as an adjunct to assist the monarch in defending his subjects and ruling over them. But the new constitution of the English government vested so much power in elite citizens via their institution of Parliament that now it was their knowledge that mattered most. As far as the state was concerned, it was no longer the education of princes but the education of gentlemen subjects—citizens—that was paramount.

In 1693, in the immediate aftermath of the new political settlement, two works appeared that focused directly on the formation of properly informed citizens in England's new situation. One, Robert Molesworth's *Account of Denmark as it was in 1692,* was written with a powerful anti-Catholic bias and later became an influential text for Radical Whigs. The other, *Some*

Thoughts Concerning Education by John Locke, was widely read and shaped British ideas about citizenship and education for generations. In both works, the public dimension of education—the necessity of creating and molding an informed citizenry—was a central theme.

Like many libertarian authors who had preceded him, Molesworth castigated Roman Catholic tyranny while fusing Protestantism and freedom. His starting point was an attack on the Jesuit schools that were frequently viewed as desirable models. In these schools, "the Queen of all Virtues," he said, was "*Submission* to Superiors, and an entire blind *Obedience* to Authority." The inculcation of those "*passive Doctrines*" meant that "the Spirits of Men are from the beginning inured to Subjection, and deprived of the right Notion of a generous and legal Freedom." So powerful was the effect of this preparation for tyranny that "most have the Misfortune to carry these slavish Opinions with them to their Graves." Indeed, those who were raised in this monstrous system of bondage "not only endure it, but approve of it likewise."[67]

Jesuit schools were merely an extreme example of the general threat posed by clerical control of education. In England, as in Greece and Rome, Molesworth argued, "*Philosophers* instead of *Priests*" should educate the youth because they understood that their purpose was to train their charges for "Exercise and Labour, to accustom them to an active Life." The academies of classical times were not based on the values of obedience and submission; "they recommended above all things the Duty to their Country, the Preservation of the Laws and the publick Liberty." The virtues they taught served the public good: "Fortitude, Temperance, Justice, a Contempt of Death." The whole purpose of this approach was to create citizens who would be "as useful to the society they lived in as possible."[68]

In practical terms, this meant that schools should not be run by the church, whether Catholic or Anglican. Churches had interests that were separate from the public interest, and they would advance their own fortunes at the expense of the public good. Church schools also committed too much of their students' time to mastering classical languages and learning the elegant forms of Latin and Greek. "Twas not to learn Foreign Languages that the *Grecian* and *Roman* Youths went for so long" to their academies or to learn all the "dark Terms and Subtilties of the Schools," Molesworth declared.[69] It was the substance of classical history, culture, and political values that was essential, not the languages in which they were expressed. "To learn how and when to speak pertinently, how to act like a Man, to subdue the Passions, to be publick-spirited, to despise Death, Torments, and Reproach, Riches, and the Smiles of Princes as well as their Frowns"—all of these were the proper goals for the training of citizens.[70] Molesworth repudiated education by churchmen, who, he said, taught the doctrines of passive obedience and the divine right of kings. He advocated the sturdy, outspoken virtues of citizens, not the elegance or refinement of courtiers.

Molesworth's ideological reading of the ancient classics was open to criticism. One friend of King William's government pointed out that Molesworth's knowledge of Greek and Roman education and politics was faulty and naive. Even such a widely read author as Cicero had drawn attention to the actual "Licentiousness and Avarice of the *Roman* Generals."[71] But for Molesworth and his readers, the actual historical record was not the important thing. What mattered was contemporary public affairs and the future well-being of a state in which authority was vested in newly powerful citizens.

John Locke's approach to the problem was neither partisan nor polemical. Indeed, in *Some Thoughts Concerning Education,* Locke seemed to embody the classical educator-philosopher that Molesworth had idealized. At the same time, Locke joined in Molesworth's advocacy of a fundamentally secular education and also rejected the Jesuit pedagogy that was based on the competitive environment of the school. Instead, the individualistic Locke stressed the importance of private, tutorial education in which qualities of temperament, carriage, and character would be instilled in children. Instruction in particular subjects was important, but it was personal qualities to which Locke assigned the highest priority.

The audience Locke addressed was, he said, "our *English* Gentry," and his aims were political in the highest and broadest sense.[72] Firmly assigning responsibility for education to parents, not the church or the state, Locke asserted that "the Welfare and Prosperity of the Nation . . . depends on it."[73] Parental supervision of education was "the easiest, shortest, and likeliest [way] to produce vertuous, useful, and able Men in their distinct Callings."[74] But Locke was not immediately concerned with the education of people of various callings; he concentrated on "the Gentleman's Calling. For if those of that Rank are by their Education once set right, they will quickly bring all the rest into Order."[75] For the good of English society, Locke was convinced, the education of the gentry was crucial.

Locke's understanding of the gentleman's calling shaped his pedagogical ideas. The gentleman was not a decorative courtier but a citizen who required "the knowledge of a Man of Business, a carriage suitable to his Rank, and to be Eminent and Useful to his Country according to his Station."[76] Although book-learning was necessary, effective training for the gentleman's calling relied heavily on the personal supervision and example that only a father and a tutor, or "governour," could supply. Consequently, the personal qualities of the tutor were critical. He must be more than just a sober scholar; he must himself be well-bred and civil and possess a sure grasp of carriage and manners—"an Art not to be learnt, nor taught by Books" but instead learned through "good Company, and Observation joyn'd together."[77] Locke did not expect a school to teach piety or academic excellence through emulation. "To judge right of Man, and manage his Affairs wisely with them," Locke maintained, was more important than knowing Greek and Latin or philosophy and metaphysics. Able men, he noted, could be found in Asia, in the absence of Western learning.[78]

The foundation of Locke's emphasis on breeding was practical and directly related to the gentleman's role in public affairs. A young man's breeding, he maintained, "will more open his way to him, get him more Friends, and carry him farther in the World, than all the hard Words, or real Knowledge he has got from the Liberal Arts."[79] The duties of gentlemen demanded personal skills and mental qualities that would make their learning serviceable. While responsibility for this kind of preparation belonged to the father, it was the task of the tutor "to fashion the Carriage, and form the Mind . . . to . . . good Habits and the Principles of Vertue and Wisdom; to give him . . . a view of Mankind; and . . . a love and imitation of What is Excellent and Praise-worthy; and to give him Vigour, Activity, and Industry." The particular subjects of the boy's instruction—and like Molesworth, Locke had distinct priorities—were to furnish "the Exercises of his Faculties, and Imployment of his Time," not to form his character.[80] Locke prescribed a moral rather than a pious education.

When it came to the actual subjects of instruction, Locke was a modern humanist. The young gentleman should be acquainted with French and Latin, arithmetic and geometry, geography and chronology, history and law, and rhetoric and logic. Greek was suitable only for mature students who possessed a special aptitude and inclination for it. Dancing and proficiency at a manual craft such as printing, cabinetmaking, smithing, or gardening were optimal. Music he viewed as the least important of a gentleman's activities. Fencing and riding the "Great Horse" were often recommended as genteel pursuits, but Locke believed they were a waste of time more suitable for the palace grounds than the council chamber or the sessions of a quarterly court of justices of the peace. To engage in public affairs, the gentleman must be skilled in writing and speaking, not swordplay, jousting, or military parades.[81]

The conventional capstone of a gentleman's education, foreign travel, was also prescribed by Locke, but his viewpoint on travel was distinctive. Timing, he thought, was all-important. A youth under the age of fourteen years should travel accompanied by his tutor, and a young man over twenty-one years should travel on his own. In either case, the purpose was not to polish a provincial lad by introducing him to cosmopolitan fashion but to deepen the young man's understanding. Travel, Locke believed, should "open his Eyes, make him cautious and wary, and accustom him to look beyond the outside."[82] A certain skepticism and relativism, a greater understanding of human nature should be the objective, not becoming au courant with the latest styles in dress or manners.

Locke's intentions were consistent throughout. A gentleman should be educated to fulfill actively, and with integrity and wisdom, his private and public responsibilities. That he should be an informed citizen was one of Locke's basic assumptions. An ignorant man, however well-bred, could not manage his private concerns to advantage and was certainly incapable of contributing to public affairs. These were a citizen's fundamental duties, on which the welfare of the kingdom depended.

The fact that Locke ignored ordinary common people in *Some Thoughts Concerning Education,* confident that a properly functioning gentry would ensure the welfare of the kingdom, reveals the boundaries of seventeenth-century English republicanism. Like Harrington, Locke wished to broaden the base of England's government and to make it more inclusive. But this was in the context of a general European debate over royal absolutism, a system wherein the king assumed what critics believed were exaggerated powers that exposed the realm to idiosyncratic and arbitrary abuses. Such a narrowly based, brittle, unbalanced monarchical system was dangerous, they believed, for a whole array of structural reasons. To achieve the security of wise governance, political authority must rest on the representation of the full range of England's propertied ranks. Court, city, and country must join together in defining and exercising the tasks of government.

Practically speaking, the revolution settlement relied on the establishment of an expanded, indeed, a central, role for the gentry. Thus, the preparation of gentlemen for their public roles as citizens was more critical than ever before. That preparation, both Locke and Harrington agreed, began with private, individual security. The foundation of that security was the gentry's landownership. In addition, however, personal security rested on personal development under parental supervision. In contrast to classical models, the English citizen was a private person first, whose private virtues undergirded and sustained his public virtues. But as vital as the citizen's private experience was, he must also transcend his personal, private, and parochial consciousness. This was the central purpose of studying classical literature, geography, and history and of traveling. Knowledge of unfamiliar times and places and of people outside the circle of private experience created the kind of enlarged perspective that public business demanded. Although the gentleman was emphatically not raised only to serve the public, serving the public was one of his central duties. The gentleman, together with the king and the nobility, must guide, administer, and defend the commonwealth or the realm.

The definition of who was and who was not a gentleman was elastic, and the lower boundary was porous. Marriage into the gentry was not unusual for the offspring of prosperous merchants, professionals, and landowning farmers; indeed, almost anyone with sufficient means could, if he chose, adopt the manners and achieve the status of a gentleman. According to British theory, these were the men who were encompassed by the idea of an informed citizenry.

During the two centuries stretching from the accession of the Tudor monarchs to the demise of the Stuarts and the emergence of the revolution settlement in the 1690s, the people of England and Wales were both subjects and citizens. Everyone, except for the monarch, was a subject—man, woman, and child. But some subjects, privileged by wealth, birth, and gender, were also citizens, that is, subjects who possessed rights and responsibilities that were recognized publicly. Over these two centuries, fitfully, political conflicts expanded and reshaped the citizenship role for subjects. As this expansion and reconfiguration of citizenship developed, the idea that citizens must be educated and informed became embedded in English Renaissance and baroque culture.

Indeed, the irresistible appeal of Renaissance and baroque neoclassicism made the ideal of an informed citizenry pervasive in Europe as well as in England, regardless of the histories of various monarchies. French gentlemen under Louis XIV and Spanish, German, and Italian gentlemen under their several princes were also committed to being educated and informed as part of their public roles. In England, however, political history had shaped the idea of an informed citizen in three crucial areas: religious tolerance, the free press, and the boundaries of inclusion within the citizenry. As a result, the cultural implications of the idea were more extensive in England than in other countries.

Religious toleration, for example, permitted a freedom and breadth of inquiry that was generally forbidden elsewhere. As a result, clerical and lay investigations of philosophy and theology, and of approaches to piety and religious devotions, promoted the idea that John Milton had asserted in the 1640s—that competition for the minds of English subjects would allow truth to vanquish error. Moreover, the fact that the established church in England was not the only legal, legitimate church meant that being informed about religion had a wide variety of meanings. Furthermore, even the most inveterate Anglican country gentleman had to recognize that in London, and perhaps even in his own county and parish, other notions than his own were circulating. Religious toleration limited the intensity of parochialism.

Religious toleration also broadened the impact of the de facto free press policy that emerged after 1695. The fact that England had no licensing laws and no government agency to enforce any form of religious or secular orthodoxy increased the possibilities of being informed to an extraordinary degree. Only in Holland, perhaps, did gentlemen enjoy comparable access to all sorts of printed information. This is not to say that gentlemen in England were more informed than elsewhere, though that may have been true judging from England's extensive book trade and the rapid expansion of London and provincial newspapers.[83] What may have been even more significant is the fact that the idea of being an informed citizen flourished in a cultural environment where gentlemen were not only free to engage in all sorts of controversies but were politically empowered as well. Under these conditions, there was a salience to being informed that went beyond cultural style. For gentlemen, being an informed citizen was a prescription that was reinforced by the actual business of being a voter, a justice of the peace, and a vestryman as well as a frequenter of clubs and coffeehouses. Although as a matter of fact country gentlemen might be more thoroughly informed about dogs, horses, and the hunt than more elevated public issues of church and state, they inhabited a society where they dared not boast of their ignorance in political or natural history and science.

The fact that access to gentry status was not firmly closed and allowed for some entry from below further enhanced the influence of the model of the informed citizen. Not only gentlemen must be informed but also all those who aspired to mix in the circles of the gentry. As a result, the powerful process of social emulation extended the prescription of being informed outward from the aristocracy and professional gentlemen to common people in various stations. The desire for entertainment as well as the aspiration to be culturally informed fed the demand that sustained growing numbers of newspapers and booksellers. In England as elsewhere, the baroque ideal of an informed citizen was intrinsically elitist—civic education was decidedly for the few. But its influence and its appeal were broader.

In the 1690s, however, all of these implications were not yet clear. The revolution settlement was new and untested and its long-term consequences remained unknown. High churchmen wanted to reinstate orthodoxy as much as possible, and Tories and Whigs could not agree on the distribution of power between the royal administration, the Parliament, and the courts. A neoclassical meaning of an informed citizenry had been articulated and widely embraced by the nobility and gentry. But the ramifications of the idea for English society and politics had scarcely been addressed. In the generations to come, British intellectuals and public figures would elaborate on the meanings that might be attached to the idea of an informed citizenry and so reveal what a protean concept it was.

Chapter 2 🜚 Freedom and Citizenship in Britain and Its American Colonies

The Glorious Revolution and the constitutional monarchy that took shape in its immediate aftermath, which sustained provisions for religious toleration and especially freedom of the press, marked a decisive watershed in Anglo-American political history. Contemporaries recognized that momentous changes were occurring, but the consequences of the new order would not be clear for some time; indeed, the terms of the new political settlement were yet to be elaborated and established in Britain. Continuing public debates over a variety of constitutional issues, such as toleration, free speech, and the proper definition and role of British citizens, meant that no single, fixed Glorious Revolution settlement was brought to America but rather an array of dynamic issues for the colonists to assimilate and adapt to their own circumstances.

Two realities affected that assimilation powerfully. First, the fact that the Anglican establishment was comparatively weak and rudimentary in the colonies whereas various dissenting groups were more numerous and powerful gave a different character to religious toleration, pushing it in the direction of full religious freedom. Second, the British aristocracy and great gentry were not powerful, everyday presences in the colonies, so the principal agents for the importation and assimilation of British culture were usually merchants, lesser gentry, and a variety of clergymen. As a result, the colonies strayed from the English mainstream in their adjustment to the Glorious Revolution and its aftermath. Situated at the periphery of political, religious, and cultural authority, colonists often embraced an outsider's interpretation of politics and the constitution, one that was tinged with the assumptions of Radical Whigs and parliamentary backbenchers.[1] In contrast to the metropolitan British, who viewed the idea of an informed citizenry as bound up with the independent gentleman of Harrington's and Locke's writings, colonists developed a more expansive notion of simple freeholder or taxpayer citizenship. In the Carolinas and the Chesapeake and northward to the Massachusetts Bay province, actual political participation was more broadly based than in the British Isles.

The most important feature of the Glorious Revolution, the establishment of a limited, constitutional monarchy, was accepted easily and often eagerly in the colonies, where the Stuarts and Roman Catholicism had few friends. Religious toleration, too, was incorporated swiftly into colonial practices. In Pennsylvania and Rhode Island, true religious freedom was established before 1688, and in the Massachusetts Bay province, acceptance of toleration was a condition for securing the new charter in 1692. Elsewhere, as in New York, Pennsylvania, Virginia, and the Carolinas, recruiting more white settlers was usually a paramount concern, and the policy of toleration helped to persuade British Presbyterians, Quakers, and Baptists—as well as German sectarians—to cross the Atlantic. Here political pragmatism and economic interests supported Enlightenment doctrine to assure religious toleration in the colonies.

But in both Britain and its colonies, acceptance of a free press was more problematic. Massachusetts was the only colony where a press had long operated, but its printing establishment was government sponsored and supervised. The idea of censorship had always been respected and practiced. Since Parliament enacted yet another licensing law the year after Massachusetts's new charter was issued, a free press was clearly not part of the revolution settlement. As far back as 1650, six years after Milton's heroic call for liberty of the press, Boston authorities had ordered the burning of a tract published in England by William Pynchon, the leader of the Springfield, Massachusetts, settlement, because they pronounced it erroneous and heretical. Later, in 1669, the same colonial magistrates suppressed the printing of the Christian devotional classic by Thomas à Kempis, *The Imitation of Christ.* When Boston's first newspaper was printed in 1690, the authorities suppressed it immediately for political reasons. It would not be until 1712 that Boston saw its last officially sanctioned book-burning, when officials consigned a satirical mock sermon to the flames.[2]

The consistent zeal that activated Puritan authorities was not evident in the other colonies, but the belief in censorship was widespread. Governor William Berkeley of Virginia testified in 1671: "I thank God, *there are no free schools* nor *printing,* and I hope we shall not have these hundred years; for *learning* has brought disobedience, and heresy, and sects into the world, and *printing* has divulged them, and libels against the best government." Since learning and printing were threats to order, he swore, "God keep us from both!"[3] Berkeley did not need to practice censorship directly in Virginia since, like most of the colonies in the late seventeenth and early eighteenth centuries, it had no press. Nonetheless, it was the standard practice of the Crown between the 1680s and the 1720s to instruct its governors to censor the press in the traditional way by requiring the prior approval and licensing of all publications.[4]

To many political and religious leaders in Britain itself, the legitimacy of censorship still took precedence over any belief in an informed citizenry. Between 1695 and 1713, no fewer than eight bills were introduced in Parliament to control the press; they failed not on ideological grounds but chiefly because of the opposition of vested interests in the printing and book trades together with the practical obstacles posed by the existence of a multitude of presses scattered throughout Britain and the ease with which printed goods could be imported across the Channel.[5] Significantly, in 1712 when Parliament passed a law placing a stamp duty on all types of newspapers and requiring the registration and taxation of all pamphlets by the government, it was viewed as a revenue measure, not as a restraint on a free press or an obstacle to the realization of an informed citizenry.[6] The limited understanding of free speech among Britain's rulers is illustrated by the fact that the Glorious Revolution's famous Bill of Rights only guaranteed freedom of speech in Parliament—not outside of it—and even so, a member was imprisoned in 1717 for making remarks critical of the king in the House of Commons.[7] What went on in Parliament itself was initially considered secret, privileged information, and newspaper coverage of parliamentary proceedings remained substantially restricted throughout most of the eighteenth century. It was only after the American Revolution, in 1783, that journalists began to be routinely admitted to the galleries to record openly the speeches and votes of members. Acceptance of the concept of public information and knowledge increased gradually over the course of the century.[8]

Libertarian voices, however, were raised frequently against censorship and were sustained by growing constituencies of literary consumers, dissenters, and gentlemen of learning. Daniel Defoe complained that government regulation of the press was "a pernicious remedy" for its admitted "licentiousness," and he likened its effects on English liberty to "cutting off the Leg to cure the Gout in the Toe."[9] Across the ocean in Boston, where censorship collapsed in the 1720s, the sixteen-year-old Benjamin Franklin extracted the core of libertarian ideology from the *London Journal* and inserted it into one of his own 1722 newspaper essays:

> Without Freedom of Thought, there can be no such Thing as Wisdom; and no such thing as publick Liberty, without Freedom of Speech; which is the Right of every Man, as far as by it, he does not hurt or controul the

Right of another: And this is the only Check it ought to suffer, and the only Bounds it ought to know.

This sacred Privilege is so essential to free Governments, that the Security of Property, and the Freedom of Speech always go together; and in those wretched Countries where a Man cannot call his Tongue his own, he can scarce call any Thing else his own. Whoever would overthrow the Liberty of a Nation, must begin by subduing the Freeness of Speech.[10]

Such assertions, characteristic of the Radical Whig writers John Trenchard and Thomas Gordon, cropped up repeatedly in English newspapers and magazines, and American colonists often embraced them. In New York City, a few years after Franklin's essay was published, the University of Edinburgh–educated Scots immigrant Cadwallader Colden penned similar views in a tract on taxation. "It is one of the best signs of Liberty," he said, "when any of the subjects may freely write & speak their Thoughts concerning affairs in which the good of Society is concern'd." Colden, who was a member of the ruling Governor's Council and later became the lieutenant governor of the colony, defended free speech on precisely the same grounds sixteenth-century Englishmen had used to advocate an informed citizenry: "The public likewise receives Benefite from peoples discovering their different Sentiments; for by that means our Superiours may more easily foresee the inconveniencies which may attend any Project or Design."[11] That an enlightened royal official such as Colden, who was also one of the colonies' leading natural scientists, should express such views was a measure of the degree to which the new political doctrines were becoming established in America.

When American colonists adopted the ideology of free speech, they understood and accepted its limitations while celebrating its liberating possibilities. In an essay inspired by models in the *Spectator,* the young New Yorker William Smith acknowledged that licentious publications must be suppressed —even at the expense of free speech. "The Press," he argued, should "have all that Liberty which is due to it, and never be checked, but where its being unrestricted will prove an Evil."[12] By "unrestricted," however, Smith meant by libel and blasphemy laws, not by prior censorship. This kind of freedom of speech and press, he exclaimed, would make it possible for "Liberty and Science . . . [to] spread their Wings, and take the most unbounded Flights." Government would be held accountable for its actions, public fraud would be diminished, and the forces of tyranny and vice would be restrained.[13] At the same time, the benefits flowing from scientific inquiry would be protected. As Franklin put it in his popular *Poor Richard's Almanack* in 1757:

> While free from Force the Press remains,
> Virtue and Freedom chear our Plains,
> And *Learning* Largesses bestows. . . .
> This Nurse of Arts, and Freedom's Fence,
> To chain, is Treason against Sense.[14]

By the 1750s, England's free press was characterized as one of the unique benefits of the Glorious Revolution settlement by leading scholars of law and political theory in Britain and on the Continent. As the Genevan philosophe Jean Louis DeLolme later explained, "Liberty of the press, that great advantage of the English nation, does not exist in any of the other monarchies of Europe." Through this liberty, "the people" were sufficiently informed to make them capable "of influencing the motions of the government."[15]

DeLolme's language, which referred to the political power of "the people" and described England as "more democratical" than any other state, even Switzerland and the Netherlands, raises the question of who, precisely, was understood to be part of the political order that a free press would help to inform.[16] By the eighteenth century, all sides acknowledged that gentlemen were properly actors in the polity that ought to be informed; but which people belonged in the gentleman category was a matter of opinion. Some argued that the political order ought to include yeomen, tradesmen, and various other common men who made no pretense of gentility. Indeed, in some of the American colonies, property was so widely distributed and gentry status was so much a matter of personal assertion and life-style that gentility could function as only a limited barrier to political participation. In many colonies, especially New England, yeomen and tradesmen constituted the majority of voters, and therefore it was clear that even if it was relatively easy to become a gentleman, more than just the self-styled gentry needed to be informed.[17] It was partly for this reason that the liberty of the press was considered so important. Newspapers were, after all, the most popular and least expensive medium of public information available. To many observers, however, being a properly informed citizen was not a question of access to newspapers or of personal effort but of formal education for one's ordained social role.

Consequently, much of the discussion about an informed citizenry took place within the context of the prescriptions the acknowledged leaders of public life made for formal education. They were concerned, of course, with the instruction of their own progeny, but they also assumed the responsibility for directing British society as a whole; they devised schemes for the education of everyone from the great gentry to the poorest of their countrymen and countrywomen, black as well as white, and Native Americans. Because the prescriptions were tailored to the actual social and political roles people were expected to fulfill, they reveal the ways in which Britons on both sides of the Atlantic thought about the boundaries of their political nation. But since education was designed as much to promote Christianity—an inclusive, proselytizing religion—as to accomplish economic or political objectives, those boundaries were seldom clear-cut.

The Massachusetts colony, for example, was ruled by a political hierarchy of gentlemen magistrates who were landowners and merchants. But those who participated in politics, in the form of electing representatives, holding local offices, and voting in town and parish meetings, included the majority of landowners, who were themselves the majority of adult men.[18] Religious convictions had caused Puritan Massachusetts to erect a graded system of local public schools and a college, just as religious motives had prompted the authorities to undertake "house-to-house inspections" to make certain that every family owned a Bible and that all children were properly catechized.[19] But the impact of this general literacy was not confined to the religious sphere. Long after the Puritan impulse had been diluted and the orthodox magistracy was superseded by an Anglicizing imperial elite, the legacy of an educated, informed citizenry remained.

The Puritan penchant for all-inclusive, government-enforced compulsory education—which had always been exceptional—did not survive, however, and was supplanted by the English Dissenters' ideology of voluntary choice. James Burgh, the influential Dissenting schoolmaster, argued that "there could be no imposition more tyrannical, than to oblige parents to have their children educated in a manner they disapproved of." Any kind of required pedagogy, Burgh claimed, "would open a door to complete religious tyranny, and would destroy freedom of enquiry."[20] Toward the end of the eighteenth century, some secular radicals such as Joseph Priestley would be so alienated from any hint of religious establishment that they would—unlike Burgh—actually oppose all kinds of government support for education. Ultimately, they argued, government aid would enable the state to control knowledge and to enforce its own orthodoxy.[21]

Because of fears that the state would abuse its powers, such reformers preferred to leave responsibility for an informed citizenry, as for the economy in general, to the marketplace—a circumstance that would enable those parents who had the means to assure their children's education, while the poor would be left to glean what they could from charity schools. It was not that radical reformers were indifferent to the idea of an informed citizenry; in fact, they actively supported the notion as a requirement for liberty. But partly because of their preoccupation with the various disabilities the ruling establishment visited on Dissenters—who, like Catholics and Jews, were not allowed to enroll in the universities or sit in Parliament—they were convinced that anything touched by the hand of the state must be tainted. Thus, if there was to be an informed citizenry, it would have to be achieved by voluntary means, chiefly under the supervision of parents, especially fathers.

This outlook was deeply influenced by the writings of John Locke, both at the general level of political and psychological theory as well as in the particulars concerning education. But whereas Locke had emphasized the tutorial instruction of a young gentleman under his father's roof, the reformers generally favored education in schools. The advantages of cooperation and competition with fellow students could only be supplied by schools, and schools were more economical. By means of schools, a much larger portion of the propertied class, whether merchants, lawyers, clergymen, or lesser gentry, could provide their sons with a gentleman's training. Tuition, room, and board were, after all, much less costly than hiring and housing learned private tutors of the sort Locke envisioned. Therefore, privately financed schools, which were open to that part of the public capable of paying for them, flourished in the eighteenth century—Anglican public schools and clergymen's private schools as well as Dissenting academies.

These parent-centered, private arrangements for education and the formation of an informed citizenry were never directed toward what DeLolme called "the people," the "democratical" part of the nation. James Burgh's utopian essay published in 1764 did propose that schools be built at government expense in every parish in order to provide for more inclusive education, but attendance at these schools would be voluntary and in them children would be taught "religion, virtue, justice, goodness, temperance, moderation, self-government, modesty, due respect, [and] obedience to their superiors."[22] This education was not aimed at political empowerment of citizens but at the creation of what one scholar calls "a disciplined and regimented Calvinist world of publicly enforced industry and sobriety."[23] The objective of Burgh's ideal popular education, in which half the day was "spent learning useful trades and employments, the other half reading, writing and understanding accounts," was to reinforce the existing social order by improving it.[24] Burgh's own commitment to a free press was qualified in his utopia by a rule that "all immoral and obscene books, prints, pictures are ordered to be burnt."[25] Burgh was not, certainly, the only educational reformer addressing questions of popular education; however, the fact that a leading Dissenting educator who was widely read in the colonies adopted a stance supporting the existing social order is revealing. The possibilities for any reform that fostered a widely informed and empowered citizenry were profoundly limited in a society where even Dissenters, who used the most scathing invective against those who threatened to violate their civil or religious liberties, sought only to perfect the existing system, not to challenge it fundamentally.

Actually, the egalitarianism implied by DeLolme's language was scarcely part of the discussion concerning an informed citizenry. The idea that the government should actively promote the education of Britain's inhabitants in order to create an informed citizenry was virtually unknown. Because there was no place for common men in public affairs, many believed that no useful purpose was served by educating them beyond the level of the catechism and elementary numeracy. Indeed, some of Britain's political and cultural leaders believed that common people were overreaching their proper stations as it was. The press was disparaged for "prating to all qualities, ages, sexes, constitutions and parties" and for supplying general access to information so that "in Politics, every man is an adept, and the lowest mechanic delivers his opinion, at his club, upon the deepest public measures."[26] From this perspective, it was just as inappropriate for a common man to be informed or to speak on public matters as for a fishmonger to dress in silks.

At one level, these attitudes expressed the snobbery that characterized Britain's stratified yet competitive social order. But sometimes criticisms of the concept of an informed citizenry cut deeper. In 1757 Soame Jenyns, an essayist and member of Parliament, attacked the entire notion of an informed public as misguided. Ignorance, he wrote, was properly "the appointed lot of all born to poverty and the drudgeries of life." It was, he declared, "the only opiate capable of infusing that sensibility, which can enable them to endure the miseries" of their lot. "Never," Jenyns said, should they be "deprived" of their God-given ignorance "by an ill-judged and improper education," which would ruin them for their assigned roles in life and upset what Daniel Defoe ironically called "the great law of subordination."[27] This was not mere snobbery but a carefully reasoned political vision that high churchmen and Tories frequently shared.

Indeed, when reformers and their opponents debated the question of whether all ranks of Englishmen ought to be educated, nearly everyone agreed that the social hierarchy should be maintained. The principal conflict concerned whether or not a popular education regime would strengthen or subvert the status quo.[28] Given the fact that Anglican churchmen led the way in implementing popular education by operating charity schools, the immediate threat to social stability was minimal.

Among the champions of charity schools, it was the friends of hierarchy who prevailed. In an article published in the *Spectator* in 1712, Richard Steele called charity schools "the greatest Instances of public Spirit the Age has produced," but not because they would lead to a politically informed citizenry. Rather, these schools would, as Locke's treatise on education had urged, train poor children of both sexes in "Methods of Industry."[29] Although Steele noted that charity schools would instruct the "honest Artificer" in Christian principles, he emphasized the degree to which they would solve the perennial servant problem. The charity school, he asserted, was "a most laudable institution" because it was "producing a Race of good and useful Servants" who would be obedient, deferential, and loyal in addition to having "a liberal, a religious Education." In their masters' homes, they would promote virtue rather than undermine it. As one clergyman explained in a sermon, access to charity schools made being poor a kind of advantage because through these schools the poor could secure both their salvation and their livelihoods. Steele quoted the clergyman approvingly: "Their Poverty is, in Reality, their Preferment."[30]

The success of this movement was greatest in and around London and other urban centers, where by 1719 over 1,400 charity schools were in operation.[31] But opposition to popular education, brilliantly articulated by Bernard de Mandeville in 1714, was substantial. Gentlemen, opponents agreed, needed to be informed and some ordinary occupations required literacy, but for the great mass of the people, any learning beyond that which could be imparted orally on Sundays was suspect and potentially dangerous.

Mandeville attacked on all fronts. Did charity schools promote industry? Mandeville asserted that, on the contrary, they promoted "Idleness" because they kept "the Poor from Working."[32] Did charity schools reduce crime? Mandeville answered that "ordinary Rogues and our common Felons" displayed "excessive Cunning and Subtlety, and too much Knowledge in general."[33] As to the claim that popular education encouraged piety, Mandeville countered that "the most Knowing, are not the most Religious." Among a hundred "Poor Men . . . brought up to hard Labour from their Infancy, such as never went to School at all, and always lived remote from Knowledge and great Towns," Mandeville declared, there is "more Union and Neighbourly Love, less Wickedness and Attachment to the World, more Innocence,

Sincerity, and other good Qualities that conduce to the Publick Peace" than could be found among "an equal number of very good Scholars, that shall all have had University Education."[34] When it came to hard work, honesty, true humility, and Christian piety, he claimed that the poor, ignorant working man and woman already excelled.

The core of the problem, as Mandeville saw it, lay in the misguided social analysis of the charity school reformers who failed to recognize the grim realities of economic existence and social discipline. Mandeville pointed out that an "abundance of hard and dirty Labour is to be done, and coarse Living is to be complied with: Where shall we find a better Nursery for these Necessities than the Children of the Poor? None certainly are nearer to it or fitter for it. . . . Hardships, neither seem nor are such to those who have been brought up to 'em, and know no better. There is not a more contented People among us, than those who work the hardest and are the least acquainted with the Pomp and Delicacies of the World."[35] Preserving the contentment and low wages of such a labor force was vital not only for domestic tranquillity but also to enable Britain to compete successfully in international trade.[36] Charity schools were not merely harmless extravagances; they were subversive. "The Knowledge of the Working Poor," Mandeville argued, "should be confin'd within the Verge of their Occupations, and never extended (as to things visible) beyond what relates to their Calling." Mandeville acknowledged that "Reading, Writing and Arithmetick, are very necessary to those, whose Business require such Qualifications, but where People's livelihood has no dependence on these Arts," he declared, "they are very pernicious to the Poor, who are forc'd to get their Daily Bread by their Daily Labour."[37]

No educated person, Mandeville explained, would willingly "do the dirty slavish Work" that Britain required.[38] "Those who spent a great part of their Youth in learning to Read, Write and Cypher," Mandeville noted, "expect and not unjustly to be employ'd where those Qualifications may be of use to them." They looked down on labor "with the utmost Contempt" and refused to "serve a Farmer for a pitiful Reward."[39] Considering these facts of life, Mandeville believed it was "madness" for gentlemen to ruin their own labor forces and to create reservoirs of discontent by using charity schools to educate "People of the meanest Rank."[40]

Mandeville defended this blunt, unsentimental analysis by appealing to the long-term public interests of Britain. Charity schools had become a matter of fashionable indulgence among the wealthy and their privileged clergy, without sufficient consideration for the schools' deeper consequences.[41]

Mandeville knew he might be called "an Uncharitable, Hard-hearted and Inhuman, if not a Wicked, Profane, and Atheistical Wretch" for pointing out the hard social truth, but he claimed the "Publick Spirit" of the nation was at stake.[42] "Where deep Ignorance is entirely routed and expell'd, and low Learning promiscuously scatter'd on all the People," Mandeville reasoned, "Self-Love turns Knowledge into Cunning, and the more this last Qualification prevails . . . the more the People will fix all their Cares, Concern and Application on the Time present, without regard of what is to come after them, or . . . the next Generation."[43] In the short run, charity schools might promote feelings of benevolence among their contributors and improve the lives of a few poor people, but in the future, they would spawn a whirlwind of popular discontent, turmoil, and villainy.

Because he was convinced that education must be functional on economic, social, and political planes, Mandeville, like Locke, concentrated on the benefits of liberal education for gentlemen, the people whose public, political responsibilities required that they be informed. Not charity schools but professorships and universities warranted philanthropic patronage, according to Mandeville, who also urged that taxes be raised so that every county would possess at least one large school of six or more grades for Latin and Greek.[44] Concern for an informed citizenry was properly directed only toward the nation's ruling class.

A similar emphasis on the education of gentlemen prevailed in the colonies, although in Connecticut and Massachusetts, seventeenth-century statutes continued to provide for tax-supported elementary and grammar schools. In 1749 when Benjamin Franklin published his *Proposals Relating to the Education of Youth in Pennsylvania,* he did not call for a publicly supported school system to educate all inhabitants of the colony; instead, he recommended "that some Persons of Leisure and publick Spirit, apply for a Charter . . . with power to erect an Academy." Not taxes but donations and tuition would finance this academy, whose students would be groomed for leadership in Pennsylvania.[45] The bulk of Franklin's proposal, which quoted from a range of notable British and French writers on the education of gentlemen, concerned the specific curriculum that was best calculated to nurture the kind of liberally educated, virtuous gentlemen of "Good Breeding" whom theory taught should guide the colony.[46] Two years later, Franklin would propose that an "English School" be created as an adjunct to the classical academy to prepare boys for "any Business, Calling or Profession" in which no language other than English was required. Like the academy's classical department, the English school would provide a foundation for "the

Happiness both of private Families and of Commonwealths" since graduates would be qualified to engage in private affairs as well as hold public office.[47] Ultimately, this Philadelphia academy would develop into the University of Pennsylvania. The preparation of elite citizens for private careers and public service, not the education of common people, was always its goal.

Originally Franklin and his associates were guided by the British ideology of the preparation of gentlemen citizens. "Wise and good men are," Franklin wrote, "the *strength* of a state: much more so than riches or arms." Even though only a few would truly fulfill this ideal, "the influence of those few and the service in their power," he was convinced, "may be very great."[48] But unlike Locke, Mandeville, Burgh, and a broad range of English educational theorists, from the very beginning Franklin planned for the academy to promote a degree of social mobility. Franklin's original proposal stated that when the endowment was sufficient, "poor Children shall be admitted and taught gratis, what shall be thought suitable to their Capacities and Circumstances."[49] Many of these, no doubt, would become "qualified to act as Schoolmasters in the Country, to teach Children Reading, Writing, Arithmetick, and the Grammar of their Mother Tongue."[50] As a result, the academy would foster a broadly informed citizenry by serving as a kind of teachers college as well as a training ground for public officials. For a few exceptional poor boys, whom Franklin perhaps imagined were like himself, the academy could serve as a ladder for the most spectacular kind of social ascent. Ironically, Franklin's mobility model was Britain, where, he supposed, "whoever distinguishes himself . . . in either of the three learned Professions, gains Fame, and often Wealth and Power: A poor Man's Son has a Chance, if he studies hard, to rise, either in the Law or the Church, to gainful Offices of Benefices; to an extraordinary Pitch of Grandeur; to have a Voice in Parliament, a Seat among the Peers; as a Statesman or first Minister to govern Nations, and even to mix his Blood with Princes."[51] In this mobility fantasy, Franklin never imagined that the poor generally would participate; but in contrast to Mandeville and most British theorists, he did not confine the poor to permanent and complete disenfranchisement by closing the portals of gentility to them.

Franklin's tribute to British social mobility may have been exaggerated, but it did underscore a reality that theorists did not often acknowledge: that, in fact, British society was accommodating social mobility and the ranks of those who called themselves gentlemen were growing. In the colonies, such mobility was even more widespread than in Britain, and although not everyone could or would label themselves as genteel, property was so broadly distributed among white men that scarcely any of them regarded themselves as members of that servile, disenfranchised class, the poor. As a result, the connotation of an informed citizenry, which in Britain meant gentlemen only, was much looser in the colonies. Another mid-century educational project, this one in the colony of New York, revealed how justifications for establishing academies and colleges to prepare colonial elites could supply the foundation for a more inclusive ideology of an informed citizenry.

In this case, the arguments of Dissenters and Radical Whigs were called into play. Although these writers accepted social stratification and the privileges of wealth, they believed such inequalities should be based more on merit than preferment, and they were willing to criticize the status quo. In their view, an informed citizenry ought to be more comprehensive and comprise more than just liberally educated gentlemen. Using the writings of John Locke and Robert Molesworth as points of departure, they argued that free inquiry, a free press, and tolerance of political criticism were integrally connected to liberty. Reaching back to ideas that had been voiced in the Renaissance by authors such as Robert Crowley, who had defended the right "to speak against the faults of all degrees without exception," and John Milton, who had called on governments to refrain from censorship, they asserted the necessity of an informed citizenry. Just as critical inquiry was vital for establishing religious and scientific truths, from this perspective a politically informed citizenry, one that was equipped to evaluate public policy, was vital for the well-being of the state and the liberty of its people.

By mid-century, this viewpoint, which valued a politically informed citizenry over a realm populated by subjects indoctrinated in religious and political conformity, was part of the Anglo-American discussion, even turning up occasionally in such respected British periodicals as Addison and Steele's often-reprinted *Spectator* and Bolingbroke's *Craftsman*.[52] In New York, William Livingston and his associates produced a fully elaborated statement of this position in 1753 in the *Independent Reflector*, a magazine inspired by the *Spectator*. Here, in an article entitled "The Advantages of Education, with the Necessity of instituting Grammar schools for the Instruction of Youth, preparatory to their admission into our intended College," they went well beyond Franklin's conventional justification for the Pennsylvania academy. Whereas Franklin had blandly sought to prepare liberally educated civic leaders, Livingston and his coauthors boldly asserted the civic necessity of an informed citizenry: "Knowledge among a People makes them free, enterprising and dauntless; but Ignorance enslaves, emasculates and depresses them." Here, they declared, lay the only sure security for the preservation of

British liberties: "When Men know their Rights, they will at all Hazards defend them, as well against the insidious Designs of domestic Politicians, as the undisguised Attacks of a foreign enemy." The natural ignorance that Mandeville and Jenyns had praised as a necessary bastion of social peace was here said to open the way to tyranny: "While the Mind remains involved in its native Obscurity, it becomes pliable, abject, dastardly, and tame: It swallows the grossest Absurdities, submits to the vilest Impositions, and follows wherever it is led." Anyone who dared to contemplate an opposing view was faced with the irrefutable evidence of world history, all of which confirmed the necessity of an informed citizenry: "He must be a Stranger to History and the World"—an ignorant provincial—"who has not observed, that the Prosperity, Happiness, Grandeur, and even the Strength of a People, have always been the Consequences of the Improvement and Cultivation of their Minds."

In menacing, even apocalyptic tones, Livingston and his colleagues warned that wherever the improvement and cultivation of a whole people's minds were neglected, "triumphant Ignorance has opened its Sluices, and the Country has been overflowed with Tyranny, Barbarism, ecclesiastical Domination, Superstition, Enthusiasm, corrupt Manners, and an irresistible confederate Host of Evils, to its utter Ruin and Destruction."[53] Given the New York colony's paucity of educational institutions and lack of a college, it, like most of the colonies, was imperiled.

This full-blown polemic on behalf of an informed citizenry was not a complete rebuttal of conservative voices like Jenyns and Mandeville since all agreed that gentlemen should be politically informed. The *Independent Reflector* articles never actually specified that yeomen or journeymen, let alone laborers or women, should be informed. Livingston and his Radical Whig mentors were also not prepared to level all ranks and abolish deference to men of property, learning, and leisure. But their views contrasted with those of Tories, and conservatives generally, who emphasized the narrowly functional and religious objectives of popular instruction, aiming always to provide only as much education as was consistent with due subordination. The two viewpoints were not yet wholly incompatible, but their tendency and thrust clearly diverged.

In reality, the Livingston argument anticipated the innovative path along which the colonists were moving. Livingston and his associates were advocating establishing a college, like Harvard, Yale, or the College of William and Mary, in order to produce generations of genteel, cosmopolitan leaders; but at the same time, they expected that the new institution would "make a vast Alteration in our Affairs and Condition, civil and religious." The fruits of learning and of cultivating enlightened, liberal values would not be confined within college or council chamber walls: knowledge "will, more or less, influence every Individual amongst us, and diffuse its Spirit thro' all Ranks, Parties and Denominations."[54] This suggestion of an inclusive, even comprehensive, conception of a citizenry comprising "all Ranks" was unusual in the 1750s, and it is all the more remarkable because it was expressed in one of America's most heterogeneous colonies. What was crucial in this viewpoint was not the belief that elite education supplied benefits to the whole society, a view that had been a commonplace since the Renaissance. What was new, and potentially radical, was the idea that the very same values, ideas, and information might penetrate and permeate the entire social order, if only in attenuated form, and that the minds as well as the manners of the lower ranks mattered.

The idea that the minds of the lower ranks figured crucially in the political balance was clearly unconventional and marked a boundary in democratic thought. At the same time, however, it is important to note the implicit assumption that women, blacks, and Native Americans were excluded from all political consideration. The idea of an informed citizenry was not being extended by Radical Whigs, or anyone else, to include members of these groups. Indeed, relatively little was written about educating blacks or Native Americans, and those who wrote about women's education at most saw it as a means to prepare pious, genteel, apolitical wives and mothers. Actually, the prescriptions for informed women, blacks, and Native Americans were predicated on the same kind of subordination that characterized justifications for charity schools.

For women, the possibilities for education included preparation for the short-term goal of competing successfully in the marriage market or more substantial training for lifelong virtue and sound household management. Essays in the *Spectator* that criticized women's education urged that they learn more than merely the ornaments of needlework, dancing, and the French language—which focused on appearances—and read more books in order to acquire "common Sense."[55] Mandeville, who admitted that "there is no Labour of the Brain, which Women are not as capable of performing, at least, as well as the Men" and that "there are many Examples of Women that have excelled in Learning, even in War," still argued that this was "no reason we should bring 'em all up to *Latin* and *Greek,* or else Military Discipline, instead of Needlework and Housewifery."[56] The purpose of being educated or informed was not so that one could realize one's latent abilities to the fullest but so that one could perform one's assigned social role. For women, that role was domestic. As Benjamin Franklin, a self-educated man who rejected his father's place in society, put it in an essay on women's education, a mother should educate her daughters so as "to make them like your self."[57] Except for female monarchs, before the late eighteenth century, no one proposed that women should have a public, civic role.

Those who proposed the systematic education of African Americans used the contemporary charity school as the model. In Philadelphia, the evangelist George Whitefield's preaching awakened black and white interest in literacy and religious training, and in the late 1740s and the 1750s, Anglicans created black charity schools.[58] The sponsors of the schools believed that catechizing blacks and teaching them to read would "make them more faithful and honest in their Masters Service."[59] As in Mandeville's critique of English charity schools, however, Franklin noted that some opposed the schools because of their conviction "that Reading and Knowledge in a Slave are both useless and dangerous."[60] After Franklin visited a "Negro School," he commented that "their Apprehension seems as quick, their Memory as strong, and their Docility in every Respect equal to that of white Children," but he did not suggest that anything other than a servile role would ever be expected of the pupils.[61] Indeed, in view of prevailing expectations about property, independence, and citizenship, it would have been no more possible for Franklin to have imagined a public role for African Americans than it would have been for him to have imagined a public role for women.

For Native Americans, the goal of education was not, as for the poor and slaves, to mold them into good Christian servants, but neither was it in any sense to help them fulfill any public or civic role. Evangelism and a measure of acculturation or "civilization" were the objectives pursued by the Anglican Society for the Propagation of the Gospel (SPG) and various Dissenting missionaries.[62] When the Reverend Henry Barclay ministered to Indians in the 1730s for the SPG, he taught reading and writing in their own language as well as the catechism.[63] A few years later, a New England missionary, the Reverend John Sergeant, proposed instructing Indians in *"the English Language . . . and thereby instilling into their Minds and Hearts, with a more lasting Impression, the Principles of Virtue and Piety."* Sergeant's plan, which promoted the education of girls as well as boys and stressed manual labor along with book-learning, was aimed at supplanting Native American culture with English customs. Sergeant viewed Indians as "greatly *debased . . . a base ungrateful People,* insensible of Kindnesses done them," which was all the more reason "to promote *Humanity* among them." Because it was necessary "to change their whole Habit of thinking and acting," there was no hope of incorporating them into the body politic at any time in the near future or even of converting very many of them to Christianity. New England missionaries' efforts were propelled as much by their desire to save their own Anglo-American souls as by their desire to rescue Indians from damnation.[64]

What set the education of Native Americans apart from that of the poor, African Americans, and women was not that they were outsiders to the public councils and therefore had no role as citizens, a condition shared by all of these groups. Instead, it was the fact that promoters of the education of Native Americans actively encouraged them to attend college. Whether at Harvard or at the College of William and Mary, the aim in all cases was to produce Native American missionaries, but the effort was a resounding failure.[65] As Benjamin Franklin explained regarding some abortive mid-century attempts to send Indians to college, the families of the students found that they became "absolutely good for nothing[,] being neither acquainted with the true methods of killing deer, catching Beaver or surprizing an enemy."[66] Being informed in the British sense did not help to fulfill the requirements of Indian citizenship.

Efforts to convert and educate Native Americans were part of a broader attempt to assimilate subordinate and alien peoples in the prescribed customs and values of Anglo-American society, even though they would not be included among the citizenry as political actors. The assimilation of another prominent group of aliens—the Germans of Pennsylvania—however, had immediate public consequences because they owned property and could vote. Significantly, it was urgent that through education the language barrier be removed in order to make German men into informed citizens.

Benjamin Franklin framed the problem in a 1753 letter to an English reformer. The difficulty was not that these people were Germans but that "those [Germans] who come hither are generally of the most ignorant Stupid Sort of their own Nation, and as Ignorance is often attended with Credulity when Knavery would mislead it, and with Suspicion when Honesty would set it right; and as few of the English understand the German Language, and so cannot address them either from the Press or Pulpit, 'tis almost impossible to remove any prejudices they once entertain." Since most German Americans were Anabaptist sectarians, Franklin noted, even "their own Clergy have very little influence over the people." These Germans created a political problem not because they were unruly but because they voted "in droves, and carry all before them." Their ignorance had created the classic problem of citizenship in a representative government. Franklin was "not against the Admission of Germans in general, for they have their Virtues," but he feared that by becoming the tools of political knaves, they would put Pennsylvania government at risk.[67]

Franklin proposed that English-language schools be established among the Germans as the primary means to solve this problem. To entice parents into enrolling their children, he insisted, the schools must be free.[68] For the "vulgar," the curriculum "should be calculated rather to make them good citizens than what is called good scholars." At the highest educational level, the senior German clergyman in Philadelphia would be appointed as a "German Professor of Divinity" at a projected Pennsylvania college. His presence, it was hoped, would draw young German clerics to study in Philadelphia, an experience that would "anglify" them. As in William Livingston's New York college proposal, not only gentlemen citizens but also vulgar citizens mattered. The core principles driving this Anglo-American scheme for German assimilation were political: "A free people can be governed only by reason, virtue, glory, honor, and the like, which are the results of education, without which, therefore, they cannot be governed at all. When men are free to speak and act they must be instructed how to speak and act rightly, otherwise they will use their liberty against those from whom they received it."[69] In the colonies' multicultural setting, where the broad distribution of property provided a major political voice for the vulgar citizenry, schooling often appeared to be the best means to furnish suitable political education.

The mainstream of eighteenth-century British political thought held that the nation's political well-being required the foundation of an informed gentleman citizenry. The prevailing assumption was that, as in the cases of the poor, Africans, and Native Americans, "Poverty and Want . . . debase the Minds of Men," so that "Ignorance and Barbarity" were linked naturally to "Despotic Power."[70] For this reason, generally speaking, those who were not gentlemen citizens should be kept subordinate at all times. Mandeville had warned of the corrosive economic and social effects of raising people's expectations above their stations. In a standard sermon commemorating the execution of Charles I, the bishop of Peterborough used that historical example to show that when the ignorant "common People . . . were taught Grievances, and a Right to have them redress'd in their own Way," the result had been "Insurrections and Rebellion."[71] This was one of the dangers that charity schools were supposed to allay. Common people should be sufficiently educated so as to value subordination and deference over the siren calls of demagogues, but they should not be so well informed that they would dare to judge public affairs on their own. As one early eighteenth-century commentator observed: "The people are not competent judges of the actions of magistrates." There existed, he asserted, "mysteries of state, to the bottom of which the people are not able to dive."[72]

Many authors from all along the political spectrum doubted that the "meaner sort" could ever be so thoroughly indoctrinated as to resist corruption; however, it became conventional to differentiate "the people" from the poor instead of conflating the two. "The people" came to mean those who possessed sufficient property to be independent of patronage jobs, especially ministerial patronage.[73] Employing this kind of definition, authors could contemplate a greater degree of "popular" political engagement. The voices that articulated this broader definition of the citizenry came from several points on the political spectrum and never united in a single description of who, precisely, ought to possess a political voice and must therefore become informed. Collectively, however, they revealed that by the middle decades of the eighteenth century the movement away from the idea of a citizenry composed exclusively of gentlemen was firmly established on both sides of the Atlantic.

In New England, where common farmers and tradesmen had long voted on public affairs in addition to making decisions about the hiring, firing, and salaries of clergymen, the nature of popular citizenship was a frequent topic of election sermons. Often the legitimacy of the people's voice was acknowledged by warnings against excess or error. In 1720, for example, a Massachusetts political homily noted that "the people, through ignorance and want of judgement, may think that amiss in rulers which is not so."[74] Twenty years later, a similar remark cautioned that "the common people are not always able to judge what is just and righteous in a public administration." At the same time, however, clergymen legitimated the popular voice even if it was imperfectly informed, pointing out that "although the ignorance of the people should make them very cautious" in judging their rulers, "everyone can feel when he is oppressed and injured, or done justly by."[75] The solution to popular ignorance and lack of good judgment was not the disenfranchisement of the people but access to better information.

As early as 1711, Joseph Addison had argued in the *Spectator* that newspapers "would be of great Use were they thus calculated to diffuse good Sense through the Bulk of a People, to clear up their Understandings, [and] animate their Minds with Virtue." For the good of society, he argued, "Knowledge" should not be reserved for learned elites by being "bound up in Books and kept in Libraries and Retirements"; it should be positively "obtruded upon the Publick, . . . canvassed in every Assembly, and exposed upon every Table."[76] Later, Benjamin Franklin addressed the same problem from a different angle, asserting that books, despite being expensive, should be made more widely available through the establishment of public libraries. Franklin's objective was not specifically political, but he did seek to promote an informed citizenry by encouraging the "more general Use and Esteem" of "valuable Books," which would "have very good Effects on the Minds of the People . . . and furnish them with the most useful kind of Knowledge, that which renders Men benevolent and helpful to one another."[77] The flowering of enlightened arguments such as those of Addison and Franklin was an indication that ideas about the solution to the problem of an ignorant people were shifting away from keeping them ignorant and submissive and toward informing and enfranchising them.

By the 1740s, for example, English newspapers carried essays advancing the view that even nonvoters, men of the "meaner sort," should have the right to hold opinions on public affairs and ought to be allowed to protest against governments and laws they deemed improper. The idea that every man who paid any kind of tax had the right to hold political opinions, whether or not he owned a freehold, was gaining currency.[78] According to the influential Viscount Bolingbroke, men "of all degrees" belonged to the political nation, and Tory patriots agreed that anyone engaged in "honest labour and industry" should be included.[79] In New York, Cadwallader Colden directly confronted the bullionist argument that "the Power & strength of a Nation consists in its riches & Money." Although Colden recognized that "money can do great things," he believed that "the Power of a Nation consists in the knowledge & Virtue of its inhabitants."[80] This optimistic Enlightenment outlook, which ran contrary to the caustic assumptions of Mandevillean and mercantilist political economy, seems to have enjoyed more general support in the colonies than in Britain, but it was gaining ground everywhere.

In Massachusetts, a young Harvard-educated lawyer, John Adams, an avid reader of English history and political theory—especially the Radical Whig writers—explained his own understanding of the English idea of an informed citizenry in a memorandum he entered in his personal diary in 1761. His was an extreme interpretation that contrasted an English Protestant ideal with an anti-Catholic caricature. In Adams's view, "English Law" required "some Acquaintance with Letters, . . . that a Man may fill any station whatever." Ignoring the fact that several of the Enlightenment's most influential writers on the education of the laity, including the noted Frenchman Charles Rollin, were Roman Catholics, Adams contrasted this mandatory British literacy with "the Countries of slavery, and Romish superstition," where, he claimed, "the Laity must not learn to read, least they should detect the gross Impostures of the Priesthood, and shake off the Yoke of Bondage." Adams concluded that "in Protestant Countries, and especially in England and its Colonies, Freedom of Enquiry is allowed to be not only the Priviledge [*sic*] but the Duty of every Individual."

In the privacy of his diary, Adams superimposed the ideals of Puritan Massachusetts over those of the mother country. "The English Constitution," he claimed with some originality, "is founded, tis bottomed And grounded on the Knowledge and good sense of the People." By "the People," Adams seems to have meant not merely all property holders or even all taxpayers but all free men. Describing a citizen's responsibility, he declared: "I must judge for myself, but how can I judge, how can any Man judge, unless his Mind has been opened and enlarged by Reading." This yeoman's son, who practiced law out of a room in his father's farmhouse, described his own situation as if it were everyman's. Although he was an aspiring college graduate and had been admitted to the Boston bar, he was still close to the ordinary men of his locale. It was his conviction, based on observation as well as ideology, that "a Man who can read, will find in his Bible, in the common sermon Books that common People have by them and even in the Almanack and News Papers, Rules and observations, that will enlarge his Range of Thought, and enable him the better to judge who has and who has not that Integrity of Heart, and that Compass of Knowledge and Understanding, which form the Statesman."[81] Such a declaration, had it been made publicly, would have seemed naively optimistic to many leaders in Massachusetts and the other colonies and would have been condemned as absolutely radical in England. But for John Adams in 1761, the people, indeed the common people, were not an intellectual abstraction; they were bone of his bone, flesh of his flesh, and he believed he understood their minds as well.

To the London-trained Boston jurist Benjamin Prat, the principles of Bernard de Mandeville made much better sense in 1760 than those of Adams, which he would have viewed as dangerous foolishness. Echoing remarks made by Governor William Berkeley of Virginia a century earlier, Prat declared publicly that "it is a very happy Thing to have People superstitious. They should believe exactly as their Minister believes. . . . They should not so much as know what they believe. The People ought to be ignorant. And our Free schools are the very bane of society. They make the lowest of the People infinitely conceited."[82] Like most Englishmen, Prat recognized that being informed was a key ingredient of hegemony, just as ignorance sustained the submissiveness of ordinary people. Among those like Prat who supported the existing political hierarchy, Mandeville's maxim, "Should a Horse know as much as a Man, I should not desire to be his Rider," explained the need for popular ignorance.[83]

But by the 1760s, views such as Prat's were routinely challenged. Several years after Adams composed his private encomium to an informed citizenry of common men, the Dissenting schoolmaster James Burgh published views that were rooted in the same Radical Whig tradition and expressed similar tendencies. Like Adams, Burgh argued that "Protestant Religion" had triumphed "over popish delusion" by means of "the exercise of the unalienable right of private judgment, and liberty of publication." He, too, denied what he characterized as "the common cant of our ministerial slaves, 'That private persons are incompetent judges of the conduct of their governors.'" Burgh dismissed with scornful irony the notion that "the brain of a statesman [was] made of materials different from that of a citizen" or that one must be a "master of the sublime geometry, or the Newtonian philosophy" in order "to judge of political subjects." Burgh did not go as far as Adams in praising the benefits of reading for common men, but he did argue that "plain sense, applied to *general,* instead of private concerns," was mostly what was needed "to judge whether the interests of one's country is [*sic*] properly attended." To govern well, a leader did not need rarefied learning or esoteric experience but the down-to-earth traits of "common sense, common honesty, and a moderate knowledge of history."[84] Although Burgh did not define precisely who he meant by the term "citizen," he seemed to include not only merchants and manufacturers, whom he claimed had "as much occasion for extensive *knowledge,* and liberal *sentiment,* as the man of estate," but all English subjects. He argued that "the subjects in a free country have a right to consider themselves as on the same foot with the stockholders in a trading company"; therefore, when a subject had grievances, like a stockholder he possessed the right to make "England ring with his complaints."[85] Burgh's apparent readiness to acknowledge a broadly inclusive citizenry converged with Adams's support for the political enfranchisement of common men in Massachusetts.

Opponents of these radical views regarded them as unconstitutional and stigmatized writers like Burgh as republican subverters of monarchy. For their part, Radical Whigs defended their version of the monarchy and the rights of Englishmen as the true constitutional legacy of 1688. In fact, however, they had reinterpreted the Glorious Revolution according to republican assumptions that undermined Britain's political status quo. When the London-based Society for Constitutional Information published its *Address to the Public* in 1780, it began with the premise that English liberty depended upon a politically informed citizenry that comprised all Englishmen. "The universal right of suffrage," it claimed, was one of the ancient rights of Englishmen. Going far beyond anything that John Adams had articulated twenty years earlier, the society declared that "as every Englishman has an equal inheritance in this Liberty; and in those Laws and that Constitution which have been provided for its defence; it is therefore necessary that every Englishman should know what the Constitution IS; When it is SAFE; and when ENDANGERED." The best way for the people to know their constitutional rights was to exercise them constantly. But until they were fully restored and in use, the Society for Constitutional Information proposed to distribute its tracts gratis throughout Great Britain.[86]

To mainstream British political thinkers, organizations like the Society for Constitutional Information represented a dangerous, radical fringe that, insofar as it was legally possible, ought to be harassed and suppressed for attempting to subvert the political order. It would, in fact, be more than a century before the doctrine of universal male suffrage and equal rights achieved victory in Britain. In the American colonies, however, the ideology of the Radical Whigs followed a different trajectory. In the next generation, John Adams, the youthful country lawyer who privately celebrated a republican interpretation of the English constitution, would move from the furthest periphery of political power to its center as he joined a cadre of American leaders who subscribed to similar beliefs. In the minds of most public men in Britain and its colonies, the idea of an informed citizenry was still clothed in a gentleman's suit; whether those garments would continue to serve the notion had become the question.

Chapter 3 ❦ Bulwark of Revolutionary Liberty ❦ The Recognition of the Informed Citizen

By the middle of the eighteenth century, even before the imperial conflict between Britain and its American colonies began, Radical Whigs and others had articulated the idea of an informed citizenry in various ways. Moreover, such widely supported ideals as free speech and press and religious liberty, together with the general Enlightenment belief that increases in knowledge were progressive and beneficent, reinforced the notion of an informed citizenry. Belief in social hierarchy remained powerful, as did the sense that society, like nature, must be stratified, but the Mandevillean argument that social peace required keeping the lower classes ignorant found few spokesmen. Bringing the light of learning, including the knowledge of the gospel, to all Englishmen was a goal commanding general assent.

From a political standpoint, however, the idea of an informed citizenry remained inconsequential in the American colonies as well as in Britain. The central preoccupations of Georgian politics lay elsewhere—in the tensions between Crown and Parliament, in debates over balanced government, and in the pronounced concern over corruption that was associated with Robert Walpole's parliamentary regime. Moreover, the meanings of the high principles that surrounded the informed citizen ideal—free speech and press, religious liberty, and the general expansion of learning—were contested. Learning and popular literacy were defended by high churchmen as measures promoting moral improvement and piety, whereas secular voices supported learning as a means to erase superstition and mindless credulity among common folk.

Understandings of the concept of religious liberty were even more vexed. To secular-minded Deists, it meant the total separation of church and state and an end to centuries of tax-supported religion. For the established Anglican clergy, religious liberty carried no such implications; it merely meant that no one would be forced to worship contrary to the dictates of conscience and that Christian worship of all varieties would be freely permitted. Among Protestant sectarians, no single viewpoint ruled, and some were ready to endorse church taxes, provided they were distributed according to the taxpayer's religious preference.

The meaning of free speech and press, principles that were interwoven with the idea of an informed citizenry, was similarly controversial. After Britain's licensing law for publications lapsed in the 1690s, freedom of the press came to mean the absence of European-style prior censorship. Publishers could print anything they wished; however, afterward they might be sued for libel by individuals or punitively by officials of the state and the church for the crimes of seditious or blasphemous libel. By mid-century, in the New York colony at least, the Zenger case had advanced the proposition that publishing the truth was protected, even against prosecution for seditious libel. And although Radical Whigs on both sides of the Atlantic believed that some kinds of false and malicious speech should be prohibited, they were moving toward a more extended view of a free press than merely one unencumbered by prior censorship. But there was no agreement as to the limits of free speech and press. Like religious liberty, freedom of speech and freedom of the press were among the celebrated "rights of Englishmen," and they supplied a grounding for the idea of an informed citizenry. But it was a rather uncertain foundation because the conceptions of these principles were ambiguous, indefinite, and fluid.

Still, by mid-century, sentiment that broadly favored some vague idea of an informed citizenry was growing. Indeed, in Britain, scores if not hundreds of charitable endowments helped to support schools and colleges and assisted in the education of well-connected and talented but needy boys. But the creation and maintenance of an informed citizenry was not considered a public responsibility. The Church of England was expected to promote "Christian knowledge"—priests were to catechize their flocks—but otherwise the education of children and youth was purely the private responsibility of families. As with other potentially marketable skills for which British parents purchased their children's apprenticeships, instruction in reading, writing, arithmetic, and all other subjects was a private matter.

Conditions in the American colonies generally reflected patterns in Britain, although from the perspective of Enlightenment ideals, there were some discouraging differences. Charitable endowments were rare in America; in addition, there were hundreds of thousands of African slaves and Native Americans who could not be included in social calculations regarding free speech and press, religious liberty, or an informed citizenry.

Indeed, to many masters of slaves, the Mandevillean belief in the social necessity of keeping the laboring class ignorant still made sense. Slavery, moreover, was an established institution in every colony.

On the other side of the balance, however, were the exceptional practices of Puritan New England, that is, Massachusetts and Connecticut. In these colonies, in contrast to other political jurisdictions in the British Empire, public authorities laid taxes to support free schools for all free boys. The objective of these seventeenth-century policies had been essentially religious, based on the conviction that an ignorant people were sinful and unconverted and would provoke God's wrath, but by the mid-eighteenth century secular and civic justifications were made as well. Moreover, the results of these education policies, which were also related to New England's broad diffusion of property and its literate heritage, struck many observers. In 1765 the young Massachusetts attorney John Adams boasted "that all candid foreigners who have passed through this country, and conversed freely with all sorts of people here, will allow, that they have never seen so much knowledge and civility among the common people in any part of the world."[1]

New England's Puritan legacy, observers agreed, gave the region a more educated common standard than other colonies had, but the differences were matters of degree rather than kind. In New York City, a gentleman complained in the 1750s "how common it is to see a Shoemaker, Taylor, or Barber, haranguing with a great deal of Warmth on the public Affairs." Though armed only with "Knowledge from the News-Papers," a tradesman would "condemn a General, Governor, or Province with as much Assurance as if he were of the Privy council."[2] To a British gentleman, the tradesman's effrontery was more striking than his access to information, but these remarks suggest that common citizens in New York City were, at least in their own eyes, informed politically.

The observations of Anglican clergyman Jacob Duché of Philadelphia supply further evidence that even in regions where there was no New England–style school establishment, ordinary men valued being informed and often saw themselves as informed citizens. "The poorest laborer upon the shore of the Delaware," Duché reported, "thinks himself entitled to deliver his sentiments in matters of religion or politics with as much freedom as the gentleman or scholar." Deferential manners, Duché said, were diminished since "cringing servility" was not the regional style. And although Duché believed "literary accomplishments here meet with deserved applause," he pointed out that "such is the prevailing taste for books of every kind, that almost every man is a reader; and by pronouncing sentence . . .

upon the various publications that come in his way, puts himself upon a level, in point of knowledge, with their several authors."[3] Farther south, learning was said to be less widespread among common white men. Yet a 1762 North Carolina statute held masters accountable for the literacy of even their black apprentices, and in Virginia, justices of the peace "consistently held parents and masters responsible for the education of their children and servants."[4] As in Britain, schooling was generally "used as a vehicle for personal advancement."[5] Although John Adams was speaking of white male New Englanders in 1765 when he asserted that "a native of America who cannot read and write . . . is as rare as a comet or an earthquake"[6] and the literacy levels of colonial women lagged behind those of men, scholars agree that American literacy rates surpassed those in England, attaining or exceeding levels in Presbyterian Scotland.[7] This cultural foundation, which combined widespread literacy and property holding with broadly expressed feelings of empowerment among ordinary householders, gave special cogency to the idea of an informed citizenry in colonial America.

Still, the idea of an informed citizenry was rarely advocated or even expressed in the mid-eighteenth-century colonies. The Americans, like the British, were preoccupied with other issues. Newspaper columns traced the course of foreign warfare and the politics of the court and Parliament, while colonial leaders expended their energy on contests over frontier land, commercial advantages, patronage partisanship, and sectarian issues.[8] Whether or not the citizenry should be informed, by whom, and in what ways seemed to have no immediate relevance. Americans were thoroughly prepared for the idea to take hold—intellectually, culturally, socially—but throughout the 1750s concern for an informed citizenry remained latent.

Between 1763 and 1775, the idea of an informed citizenry was activated. The catalyst was a series of parliamentary acts and administrative policies the British initiated in their efforts to reform the imperial system. The new British measures, which affected overseas trade, imported consumer goods, western lands, newspapers, and all legal transactions, aroused repeated protests from the elite political classes in the colonies. Planters and merchants were joined by almost everyone with a college degree or a claim to gentry status as well as master tradesmen like shipbuilders, printers, and iron masters. When these self-styled gentlemen sought to mobilize opposition to the measures via legislative resolutions, public meetings, newspapers, and pamphlets, they discovered the importance of the idea of an informed citizenry. They seized and elevated to prominence a concept that had hitherto lain inert in the background of Whig thought. What had been merely a last resort of liberty in Radical Whig doctrine was suddenly of central practical as well as theoretical importance.

The unself-conscious, only partly deliberate way in which the idea emerged into prominence is evident in Boston's Radical Whig politics. Almost without exception, the men who led Boston and Massachusetts into the Revolution did not see themselves as social or political innovators before 1775. As in the other colonies, they were mostly men of affairs who enjoyed the privileges of gentility and backed the social order as it was. From their perspective, the British ministry and Parliament, not themselves, were the sources of innovation. Indeed, when Boston's leaders first began to protest British innovations in tax law and administration, they generally confined their discussion of grievances to legislative chambers and the occasional newspaper essay or pamphlet. They intended to include within the boundaries of legislative debate a limited audience of gentlemen only, not the public at large. But a significant exception occurred at the public Boston town meeting of May 1764, at which the assembled voters and other inhabitants—a socially inclusive gathering of free men—discussed and then approved a remonstrance against the Revenue Act of 1764.[9] Conscious that their protest would find more support in the town meeting than in the province legislature, the "gentlemen" merchants who felt the grievance most keenly brought their case into this inclusive local forum. What was unusual here, though not unprecedented, was the fact that a town meeting, which was normally concerned with local administration and finances, had been employed to engage a broad array of citizens in rendering a judgment on imperial policy.

It is unlikely that any of those who supported this tactical move in 1764—even Samuel Adams—was completely aware of its full implications. By bringing the issue out of the closed, exclusive, centralized forum of the legislature and into the open, inclusive local town meeting, Boston Whigs did more than gain a majority vote. Indirectly and apparently without specific intention, they resorted to the model of political action that would soon dominate the resistance movement—that is, an appeal extending beyond the time-honored circles of political gentlemen to include all men who held property and even many who did not. The Radical Whig gentlemen who led Boston politics were discovering in 1764 what leaders in other colonies would soon recognize: that by engaging the citizenry-at-large in their protests, their opposition became formidable to the royal administrations in their colonies and perhaps even to the ministry and Parliament.[10] The recognition of this political reality, more than any other single factor, convinced revolutionary leaders, who had not previously devoted much attention to the subject, that an informed citizenry was a vital matter of practical politics.

The revolutionaries came to appreciate both the practical and theoretical importance of an informed citizenry. Most immediately, practical politics required that citizens be properly informed, that is, indoctrinated in the facts and interpretations that would reinforce support for resistance measures. More generally, they should be informed concerning Whig theory in the manner that William Livingston's *Independent Reflector* had prescribed so that they would always know their rights and not fall prey to the machinations of tyrants. To achieve that goal, John Adams, the obscure young country lawyer who burned to distinguish himself by serving his country, published an unsigned, untitled, four-part essay in the *Boston Gazette* in 1765. In it, Adams both elaborated and went beyond the themes that Livingston had proclaimed a decade earlier in New York. So powerful and evocative was Adams's rhetoric that Thomas Hollis, the English Radical Whig, titled the essay "A Dissertation on the Canon and Feudal Law" and had it republished late in 1765 in the *London Chronicle* and in 1768 as a separate pamphlet.[11] This "Dissertation," which was aimed directly at the Stamp Act, examined familiar Radical Whig historical and political ideas, with an emphasis on the need for an informed, knowledgeable citizenry.

Adams began with a quotation from the widely read, liberal English divine, Bishop John Tillotson, who had said that "Ignorance and Inconsideration are the two great Causes of the Ruin of Mankind." For Adams, this maxim conveyed powerful political implications. In the "early Ages of the World," Adams explained, when absolute monarchy was "the universal form of Government, . . . the People . . . were little higher . . . in the scale of intelligence than the Camells and Asses and Elephants."[12] In contrast, history demonstrated "that whenever, a general Knowledge and sensibility have prevailed among the People, Arbitrary Government and every kind of oppression have lessened and disappeared in Proportion."[13] History proved that the connection between tyranny and ignorance was just as strong as that between liberty and learning.

In the minds of Radical Whigs like Adams, the Protestant Reformation was the crucial dividing line in modern history. Before Luther and Calvin, an alliance between monarchies and the Roman Catholic Church maintained popular obedience through popular ignorance. The chains of church and state kept "the Minds of the People" in "a State of Sordid Ignorance and staring Timidity, . . . infusing into them a religious Horror of Letters and

Knowledge of every Kind." Bound by feudal tenure to follow their lords "wherever they commanded, and in a state of total Ignorance," the people for centuries saw no alternative to tyranny. "Ignorant as they were of Arts and Letters," they "could not frame and support a regular system of opposition." But the Reformation cracked the iron grip of oppression so that "Knowledge gradually increased, and spread among the People," until, by the time of the Stuarts, tyranny was forced to retreat.[14]

The Puritans who founded New England represented the culmination of this historic process. Adams noted that the king himself had recognized "that they were more intelligent, and better read than even the members of the Church." For this reason, Charles I and his officials persecuted Puritans "for no other crime than their knowledge, and their freedom of enquiry and examination."[15] Adams celebrated the founders of New England as heroes in the historic struggle for knowledge and liberty. "Intelligent in general, and many of them learned," they had left libraries to posterity "in which the wisdom of the most enlightned [*sic*] ages and nations is deposited," though written in languages that, sadly, "their great Grand sons can scarcely read."[16]

The founders had been fully aware of the difficulties of perpetuating an informed citizenry, as Adams's interjection about grandsons suggested, and had therefore made institutional provisions for its maintenance. They established fee simple land tenure because it would create a yeomanry with "a very general contempt and detestation of holdings by quit rents."[17] This New England yeomanry possessed "an hereditary ardor for liberty and thirst for knowledge"[18] that was undergirded by the schools and colleges Puritan leaders had established by law. "The education of all ranks of people was made the care and expence of the public,"[19] Adams explained. "To propagate and perpetuate knowledge," Puritan settlers not only set an example in their own time but created lasting foundations. Warming to the subject, Adams exclaimed "that they have left among their posterity, so universal an affection for those seminaries [Harvard, Yale], and for liberal education, that the meanest of people contribute chearfully to the support and maintenance of them."[20] According to "A Dissertation on the Canon and Feudal Law," an informed citizenry, maintained from common school to college, was New England's glorious heritage.

But why, then, among such an enlightened people, was liberty in danger? Here Adams sketched a portrait of Mandevillean malevolence that must have resonated with such English Radical Whigs as Thomas Hollis. "There has been among us a party for some years," Adams charged, "consisting chiefly not of the descendants of the first settlers of this country but of high churchmen and high statesmen, imported since." These worldly interlopers were tearing at the institutional fabric that preserved New England's liberty. They "affect to censure this provision for the education of our youth as a needless expence, and imposition upon the rich in favour of the poor." The school system that defended New England liberties by educating its people was now being denounced "as an institution productive of idleness and vain specula-tion among the people, whose time and attention it is said ought to be de-voted to labour, and not to public affairs or to examination into the conduct of their superiours." In short, liberty and its companion, an enlightened cit-izenry, were in danger because this "party . . . and certain officers of the crown, and certain other missionaries of ignorance, foppery, servility and slavery" were actively defiling New England's hard-won, sacred heritage.[21]

Here Adams presented the issue in stark political terms. It was important that the people possess general knowledge in order to understand natural philosophy and religious truth and maintain a decent level of civility, but more immediately, it was absolutely critical that they acquire knowledge in order to participate in politics. "The people," Adams proclaimed, "have a right, an indisputable, unalienable, indefeasible divine right to that most dreaded and envied kind of knowledge, I mean of the characters and con-duct of their rulers."[22] This was not an informed citizenry educated in the docile servitude of high church catechisms; it was a *politically* informed citi-zenry that knew its rights and jealously defended them. On this point, Adams was adamant: "The preservation of the means of knowledge among the lowest ranks, is of more importance to the public, than all the property of all the rich men in the country."[23] The argument that the rich should not be taxed to pay for poor men's education was nonsense; since public liberty protected their property, the rich ought "to contribute in the same propor-tion."[24] Liberty itself was at stake for the rich no less than for the poor.

In "Dissertation," Adams's panegyric to the Puritan settlers of New England and the institutions they founded began with a firm grounding in historical fact: the public education laws and the creation of Harvard College in the 1630s. But when he put the final part of his institutional argument into place—an assertion of the necessity of free speech and press—he replaced the historical record of orthodox authoritarianism that was actually New England's official seventeenth-century policy with fictions of enlightened liberality. "None of the means of information are more sacred, or have been cherished with more tenderness and care," he announced, "than the Press."[25] It was true, of course, that the Massachusetts Bay General Court had, with the publishing of religious and government publications in mind, sponsored

ient of a press in the 1630s; but on this foundation, Adams
press tradition. Ignoring the actual censorship practiced by this
sponsored printing office, as well as the fact that Puritan magis-
suppressed Boston's first newspaper in 1690, Adams asserted
been taken that the art of printing should be encouraged, and
be easy and cheap and safe for any person to communicate his
thoughts to the public." Completing his transformation of New England's
actual legacy to make it conform to Radical Whig principles, Adams admonished his fellow countrymen not to be "intimidated . . . from publishing
with the utmost freedom, whatever can be warranted by the laws of your
country; nor suffer yourselves to be wheedled out of your liberty, by any pre-
tences of politeness, delicacy or decency."[26] The British must never be permitted to believe that Americans were, as their enemies had represented
them, "an ignorant, a timid and a stupid people."[27]

The best course of action was to cultivate, stimulate, and set in motion
New England's informed citizenry. Adams's vision was comprehensive. "Let
us," he exhorted, "tenderly and kindly cherish . . . the means of knowledge."
His concern was not directed at any one class of people but at all citizens, at
least all free men: "Let every order and degree among the people rouse their
attention and animate their resolution. Let them all become attentive to the
grounds and principles of government, ecclesiastical and civil. Let us study
the law of nature; search into the spirit of the British constitution; read the
histories of ancient ages; contemplate the great examples of Greece and
Rome; set before us the conduct of our own British ancestors, . . . [and] our
own more immediate fore fathers."[28] Since the liberties of all were at stake,
the responsibility for defending liberty belonged to everyone. At the same
time, however, those who dispensed knowledge at the bar, in colleges, and in
the pulpit, "the proper patrons and supporters of law, learning and religion,"
bore a special obligation to disseminate an understanding of law and liberty
among the people at large. Ultimately, Adams's vision of the informed citizenry in 1765 was hierarchical, with the learned few broadcasting knowledge
to the many. With this goal in mind, he concluded by declaring that "every
sluice of knowledge be open'd and set a flowing."[29]

For colonial opponents of the Stamp Act, Adams's arguments touched
a sensitive nerve. Adams himself had declared that this act of Parliament was
deliberately "form'd to strip us in a great measure of the means of knowledge,
by loading the Press, the Colleges, and even an Almanack and a News-Paper,
with restraints and duties."[30] Although economic distress, as noted in
Adams's locally influential Braintree Resolves of October 1765, together with

the larger principle of "no taxation without representation" were the chief arguments against the Stamp Act, Adams had elevated the issue of an informed citizenry to a prominent place in Radical Whig discourse. At the theoretical as well as the practical level, Adams's "Dissertation" voiced a new recognition of the need to engage the general citizenry in imperial politics.

Of course, no avalanche of rhetorical pronouncements or specific measures occurred in New England or elsewhere in 1765 and the ensuing years to mark this new consciousness. But a few significant milestones emerged. In November 1764, when members of Virginia's House of Burgesses were voicing opposition to the recent Revenue Act, they voted to erect a public gallery in their legislative chamber to permit newspaper reporters and the public to learn the substance of their debates. Now, in the wake of the Stamp Act, Massachusetts followed. In May 1766 the Boston town meeting instructed its representatives to "make the debates in the house of representatives as public as those in the House of Commons in Great Britain," and in June the legislature accommodated the request by adding a public gallery.[31] "So Noble a School of Political Learning," John Adams believed, would encourage a "spirit of virtue."[32] What Boston's Radical Whigs had begun in the town meeting of May 1764—engaging the public in imperial politics—was developing into a new orthodoxy.

Allowing the public to attend legislative debates and permitting newspaper accounts of those debates to circulate among the people, as had long been the practice in Britain, were important affirmations of the belief in an informed citizenry. But in themselves they did not extend the actual boundaries of an informed citizenry to include common householders. The process of inclusion was less a question of making procedural gestures like opening legislative debates to public view than it was a matter of mobilizing ordinary men. In such a mobilization, the interaction of ideology, events, and rhetoric proved crucial. The Revenue and Stamp Acts energized the idea of an informed citizenry and began to broaden its scope, but the process was interrupted and incomplete.

The publication of John Dickinson's *Letters from a Farmer in Pennsylvania* during the fall and winter of 1767–68 propelled the idea forward. Like Adams's "Dissertation," Dickinson's *Letters* first appeared serially in a newspaper, initially in Philadelphia and then in nineteen papers all along the eastern seaboard. By the time it was published as a pamphlet, Dickinson's *Letters* was a sensation, having reached tens of thousands of readers, a more extensive audience than any other political writer had ever reached with a single effort in the colonies.[33]

The unexpected and unprecedented appeal of Dickinson's *Letters* was based on three interrelated elements: its timing, its content as political argument, and its rhetorical approach. Of these, the argument and the rhetoric were most important since the writings of many other contemporary colonial newspaper spokesmen kindled no such flame. What made Dickinson's constitutional argument so attractive was his readiness to combine a seemingly conciliatory doctrine of loyalty to Britain—accepting parliamentary regulation of external affairs including trade and foreign relations—with an unequivocal denial of Parliament's right to tax the unrepresented American colonies. Dickinson's reasoning promised the colonists exactly what they wanted—participation in the imperial commercial system as well as continuity with the pre-1763 status quo on taxation and provincial government.[34] Had British leaders been ready to accept Dickinson's position instead of ridiculing it, the conflict could have been resolved to the satisfaction of most politically active colonists.[35]

Yet even though Dickinson's argument possessed the essential ingredient for popularity, being a clever formulation of existing but not yet fully articulated beliefs, it was his rhetorical strategy that propelled *Letters* toward its exceptional popularity. Employing an epistolary style borrowed from innovative and widely read novelists such as Samuel Richardson, Dickinson invented for himself an ideal persona for appealing to prosperous American planters, merchants, farmers, and professional men.[36] From the gracious informality of his opening line, "My Dear Countrymen, I am a *Farmer* settled after a variety of fortunes near the banks of the river *Delaware,* in the province of *Pennsylvania,*" to his closing affirmation, "I am resolved to contend for the liberty delivered down to me by my ancestors; but whether I shall do it effectually or not, depends on you, my countrymen," Dickinson's voice was direct, familiar, and morally engaged. Deftly mixing the vocabularies of feeling ("alarming," "dreadful," "fervent," "miserable," "love," and "rage") and of constitutional rights ("authority," "duty," "freedom," "institutions," "obedience," "privilege," "regulation," and "violation"), the sober Pennsylvania farmer invited his readers to share his sense of injustice.[37]

Central to the legitimacy and authority of the farmer was his self-proclaimed stature as an independent, informed citizen, which he announced in the opening paragraph of his first letter. "I received a liberal education and have been engaged in the busy scenes of life," he explained, "but am now convinced, that a man may be as happy without bustle as with it." The farmer was no rustic but an educated gentleman who had deliberately retired to a rural setting, where, he said, "my farm is small, my servants are few and good,

[and] I have a little money at interest." Disclaiming all ambition—"I wish for no more"—and dwelling far from the world of patronage and privilege, Dickinson's farmer embodied the political ideal of personal independence.

But the farmer was not only independent, he was informed. Building on his liberal education, and "being generally master of my time, I spend a good deal of it in a library, which I think the most valuable part of my small estate." Through his reading and conversations with "two or three gentlemen of abilities and learning," the farmer conceded, he had achieved "a greater knowledge in history and the laws and constitution of my country, than is generally attained by men of my class, many of them not being so fortunate as I have been in the opportunities of getting information."[38] This gentleman farmer did not mean to boast—he had merely been "fortunate" in his retirement—but his modesty did not conceal his self-assurance.

The idealized construction of Dickinson's informed citizen, a gentleman with whom all sorts of actual and aspiring colonial gentlemen could identify, combined with his novelistic diction to give *Letters from a Farmer in Pennsylvania* its extraordinary influence. In contrast to Adams's "Dissertation on the Canon and Feudal Law," instead of making the argument for an informed citizenry, Dickinson appealed to the idea by personifying it while capitalizing on its general prevalence among the politically active. Although Dickinson was more conservative than Adams in the sense that he paid no particular attention to the common people as informed defenders of liberty, his writing reached a broader segment of literate Americans than any previous political tract and thus, both in substance and impact, marked an important stage in the enhancement of the ideology of the informed citizen.

By 1770, when Parliament placated the colonies by repealing most of the Townshend duties, which the Pennsylvania farmer had opposed, the importance of an informed citizenry was widely appreciated. The structure of the political conflict had, to a significant degree, dictated that Radical Whigs would use the idea to justify their mobilization of the general populace. Since royal officials saw no threat to liberty in imperial policy, promoting colonists' access to political information was less important to them than strengthening British political ties, a strategy that was both practical and congruent with the ideology of parliamentary and Crown supremacy over the colonies. Radical Whigs in the colonies also tried lobbying in Britain, but they found it a discouraging experience and therefore looked more and more to mobilizing their own constituents. Although few contemporaries recognized fully the long-term implications of this alteration in the structure of politics, the active engagement of common farmers and tradesmen profoundly changed the character of public life. Increasingly, the beliefs of common people were beginning to influence events, sometimes decisively. As Benjamin Franklin argued in 1773, "Much of the Strength of Government depends on the *Opinion* of the People."[39]

The idea of an informed citizenry became inseparable in certain respects from the emerging conception of public opinion, a force that came to be recognized as powerful and unruly. Because the information that circulated publicly shaped public opinion, partisans on both sides of the imperial conflict searched for ways to influence it. Controlling a newspaper was one time-honored approach; in Massachusetts, the royal lieutenant governor, Thomas Hutchinson, secretly sponsored a newspaper, the *Censor*, hoping to reinforce government support among the commercial and political elite without arousing still more of the popular engagement in politics that the royal administration believed was both dangerous and illegitimate. But after less than a year (1769–70), Hutchinson and his associates gave up the project.[40] Thereafter, they would rely more on the levers of authority and patronage and less on public opinion, except insofar as it could be influenced by appeals to deference coming from the lips of such learned and respected officials as the governor, judges, and justices of the peace.[41] Owing to a mixture of ideological considerations—the British administration did not believe in an active citizenry—and pragmatic calculations as to how best to enhance their power, royal officials sought to influence public opinion by shows of authority and by the power of their London connections, not by a broad program of informing the public.

In Massachusetts, the Radical Whigs moved in precisely the opposite direction. In March 1771, the Boston town meeting voted to commemorate the Boston Massacre with an annual oration that would "impress upon our minds the ruinous tendency of standing Armies in Free Cities, and the necessity of such noble exertions in all future times . . . whereby the designs of the Conspirators against the public liberty may still be frustrated."[42] These orations, which continued through 1785, provided basic instruction in Radical Whig ideology to several thousand auditors annually. Every year, the speeches were subsequently published as pamphlets, thus their political instruction circulated beyond Boston's immediate environs.[43] One town, Braintree, copied Boston's example by voting to set up its own "oration or lecture in some branch of Government," to be given by a college graduate, in the first instance, John Adams.[44] For the most "advanced" Radical Whigs, the development of an informed citizenry—informed according to correct principles—had become an urgent priority.

But for most of Massachusetts, not to mention the rest of the colonies, the issue of an informed citizenry remained comparatively abstract and remote. To counter this inattention, Samuel Adams conceived the idea of the Boston Committee of Correspondence in 1772. The impetus for the creation of the committee was the royal administration's decision to include the salaries of the judges of the Massachusetts Superior Court of Judicature on the government's civil list, which meant that they would be paid by Parliament rather than the Massachusetts legislature. However, the larger purpose of the committee was to create a general political awakening in Massachusetts. The pamphlet that the committee produced, which the Boston town meeting voted to print and distribute to the province's 260 towns and districts, was a basic textbook of Radical Whig political theory.

This "Boston Pamphlet," as it came to be called, began with a Lockean statement of natural rights. It went on to explain British constitutional rights generally, especially safeguards against tyranny, before concluding with a detailed list of grievances against the royal government in Boston and the imperial government in London. Strictly speaking, the "Boston Pamphlet" brought little of substance that was new to the ongoing controversy between the friends of government and the Radical Whigs. What was novel was the concept of collectively instructing the broad mass of "voters and inhabitants" through the local town meetings they attended. The pamphlet was written in clear, accessible prose, free of Latin phrases, and was intended both to circulate among local leaders and to be read aloud, which it often was, in town meetings.[45]

Boston's invitation to every town to consider the pamphlet and to issue statements of local political sentiments generated an unprecedented volume of grassroots political expression. Scores of town meetings took up the proposal, appointing local committees to draft statements and then formally voting on whether these statements expressed their communities' views. The statements were then transmitted to Boston, where during the first half of 1773 they were printed in the *Boston Gazette* week after week.[46] Quite deliberately, the activities of the Boston Committee of Correspondence were creating the kind of politically informed yeoman citizenry that John Adams's "Dissertation" had idealized. Whereas Dickinson's learned farmer had instructed property holders in political principles and constitutional law, the Boston committee engaged local notables as well as common farmers and tradesmen in a colloquy so that a broad, popular political education would occur in town meetings. When a New York Whig complained to a member of the Boston Committee of Correspondence about the obstacles to mobilizing opinion in that colony, the Bostonian responded sharply: "You complain of the ignorance of the common people, you may as well complain of the roughness of a desart [*sic*]! Our people would have known as little as yours had we taken as little pains to instruct them."[47]

The strenuous efforts of the Boston Committee of Correspondence, together with the resolutions of nearly 150 towns, could not alter royal policy regarding the salaries of the judges of the superior court, but they did propel the idea of an informed citizenry toward realization in Radical Whig terms among the wide range of men who participated in town meeting politics.[48] Several years later, in the spring of 1776, Samuel Adams would recall that when apathy and inattention to public affairs had seemed to prevail in Massachusetts, the Boston Committee of Correspondence had "raised the Spirits of the People, drawn off their attention from *picking up pins,* and directed their Views to great objects."[49] From the perspective of Radical Whigs, an informed citizenry was effectively one that was active in defense of constitutional rights.

By the summer of 1773, one notion of an informed citizenry had emerged from the vocal expressions of the Massachusetts towns. But elsewhere in the colonies, the importance of the principle of an informed citizenry, and the actual presence of such a citizenry, was less clearly established. Dickinson's *Letters* had been prompted by the Townshend Acts, and following their repeal, little attention had been paid to the subject of an informed citizenry outside of Massachusetts. Only after colonial leaders learned the provisions of the Tea Act in the autumn of 1773 did they generally seek to mobilize opposition. As in the earliest protests against the Revenue and Stamp Acts, the Tea Act resistance was initially concentrated in the commercial communities of the major ports and focused narrowly on nullifying the provisions of the Tea Act, not the long-term question of the value of an informed citizenry.

Indeed, even after the Boston Tea Party and the ensuing mobilization of continental resistance to the Coercive Acts in 1774, self-conscious attention to an informed citizenry commanded little direct concern. In part, this was because British measures made it easy for Radical Whigs to organize opposition in the legislative bodies they came to control and to shape public opinion through newspapers, speeches, and resolutions. To the extent that they needed an informed citizenry, during 1774 and 1775 Radical Whigs felt they had one. Moreover, as time went on, they faced diminishing competition for local and colony-level control. The only political competition they encountered came from leaders whose conceptions of political order were based on a common citizenry that was informed to be deferential and obedient rather than querulous and challenging. The broadest effort these loyalist leaders could imagine to inform the citizenry was to publish pamphlets, which they did. Such authors as Jonathan Boucher, James Chalmers, Joseph Galloway, Daniel Leonard, and Samuel Seabury tried to persuade the colonists of the wisdom of restraint. They sought in 1775 and 1776 to inform the citizenry from a more prudent and cautious perspective. But their writings circulated narrowly in the colonies because at the time they appeared, neither their monitory tone nor their usually pragmatic arguments possessed wide appeal. None of these writers who urged submission to Parliament spoke the language of reactionary or even conservative populism in arguing their cases. Rather, they delivered conservative messages from conservative postures.

This is not surprising since most of their Radical Whig opponents were similarly conventional and also delivered their views in a genteel, educated voice. But the work of one pamphleteer exploded like a comet when it struck the colonies in 1776—that of Thomas Paine. Paine's anonymous pamphlet, *Common Sense,* appeared first in Philadelphia in January 1776 and was then reprinted up and down the coast until by the end of the year it had gone through nineteen American editions, with a total of perhaps 150,000 copies printed.[50] Both in form and in content, *Common Sense* was a new phenomenon.

The innovations in Paine's pamphlet presumed an audience of politically interested common men, not an elevated citizenry of gentlemen and masters of businesses. Placing himself on an equal footing with common citizens, the author chose a stance that would enable him to speak to his audience on a level plane without flourishes. In *Common Sense,* there was none of John Dickinson's polite condescension or the "Boston Pamphlet"'s stern formality. Instead, Paine addressed his readers as one common man using everyday language and homely illustrations to speak to other common men. The language and tone that some college-educated Radical Whigs, like John Adams, rejected as vulgar in *Common Sense* were actually keys to its influence. Repetition of the word "bloody" and references to William the Conqueror as a "French bastard" offended genteel taste, but it was just this kind of bold, plain language that gave *Common Sense* its pungent magnetism.

The substance of *Common Sense* was even more of a departure because instead of attacking particular violations of the vaunted British constitution, it laid an axe to the entire political system, root and branch, pronouncing it too rotten, too corrupt to ever be corrected. Paine's solution, obviously, was total independence, not some kind of patched-up accommodation. The time to act was now, when American human and natural resources were sufficient and Britain, beset by decay and corruption, was in a weakened state. As Paine viewed it, the present was the optimum time to act in a struggle that could only end in American victory. Like the Pennsylvania farmer a decade earlier, Paine told his audience what it wanted to hear at a time when no "responsible" Whig was ready to embrace warfare with such cheerful enthusiasm.

The vigor of Paine's arguments, which displayed more ardor than logic, enhanced their appeal. The fact that Paine also vented moral outrage, reproaching Britain angrily as a selfish, tyrannical parent, also struck a responsive chord.[51] For a decade, Americans had been trying conscientiously to find a way to reconcile their rights and their interests with loyalty to Britain; but in 1775 the king had classed them as rebels subject to military conquest. *Common Sense* depicted a corrupt and haughty Britain making war on plain, well-meaning, honest Americans. British policy was outrageous.

Paine's pamphlet was oriented toward a literate but not well-educated, well-informed, or critically sophisticated audience. Yet it mobilized American men as never before. Its extensive circulation—into perhaps 100,000 households in 1776—is clear evidence that the idea of common men being politically informed enjoyed general currency. No longer, it seemed, would it be necessary to argue that the citizenry should be informed, as Radical Whigs had done since 1765; the extraordinary popularity of *Common Sense* proved that common men embraced this belief widely. But the success of the idea and its apparent realization in 1776 raised some complicated questions. What, exactly, should gentlemen and common men know, and how should they be informed? There was no consensus on what being informed meant.

During the surge of patriotic ardor that sustained American public life from Lexington and Concord through the Declaration of Independence, only a few revolutionary leaders recognized the concept of an informed citizenry as a pressing issue. But their thoughts prefigured debates that would lie ahead. John Adams saw dangers in *Common Sense* itself because, although he applauded Paine's proindependence conclusion, the pamphlet attacked the notion of balanced government that Adams regarded as essential for preserving liberty. Paine had misinformed his vast audience by misrepresenting the British constitution and by rejecting principles that would be vital to the future of the American republic. From John Adams's perspective, *Common Sense* was a useful but dangerous pamphlet because it rejected time-tested principles of constitutional liberty in favor of naive democratic ideas like unicameralism.[52] Such ill-informed rhetoric, Adams believed, was pernicious.

But in 1776, few revolutionary leaders shared Adams's fastidious concerns. Instead, it was the major themes relating to the conception of an informed citizenry, ideas that Adams had laid out in "A Dissertation on the Canon and Feudal Law," that were widely expressed. Tyranny was bound up with luxury, corruption, and ignorance. Monarchy was said to require an ignorant population, whereas republics could survive only if their citizens were informed. The revolutionary struggle pitted republican industry against monarchical idleness, virtue against vice, and knowledge against ignorance. As the provincial congress of Massachusetts succinctly proclaimed in January 1776, using language composed by John Adams himself: "As a government so popular can be supported only by universal knowledge and virtue, in the body of the people, it is the duty of all ranks to promote the means of education for the rising generation, as well as true religion, purity of manners, and integrity of life among all orders and degrees." The congress ordered that this resolution be read at every court opening and every annual town meeting and urged the clergy of Massachusetts to read it to their congregations after the next Sunday service.[53] Later that year, Pennsylvania and North Carolina, acting from similar motives, would each include a provision for the support of public schools and universities in their new constitutions.[54] The necessity of a virtuous and informed citizenry was officially recognized as a fundamental principle of this republican revolution.

It was easy enough to affirm and publicize the vital importance of an informed citizenry in revolutionary assemblies, where the idea was supported by general consensus. For many revolutionary leaders, this idea was only one dimension of long-held Radical Whig, Protestant, and Enlightenment beliefs. The chief function of legislative resolutions was to raise to prominence some of the latent assumptions of mid-eighteenth-century American political culture. However, with this heightened recognition of the need for an informed citizenry came the realization that ways and means must be found to implement the idea in practical terms. Once the process of forming republican governments was under way, it became evident that reliance on an informed citizenry was so crucial that systematic steps must be taken to assure its existence among the broad base of common property holders. Enunciating principles was a necessary first step, but it was not sufficient in itself. Measures must be taken to make an informed citizenry a permanent feature of the new society.

In states like Massachusetts and Connecticut, which already supported common and grammar schools in addition to their colleges, Harvard and Yale, new institutions were not required. What was needed was a fresh commitment to the old ones. Indeed, everywhere exhortation was cheaper and easier than innovation. The institutions that could nourish an informed citizenry—the family, the church, the press, and the post office, as well as schools—were promoted rhetorically. Samuel Adams laid out some of the key arguments as early as November 1775 after he learned "that some of our Towns have dismissd [*sic*] their School masters, alleging that the extraordinary Expence of defending the Country renders them unable to support them." This was wrongheaded, Adams declared, and he urged "the leading Gentlemen [to] do eminent Service to the Publick, by impressing upon the Minds of the People, the necessity and Importance of encouraging that *System of Education,* which . . . is so well calculated to diffuse among the Individuals of the Community, the Principles of Morality, so essentially necessary for the Preservation of publick Liberty." Adams spoke with a sense of urgency, both for the present and for perpetuity: "No People will tamely surrender their Liberties, nor can they easily be subdued, when Knowledge is diffusd [*sic*] and Virtue preserved."[55]

A free press was no less important than schools. As early as October 1774, the Continental Congress spelled out exactly why it was so critical, explaining that "besides the advancement of truth, science, morality, and arts in general, in its diffusion of liberal sentiments on the administration of Government, its ready communication of thoughts between subjects, and its consequential promotion of union among them," the press "shamed or intimidated" public officials into behaving properly.[56] Moreover, because, as Thomas Paine put it, the press's influence "over our manners and morals" was so extensive, the issue of its control was vital.[57] When George Mason and Thomas Jefferson prepared Virginia's Declaration of Rights in 1776, they emphasized that "freedom of the Press is one of the greatest bulwarks of liberty" and that "printing presses shall be free."[58] Linking an informed citizenry to a free press, a Congregational clergyman declared that a free press was an "eminent instrument of promoting knowledge, and great palladium [protection] of public liberty."[59]

The institution of the post office was another necessity for an informed citizenry. During the Revolutionary War, Thomas Jefferson complained that "so many falsehoods have been propagated that nothing is now believed" unless it came with a pedigree. As a result, "our people merely for want of intelligence which they may rely on are becoming lethargick and insensible." In light of this wartime experience, leaders like Jefferson, Adams, and other congressmen came to recognize that "the speedy and frequent communication of intelligence is really of great consequence"[60] and that a post office, though usually financed by trade correspondence, was a political requirement even more than a commercial one.

Revolutionary leaders everywhere recognized that social and political institutions must play crucial roles in the formation of an informed citizenry. At the same time, however, nearly all institutions had problems that were more intractable and entirely different from the logistical obstacles that interfered with the prompt, reliable operation of the post office. Churches, for example, had long been viewed by leaders from all points of the political compass—whether monarchist or republican—as fundamental agencies for promoting the morality and enforcing the integrity that Radical Whigs, now republicans, understood to be vital to the new political order. But whereas monarchists could rely on established churches to not only instruct the people in morality in the parishes but also control the schools, colleges, and universities, republicans were moving to end religious establishments.[61] Terminating the institutional arrangements connecting church and state put moral education in jeopardy. Among some New England clergymen who were otherwise enthusiastic supporters of the Revolution, fears mounted: "Let the restraints of religion once be broken down, as they infallibly would be by leaving the subject of public worship to the humors of the multitude," a Massachusetts preacher warned the legislature, "and we might well defy all human wisdom and power to support and preserve order and government in the state."[62] This was not groundless panic; all of recorded history seemed to prove that order and morality required the integration of church, state, and schooling. The unconverted, rationalistic John Adams, imbued as he was with New England traditions, believed that these links were necessary to maintain personal and social morality.[63]

But the tendency of the states, now freed from British control, was to deny any one church the sole or even primary responsibility for educating children and youth.[64] Instead, the states turned first to the family, falling back on that most basic and traditional agency of order. Even in states like Pennsylvania and North Carolina, where revolutionary constitutions prescribed the establishment of public schools, attendance was voluntary and parents were expected to pay their children's tuition costs. The combination of serious concern for education with the reality of institutional disarray was illustrated by the difficulties that revolutionary leaders encountered as they tried to provide the best and most suitable education for their own children—mostly boys but also girls—before and during the war. Not only did these parents, principally fathers, have to devise curricula for their children, they also had to contrive the means of their instruction. Outside of New England, education was a highly individualized rather than a communal undertaking, and there were no well-worn paths to follow.

In England, educational goals were synchronized with a system of social stratification that did not quite match American expectations at any level, from great planters and transatlantic merchants to tradesmen and yeoman farmers. The British mixture of objectives of learning—ornament, public service, gentility, and practical utility—never seemed to fit satisfactorily. James Maury, the Anglican priest and Virginia schoolmaster who prepared Thomas Jefferson for the College of William and Mary in his log cabin schoolhouse and who gave the question of a planter's education considerable thought, concluded that none of the English models suited the needs of Virginians. The "English Gentleman of the upper Class" as well as the "Nobleman" were far above material pursuits and thus could properly become deeply engaged in classical studies, leaving their "studious Leisure and Philosophic Repose" only to answer their country's "pressing Calls" to public service. But Virginia's leaders were enmeshed in material pursuits and considered it a waste of time to study Greek and Latin. Maury did not completely renounce the study of classical languages; he pointed out that some students, like young Jefferson, thrived on it. But for the majority of Virginia planters', lawyers', and merchants' sons, he prescribed such "useful and necessary Studies, as English Grammar, reading, writing, arithmetic, History, Geography, Chronology, the more practical Parts of the Mathematics, Rhetoric, Eloquence & other Species of polite & useful Learning" such as English literature. Thus educated, Virginians could improve their property, serve their country, speak in public assemblies, and engage in conversation that rose above the subjects of cards, dice, horses, and cockfighting. The particular social roles and standing of Virginians had no true British equivalents. As Maury concluded: "Because the Genius of our People, their Way of Life, their Circumstances in Point of Fortune, the Customs & Manners & Humors of the Country, difference us in so many important Respects from Europeans, . . . a Plan of Education, however judiciously adapted to these last would no more fit us, than an Almanac, calculated for the Latitude of London, would that of Williamsburg."[65] Even before the imperial conflict turned the colonists toward independence, a recognition of American distinctiveness was emerging in the search for new models of an educated citizen.

Maury's judgments about education in Virginia and England were based on secular considerations, not morality. But for American parents, morals were often a paramount concern, and vanity and extravagance, if not outright debauchery, came to be seen as hallmarks of English education. As Landon Carter, a leading planter, remarked in 1770, "every body begins to laugh at English education" because it had become "the learning of the foppishness of the fancy."[66] Such ridicule was combined with a sense of anxiety as parents contemplated the proper education of their children.

The experiences of Henry Laurens, the South Carolina patriot leader, are especially revealing because, as a widower, he had to supervise his daughters' education as well as that of his sons and because South Carolina possessed only scant provisions for any kind of education. Consequently, Laurens's pursuit of his children's education, which was not limited by expense, showed that for even the most privileged Americans, institutional deficiencies, as well as the absence of clear models, obstructed the formation of an informed citizenry. Laurens's difficulties dated from at least as early as 1763, when he attempted to hire a teacher for Charleston's "provincial Free School," which had been created by the colony's legislature in 1712. The teacher was expected to instruct children in "writing, arithmetic, merchants accounts, navigation, surveying," decimal fractions, and "other practical parts of the Mathematics."[67] But even with a teacher of "sound moral principles," the school remained weak. No history, geography, or foreign or classical languages were being taught. Seven years later, at which time Laurens's oldest son was tutoring his eleven-year-old daughter in French and English grammar, Laurens complained that his own colony was "perhaps the worst off at present for Schools of any province in America."[68] Laurens, who believed deeply in an elite version of an informed citizenry, was mortified by his fellow Carolinians' unwillingness to support the institutions that were necessary to give it a decent foundation. "The inhabitants of South Carolina," he lamented, "have almost totally neglected the education of their Youth upon a Public foundation." Content to employ tutors and send their children abroad for education, they had "refused upon divers applications even to enlarge . . . our present little Provincial School, scarcely worthy of the name of a School."[69]

At bottom, Laurens's complaint centered on the moral costs of sending children away for their education. The reason he was willing to struggle "with some of my Country Men and Neighbours, as well in our little Senate as out of Doors," was because he believed that much more than gold and silver were lost by exporting their children. "We are," he complained, "deprived of the principal Happiness which we can enjoy in this Life, that of seeing the daily Progress of our children in Knowledge and Virtue, and of a Consciousness that Nothing on our Part has been omitted to restrain, to dissuade them from vicious and dishonourable Practices." A local college, which Laurens insisted must be strictly nonsectarian, was needed to educate youth above the elementary level. But the creation of the University of South Carolina was a generation away.[70]

As a result, Laurens was forced to tread the path so many other wealthy South Carolinians had followed by educating his sons in England, where he encountered precisely the same kinds of problems in finding a suitable curriculum and moral environment that James Maury and Landon Carter had described. Britain's two famous universities, he learned, were "universally censured"; indeed, "Oxford in particular is spoken of as a School for Licentiousness and Debauchery." The private academies Laurens visited were also discouraging. "Not one in ten," he exclaimed, was "good for any Thing."[71] Finally, when Laurens did locate an acceptable school run by the Reverend Richard Clarke, his concerns centered on personal character development more than academic accomplishments: "Above all, I entreat you to keep him [his son] in due Subordination, to impress the Fear of God upon his Mind, to shew him the great difference between Good and Evil, Truth and Error, between a useful and a fine man in Society."[72] Moral and academic training were inseparable in Laurens's view, and both were essential to the formation of the "useful" man, the informed citizen.

Before independence, the scarcity and weaknesses of public institutions for creating an informed citizenry were particularly glaring in South Carolina. But once the war began, disruptions to academies and colleges made the South Carolina case more typical of conditions throughout the colonies for at least several years. Such revolutionary republicans as Robert Morris of Philadelphia and John Adams of Massachusetts, who would previously have relied on domestic institutions, now looked abroad and, like Laurens earlier, struggled to find the proper combination of moral and academic training. But whereas Laurens had chosen England for his sons' education before the war for independence, Morris and Adams turned to the Continent, basing their decision on considerations beyond the obvious political reason of being at war with Britain.

What preoccupied Robert Morris and John Adams above all was the social context and noncurricular content of the entire educational experience. "These Young Gentlemen," Robert Morris remarked in 1781, "are expected to pass their Days in America, under republican Governments, where, . . . they may probably be of some Political Consequence."[73] Accordingly, it was vital that their sons combine academic and moral training in order to acquire values consistent with the republican character of the United States. These considerations led Morris to "prefer Geneva, where as I am told, the Manners of the People are favorable to the Practice of Virtue, and being a republic, I should suppose the Stile of living may partake of that Plainess, and Simplicity, best adapted to such Governments."[74] For John Adams, who, unlike Morris, did not live in America at the time but at his diplomatic mission on the Continent and who also held the highest academic aspirations for the brilliant and precocious John Quincy Adams, the choice was Leyden, the leading republican university in the world. Here his father directed the thirteen-year-old boy in training to be a statesman not only to extract every bit of learning he could from the great professors but also to inform himself fully on the university's operation, "and especially to remark every Thing in it, that may be imitated, in the Universities of your own Country."[75] The ultimate objective of this foreign training was the building of American institutions.

Wartime conditions had created a need to send the nation's future leading citizens abroad, even though revolutionary leaders shared the Reverend James Maury's sense that a European education was incompatible with American society. To his second son, Charles, who remained in Massachusetts, John Adams's counsel was to "study earnestly, go to Colledge [*sic*] and be an Ornament to your Country." Adams, who knew institutions on both sides of the Atlantic firsthand, concluded that "education is better at Cambridge [Massachusetts], than in Europe. Besides every Child ought to be educated in his own Country." Regarding his first son, John Quincy Adams, he told his wife, Abigail, "I regret extreamly that [he] . . . is not to have his Education at home."[76] The most learned professors at the oldest universities could not create the moral environment or attract the peer group that was best suited to republican education.

Adams's colleague in diplomacy, John Jay, drew similar conclusions, arguing that domestic education was preferable because parents' "Advice, Authority and Example are frequently of more worth than the Lessons of hireling Professors, particularly on the subjects of Religion, Morality, Virtue and Prudence." The wartime experience with European institutions, like the prewar experience with British schools and universities, convinced Americans who were most knowledgeable that American institutions must be developed. Jay did admit that a few subjects, like languages, could be better learned in Europe. But in a letter written from Paris to Robert Morris, Jay frankly declared that education was better in the United States than in Europe: "I do not hesitate to prefer an American Education. I fear that the Ideas which my Countrymen in general conceive of Europe are in many Respects rather too high."[77] The republican preferences for virtue over elegance and socially useful education over ornamental education cast a shadow over European brilliance. Before the war, Henry Laurens had exclaimed after bringing his sons to England for their schooling: "Oh my Friend! how much are we to blame in Carolina, we have reduced ourselves to a Necessity of sending our Children 1,100 Leagues to learn ABC imperfectly . . . at a vast Expence of Money, some times a total Loss of Morals and Constitution, when such ABC might be better obtained at home."[78] But now that the most wealthy and ambitious citizens of the United States had learned Laurens's lesson, they resolved to work to form their children in their families and in American schools and colleges. They would seek to create an institutional environment in America that would nurture republican citizens.

The new emphasis on virtue and on the family as the best agency for inculcating it promoted a revaluation of girls' as well as boys' education. Although domestic training remained the primary focus of education for girls, some fathers began to look beyond it. Henry Laurens, who paid tuition for his daughter, Polly, to learn drawing, writing, arithmetic, and French, was committed to female domesticity. To his brother, who was supervising Polly's education, Laurens wrote: "Amidst all these finer Branches of a Carolina Ladies Education, I hope she will learn to cut out and make up a Piece of Linnen, and even a Piece of white or blue Woolen for her Negroes, to administer family Medicine, and be able by and by, to direct her Maids with Judgement and understanding, in such and many other essential Duties in Domestic Life, which She has now an Opportunity of learning from her Dear Aunt." Besides promoting these conventional skills, however, Laurens asked that Polly be directed "to peruse attentively and go twice over the History of England"[79] so as to give her a grounding for understanding politics, a subject that had generally been off-limits to women. Laurens was not suggesting that girls should be educated to participate in public affairs, as were boys; he simply believed they should not be kept in ignorance. Such a view was more fully articulated in a Boston Radical Whig magazine in which "Clio," the goddess of history, called on "Man" to "bestow his wisdom to improve" the "*Female Mind,*" which was "rich with native genius and noble sentiment." One of the benefits, Clio noted, would be "the advantage . . . to those who are under [women's] care."[80] Even before American independence, the notion of an educated, virtuous republican wife and mother, as Jan Lewis and Linda K. Kerber have explained, was taking shape.[81]

Because of the focus on the family as the incubator of the virtuous, informed republican citizen, women could not remain in total political ignorance, lacking any knowledge of history. In contrast, leaders perceived no need to improve the education of African Americans and Native Americans, who were seen as being outside the political community. At the same time that the secular Jefferson was proposing grand reforms for the education of white Virginians, his plan "for teaching Indian boys" was limited to maintaining the charity school initially financed by the Englishman Robert Boyle, at which the curriculum was confined to "reading, writing, vulgar arithmetic, the catechism and the principles of the Christian religion."[82] The old charity school model of piety and useful service continued to dominate consideration of Native American and African American education. Since these dependent peoples lacked even the indirect access to political inclusion that the role of wife and mother offered women, leaders saw no reason for them to read Catharine Macaulay's or anyone else's history of England. Their duty was to comply humbly with the authorities, not to defend their few rights or to judge their betters.

When it came to actually establishing an informed citizenry in America after independence, revolutionary leaders had no generally accepted, clearly understood models to imitate. If American leaders were going to lay the institutional foundations for an informed citizenry, they would have to invent them. The rhetorical creation and valuation of the republican wife and mother was one new approach that enhanced the public significance of family life. The freeing of religious sects by the state legislatures was an even more radical and problematic innovation since it encouraged all Protestants to pursue salvation and virtue according to their own lights in order to promote a net increase in public virtue. Both of these innovations, together with the widening state adherence to the doctrine of free speech as a means for assuring an informed citizenry, required no public expenditures; they simply freed Americans to follow republican ideals. Another innovation of far-reaching significance was potentially costly, however: the statutory commitment to public education through schools and colleges.

The fiscal implications of "public education" in the revolutionary era were ambiguous. In Britain "public" schools and colleges were open to the public for admission, but they were financed wholly out of student tuitions, fees, and private endowments, not tax revenues. In a strict sense, this was the meaning of "public education" in 1776. Indeed, when one considers the Pennsylvania and North Carolina constitutions of that year, it appears that their provisions for public schools and universities meant that they would be "public" in the British sense and that neither state intended to raise tax revenues to supply free education for its inhabitants. Rather, each state encouraged the formation of an extensive, tuition-based educational system.

The New England "public" school model, which differed from the British model, was also available for consideration. In Connecticut and Massachusetts, tax revenues and public lotteries as well as tuition charges and student fees all paid for the public education regime. Colonial statutes required towns to lay taxes to support schools, and although all towns did not always comply, in most communities the public taxed itself in order to supply "free" elementary education for boys and, increasingly, for girls as well. The public defrayed the capital cost of erecting the school building, normally a cheap wooden structure, and also paid the teacher's salary, but parents bore the responsibility of maintaining the schoolhouse, providing it with firewood, and supplying their children's textbooks. At the level of the grammar school, where Latin was taught and where a boy might prepare for college, actual public provisions fell far short of statutory requirements. Less than half of the towns that were required to support grammar schools with tax revenues did so (65 out of 144 in 1765), and many boys prepared for college with local clergymen as private tutors, as John Adams did in the 1740s.[83] At the college level, both Harvard and Yale received some capital funds and operating expenses from their colonial legislatures, but they also relied on tuitions, fees, gifts, and endowments. With the exception of a few charity scholars, the students paid for the operating costs of education. This New England model, in which "public" meant the use of tax revenues in addition to the passage of enabling legislation, would prove influential over time as states in other regions adopted some of its elements.

Thomas Jefferson proposed the most dramatic revision of the New England arrangement in Virginia in the 1779 Bill for the More General Diffusion of Knowledge. This bill was part of a comprehensive revision of state law and institutions designed to make Virginia a model republic. For Jefferson and James Madison, its principal advocates, the permanent establishment of an informed citizenry was the central purpose of the proposal. To his old mentor, the widely respected attorney and judge George Wythe, Jefferson declared that this was "by far the most important bill in our whole code." "Preach, my dear Sir," he entreated Wythe, "a crusade against ignorance; establish and improve the law for educating the common people."[84] This law originated in Radical Whig fears concerning the seductive, deceitful paths that tyrants used to seize unlawful power, as well as in the Enlightenment faith in reason and knowledge as agents for human improvement.

The bill stated that its first objective was to block the rise of tyranny, and it asserted that an informed citizenry was ultimately the only effective barrier against despotism. It proposed to "illuminate . . . the minds of the people at large, and more especially to give them knowledge of those facts, which history exhibiteth, that, possessed thereby of the experience of other ages and countries, they may be enabled to know ambition under all its shapes." Thus informed, common people would be "prompt to exert their natural powers" so as to repel tyranny. A further goal was to secure "publick happiness," which required laws that were "wisely formed and honestly administered."[85]

Since common people could not make and implement laws on their own, they needed the guidance of men possessing natural "genius and virtue," whose "liberal education" rendered them worthy to rule. For that reason, the bill called for a two-tier school system leading to college, whereby the ablest and most virtuous youths might be brought forward "without regard to wealth, birth or other accidental condition." As in New England, the whole system was to be supported financially by a combination of taxes and tuitions. At the elementary level, "all the free children, male and female," should have three years of schooling at public expense. The subjects of instruction were basic—reading, writing, and arithmetic—but the textbooks would simultaneously "make them acquainted with Graecian, Roman, English and American history."[86] This secular education for girls as well as boys, without either Bible or catechism, would establish the foundation for the republican commonwealth of Virginia.

To supply republican leaders, the bill provided for higher levels of training. Grammar schools located on 100-acre lots spaced throughout Virginia would not be mere log cabins but instead physical emblems of the permanent commitment to an informed citizenry. Each one would be constructed at state expense out of "brick or stone" with "a room for the school, a hall to dine in, four rooms for a master and usher, and ten or twelve lodging rooms for the scholars."[87] The curriculum would include Latin and Greek, English grammar, geography, and the higher levels of arithmetic such as decimals and cube roots.[88] Most of the students would pay their own way, but each year, one boy with at least two years of training would be selected from each of the local elementary schools to attend his region's grammar school at state expense if his "parents are too poor" to pay tuition.[89] Such gratis scholars would be progressively weeded out over a six-year period so that at the highest level each grammar school would have only one gratis "senior" student. One of these gratis seniors, "of the best learning and most hopeful genius and disposition," would then be sent for three years to the College of William and Mary to complete his education at public expense.[90] To assure that the college itself would be adequate to the new demands of supplying leadership, Jefferson prepared a bill to revamp its constitution, finances, and curriculum, including provisions for secular professorships in ethics/fine arts, law, history, mathematics, anatomy/medicine, natural philosophy and history, ancient languages, and modern languages.[91] By offering modest but unmistakable encouragement for state-sponsored upward mobility, Jefferson's plan departed significantly from all earlier schemes, such as that of Benjamin Franklin, with which it had other common elements. In the Virginia scheme, Radical Whig ideology and Enlightenment learning were combined.

At the same time, Jefferson's plan aimed to unite mass popular education with the perpetuation of elite, albeit enlightened, rule. "The best geniuses will be raked from the rubbish annually," Jefferson explained, thereby gaining for the state "those talents which nature has sown as liberally among the poor as the rich, but which perish without use, if not sought for and cultivated." As for those possessing merely common abilities, the public schooling would develop their political understanding: "It will avail them of the experience of other nations; it will qualify them as judges of the actions and designs of men; it will enable them to know ambition under every guise it may assume; and knowing it, to defeat its views."[92] Overall, the statutes would create a broad base of discerning, watchful citizens who would be qualified to choose wisely among their liberally educated leaders. In a state whose citizens had already selected such leaders as Thomas Jefferson, Richard Henry Lee, James Madison, George Mason, and George Washington, the reforms did not point so much to any radical change in the character of politics as to a regular process to institutionalize the nascent republican order and guard against future despots and demagogues.

In New England, where the means for informing and educating the inhabitants were well developed, Radical Whigs were confident that the informed citizenry had already proved itself in the crises of 1775 and 1776. Virtually no one believed that major reform, such as the reforms Jefferson proposed for Virginia, was necessary since the system had so recently demonstrated that it was not broken. Yet new concerns went beyond Radical Whig attention to citizens as politically informed defenders of liberty. The empowerment of common men at the moment of independence did not necessarily encourage respect for the best informed, most learned citizens or respect for men who believed in elite republican rule according to New England models or the principles of the Virginia reform.

In New Jersey, "a Prejudice against liberal Education" existed among the people, and John Adams reckoned that "there is a Spice of this every where." Elite snobbery was partly to blame, Adams thought, and he admonished "Gentlemen of Education to lay aside Some of their Airs, of Scorn, Vanity and Pride." "Gentlemen," Adams warned, "cannot expect the Confidence of the common People if they treat them ill, or refuse hautily [*sic*] to comply with some of their favorite Notions."[93] But this antagonism between men with common education and those few possessed of greater learning cut deeper than issues of style. There was "a Jealousy or an Envy taking Place among the Multitude" that was aimed at "Men of Learning." The short-term practical result of this jealousy "in various Parts of these States," including New England, was "a Wish to exclude [men of learning] from the public Councils and from military Command."[94]

From a long-term perspective, this tendency was even more ominous since it would lead to rule by parochial, self-interested demagogues. To revolutionary leaders who believed that a republic, above all other forms of government, needed the guidance of disinterested men of expanded learning and vision, the jealousy Adams identified was poisonous.[95] Day-to-day necessities in 1776 would push aside the worries of the Massachusetts delegate to the Continental Congress, but his fear "that human Nature will be found to be the Same in America as it has been in Europe, and that the true Principles of Liberty will not be Sufficiently attended to," would not only activate Virginia reformers to propose a new foundation of and for republican institutions but also motivate New Englanders.[96]

In Massachusetts, Radical Whig and Enlightenment ideas were interwoven with the Puritan legacy and clerical influence in the laying of the foundation of republican society. As in Virginia, an informed citizenry was seen as crucial. According to the patriot clergyman who preached the 1778 election sermon, "Knowledge and learning will be considered as most essentially requisite for a free, righteous government. . . . A certain degree of knowledge is absolutely to be diffused through a state for the preservation of its liberties and the quiet of government."[97] Here the Radical Whig defense of liberty merged with the Puritan and clerical concern for order. But there were also larger, enlightened aspirations: "A republican government and science mutually promote and support each other." Underlying these calls to support learning were the fears John Adams had expressed earlier. The election homily of 1778 asserted: "Every kind of useful knowledge will be carefully encouraged and promoted by the rulers of a free state, unless they should happen to be men of ignorance themselves; in which case they and their community will be in danger of sharing the fate of blind guides and their followers. The education of youth, by instructors properly qualified, the establishment of societies for useful arts and sciences, the encouragement of persons of superior abilities, will always command the attention of wise rulers."[98] Were the Massachusetts legislators "wise rulers" or "men of ignorance"? When the preacher delivered these lines, he knew he must tread carefully since most of his audience had never attended college. Yet he drew on a common social vision that was rooted in colonial experience.

Two years later, the new Massachusetts constitution, drafted by John Adams, formalized the admonitions of this 1778 sermon. Recasting the mission of government in broad republican rather than Puritan terms, the constitution of 1780 proclaimed a comprehensive public responsibility not merely for education at all levels but also for creating an advanced, enlightened, knowledgeable, and progressive society. Like the Virginia reform proposals of the previous year, the new Massachusetts constitution was designed to enable republican principles and institutions to endure; furthermore, it affirmed that they could survive only in the custody of a virtuous and informed citizenry.

The constitution emphasized the fundamental importance of the Radical Whig ideal and furnished institutional means for its support. In the opening section, the Declaration of the Rights of the Inhabitants called for "the public worship of God" because public happiness and civil order required "instructions in piety, religion and morality." Significantly, this religious establishment was justified in secular rather than sacred terms; the republican state was interested not in salvation but in order and ethical behavior. Religious instruction was said to supply social benefits, and for that reason, "the support and maintenance of public protestant teachers of piety, religion and morality" were required in every locality within the state. "Attendance upon the instructions of the public teachers," or churchgoing, was also enjoined unless it violated an individual's religious scruples.[99] The chief purpose of these institutional arrangements was to maintain a citizenry sufficiently informed in Christian principles to embrace morality and therefore civic virtue. Being morally informed was an essential element of the prescription for republican citizenship.

Political information, however, was equally important, and as in Virginia, the Massachusetts Declaration of Rights also guaranteed the "liberty of the press," which it declared to be "essential to the security of freedom in a state."[100] In addition to a free press, all of the other means that had been employed by patriots to inform the people from 1765 onward would be protected in perpetuity: "to assemble to consult upon the common good; give instructions to their representatives and to request of the legislative body, by way of addresses, petitions, or remonstrances, redress of the wrongs done them, and of the grievances they suffer."[101] These general guarantees of free press and assembly were widely adopted by the states in their revolutionary constitutions, which drew upon the Radical Whig repertoire of requirements for the preservation of a free state.

In Massachusetts, these passages in the Declaration of Rights recalled the English heritage of the recent past, whereas the provision for a religious establishment—so contrary to the letter and spirit of the Virginia reforms—blended elements of the Puritan legacy with an Anglican conservatism that linked piety and order and referred to citizens as "subjects of the commonwealth." Combining these distinct, even conflicting, traditions—Radical Whig, Puritan, and Anglican—to promote a coherent political order was problematic and would later generate divisions. But in the short term, the combination helped to sustain the revolutionary coalition.

The fifth chapter of the Massachusetts constitution, devoted to "The University at Cambridge, and Encouragement of Literature &C," was even more innovative. It expressed an entirely new enlightened vision of an informed and cultivated citizenry that would be elaborated by leaders throughout the United States for two generations and would ultimately have major institutional consequences. Here John Adams went far beyond the themes sounded in his 1765 "Dissertation on the Canon and Feudal Law" and drew on cosmopolitan Enlightenment ideas in articulating a new mission for government.

The constitutional provisions concerning Harvard were in themselves ordinary. Chiefly, the constitution guaranteed Harvard's property and its system of governance. In addition, however, the state extended the purpose of the university far beyond its original Christian and civic missions. "The encouragement of arts and sciences, and all good literature," the constitution proclaimed, "tends to the honour of God, the advantage of the christian religion, and the great benefit of this and the other United States of America."[102] Here Massachusetts was assigning a broad range of secular objectives to the university, objectives whose fulfillment would enrich the state and the nation.

What was remarkable, however, was not the portion dealing with the university; the ideal of an informed elite, after all, reached back to the Renaissance. It was the next paragraph, entitled "The Encouragement of Literature," on the education of common people—presumably common men—that was revolutionary. Here earlier Puritan and Radical Whig traditions were transformed into an Enlightenment ideal of comprehensive education that would ensure a society that was not only Christian and free but also just, humane, and progressive. According to the commonwealth's constitution:

> Wisdom, and knowledge, as well as virtue, diffused generally among the body of the people, being necessary for the preservation of their rights and liberties; and as these depend on spreading the opportunities and ad-

vantages of education in the various parts of the country, and among the different orders of the people, it shall be the duty of legislatures and magistrates, in all future periods of this Commonwealth, to cherish the interests of literature and the sciences, and all seminaries of them; especially the university at Cambridge, public schools, and grammar schools in the towns; to encourage private societies and public institutions, rewards and immunities, for the promotion of agriculture, arts, sciences, commerce, trades, manufactures, and a natural history of the country; to countenance and inculcate the principles of humanity and general benevolence, public and private charity, industry and frugality, honesty and punctuality in their dealings; sincerity, good humor, and all social affections, and generous sentiments among the people.[103]

Adams's tribute to universal education, embracing all productive and illuminating fields of endeavor, carried Massachusetts well beyond Radical Whig notions of an informed citizenry as a bulwark against tyranny. The objective was more than a defense of liberty; it was the positive creation of a progressive, enlightened, and virtuous society.

For Adams and Jefferson—indeed, the entire generation of revolutionary leaders—the success of liberty and of republican government and society rested on the crucial equation of virtue and knowledge. As they saw it, Rousseau's notion of a virtuous (and ignorant) savage was absurd because a benighted, uninformed people could not be virtuous, just as a virtuous people could not be ignorant. Within this consensus, the principal differences among patriots concerned the place of religion in a republican society. According to evangelical formulations, people who came to know Christ and embraced his message became unselfish, virtuous citizens.[104] Mainstream Protestants, too, linked good citizenship to knowledge of religious truth. According to Benjamin Rush, a Pennsylvania Presbyterian who signed the Declaration of Independence, "a Christian cannot fail of being a republican." In Rush's mind, the two were conflated inasmuch as "Republicanism is a part of the truth of Christianity."[105] To the latitudinarian president of Yale College, Ezra Stiles, the idea that "all should be taught to read the scriptures" was axiomatic. At the same time, Rush, a scientist and college founder, concluded that "without religion I believe learning does real mischief to the morals and principles of mankind."[106] Knowledge, after all, was linked to sin in the Garden of Eden, and the Devil himself was a knowledgeable fallen angel. To many revolutionary leaders, the idea of raising a wall of separation between Christianity and the new republican states seemed self-contradictory and ill-advised if the merger between knowledge and virtue was to flourish.

Thomas Jefferson and his Virginia constituents, however, saw things differently. In principle, Baptists argued, religion was a private, not a public, matter; and besides, pragmatists pointed out, religious establishments led to sectarian wrangling and infringements on freedom of worship. Both Adams and Jefferson shared an essentially secular orientation, looking to Christianity chiefly for ethical standards, not personal theological truth, but they disagreed over the relationship between organized religion and the state. Adams, whose outlook reflected that of his Massachusetts constituency, saw the need for a religious establishment, whereas Jefferson came to the conclusion that religion must be separate from the state and proudly championed a law to that end, the Virginia Statute of Religious Freedom. This statute echoed Milton in its claim "that truth is great and will prevail if left to herself, that she is the proper and sufficient antagonist to error."[107] On both sides, however, revolutionary leaders agreed that republican states bore a central responsibility for guaranteeing their own survival by making provisions to assure the existence of an informed citizenry.

Before the movement for independence began, the idea of an informed citizenry was already an established part of the Whig and Radical Whig ideologies. It was the mobilization of colonial opposition to imperial reform that made the idea relevant to everyday politics and led revolutionary leaders to invest it with more urgency than ever before. As long as colonial political opposition was confined to legislative and council chambers, the extent of political information among the population at large could be disregarded, as had long been the case in every colony. The plantation and village parochialism of farmers, who seldom looked beyond their dungheaps, had long made popular engagement in provincial or imperial politics an occasional event rather than a routine staple of colonial public life. But now the widening circles of opposition to British measures and the intensification of protests gave new meaning to the idea. Concern for the kind of information supplied to citizens, its mode of presentation, and its political content stimulated a new consciousness of being either "informed" or ignorant. Indeed, as the need to be informed assumed heightened importance among common men and women, pamphlets, newspapers, and formal public oratory gained larger, more diverse audiences. A more socially comprehensive conception of an informed citizenry emerged, together with the sense that common people possessed a more active, critical role. After Americans swept British government away between 1774 and 1776, it became immediately apparent that old customs and institutions were not fully capable of meeting republican needs for an informed citizenry. Now the need to be informed was constant, not episodic, and public engagement in the revolutionary cause was essential to its survival.

Thus in 1776, and later, revolutionaries turned to the state as the principal agency for the formation and perpetuation of an informed citizenry. Two kinds of approaches were adopted simultaneously. The first, drawing on Radical Whig prescriptions for a free state, focused on liberating the channels of information by assuring the right to free speech and press and freedom of assembly and petition. Connected to this movement was the liberation of religious sects—freedom of religion—which meant that the state would no longer interfere with pathways to virtue. Indirectly, freedom of religion promoted the formation of an informed citizenry by releasing religious energy in order to encourage virtue, just as free speech and press enhanced the circulation of information.

The second approach, using the state in a positive way to support the institutions required by an informed citizenry—schools, colleges and universities, libraries, and learned societies—represented a substantially new departure. In the case of Massachusetts, secular public institutions were designed to complement churches and clergymen in their long-standing role of promoting knowledge and virtue. In Virginia, reformers sought to bypass the old Anglican establishment and create new, secular educational institutions. Everywhere there was confidence that the state could play a positive role in establishing the foundations of an informed citizenry.

Revolutionaries were optimistic, even visionary in the cases of Thomas Jefferson and John Adams, when they looked toward the future, even though there were signs of hostility to cosmopolitan learning and its supporters from the outset. This incipient populist resistance to higher learning proved to be only one of many complications prompted by the idea of actively creating an informed citizenry. As the idea of being informed was extended beyond the Radical Whig notion of knowing one's rights and some political history and came to embrace a multitude of useful and speculative Enlightenment and Christian topics, forming a consensus as to the meaning of being "informed" became more elusive. The difficulties Christians encountered in agreeing on doctrine were a foretaste of the problem of concurring on what being informed ought to mean.

Revolutionary leaders, even those like Adams, Jefferson, and Rush who were most farsighted, were further limited by their culture and historical context in that they did not anticipate the dynamic impact of the Revolution on the concept of citizenry itself. They could not seriously entertain the idea that the political meaning of "citizen" as "freeholder" might in a generation or two be challenged. The idea that propertyless men, white or black, might be candidates for equal political rights appeared truly radical in the 1770s, and the notion of women, propertied or not, as political actors was almost unthinkable. For revolutionary leaders, an "informed citizenry" was more restricted and firmly linked to virtue than it would later prove to be.

Chapter 4 🌱 Shaping an Informed Citizenry for a Republican Future

In the decades preceding the independence movement, the issue of an informed citizenry was peripheral to the major political and cultural concerns of Britons at home and in the colonies. Voices asserting Mandevillean arguments in favor of popular ignorance and illiteracy had faded away, and there was little controversy over the purposes and value of being informed. For ordinary people, the many, the prescribed objective of being educated and informed was to perform one's allotted private role in the social and economic order piously and dutifully. For those few who occupied professional and aristocratic stations, the prescribed social and cultural duties included guiding and ruling the many. Because their rank entailed public responsibilities, informed citizenship for them required some cosmopolitan learning and a knowledge of ecclesiastical and public affairs.

But the Revolution undermined the assumptions that had sustained this consensus.[1] Now the many, not just the few, were to play active public roles and thus must be informed in order to be able to fulfill their public responsibilities. Revolutionary leaders recognized this new reality even before independence was won, and in several states—Pennsylvania, North Carolina, Georgia, and Massachusetts—constitutional provisions for the encouragement of education attested to this consciousness. Some revolutionary leaders, among them John Adams, Thomas Jefferson, James Madison, and Benjamin Rush, were so worried about the historic fragility of republican regimes that they were convinced that tax-supported, state-sponsored schools and universities were vital necessities. Others, however, felt the need to inform the citizenry less urgently and were resistant to taxation in general. They preferred a more modest role for government in which Congress or the states would merely encourage private citizens and localities to promote an informed citizenry by enabling them to create schools, libraries, and other suitable agencies. Since it was generally agreed that, as in the colonial era, leading citizens needed to be more broadly informed than common people and no agreement could be reached concerning precisely what body of information all citizens ought to command, contests over public education were enduring. Neither the form, the substance, nor the financing of public education could command unanimous agreement.

The belief that a free press was necessary in order to assure an informed citizenry was even more fundamental to the Revolution and was enshrined in state constitutions and bills of rights from the beginning. But almost everywhere politics were contested, there were controversies over the proper meaning of a free press. The legacies of the colonial and revolutionary eras were ambiguous and gave some comfort both to those who claimed that press freedom merely meant no prior censorship and to others who argued that the law of private libels was the only useful limit to press freedom. On this issue more than any other, it seemed that where one stood depended on where one sat. At different times, John Adams and Thomas Jefferson were among the most ardent defenders of the press and its freedom in principle and among its most savage critics in practice. The press of the early republic was simultaneously one of the most sacrosanct as well as one of the most excoriated agencies of an informed citizenry.

At the outset, two questions were paramount: Who, precisely, should be informed and what, exactly, should they know? Clearly, the old British charity school ideal of promoting simple literacy in order to maintain a pious and docile work force was not a revolutionary goal. Being informed, it was understood, meant a knowledge of public affairs, but whether it involved only a knowledge of one's rights so that they could be defended or more comprehensive and positive information so that the people could identify and pursue their interests generally would be a matter of contention for two generations. In the colonial era, the people "out-of-doors" engaging in political demonstrations had included propertyless artisans, laborers, boys, African Americans, and even women; now that common people were being recognized and brought "indoors" as enfranchised members of the body politic, expectations about the identity and responsibilities of citizenship needed to be adjusted.[2] Controversies over who should be informed—according to property, gender, and race—would become heated and intractable.

These tensions were exposed in discussions of free speech, education policy, and the notion of public opinion. The British rhetorical heritage of constitutional and political liberty was glorious and elevated, but it was also so broad and various that it was often invoked indiscriminately. In 1766, for example, a Connecticut newspaper had reprinted a passage from the London

press that declared that "every good Englishman will at all times be an advocate for liberty of the Press" because "public knowledge and public Freedom
depend alike on its preservation." But who was to say exactly what "public
knowledge" meant? Ribaldry, falsehood, scurrility, and invective should
not be protected. For such licentiousness "there can be no liberty, either in
speaking, writing, or printing."[3] A decade later in 1775, the newly arrived
Englishman Thomas Paine declared in the *Pennsylvania Magazine* that the
press exerted the most general "influence over the manners and morals of a
people." From the press, he said, "as from a fountain, the streams of vice or
virtue are poured forth over a country."[4]

Revolutionaries generally shared these views, grandly proclaiming their
belief in free speech as long as it remained within the boundaries of decency
and truth. As the Virginian George Mason put it in his state's Declaration of
Rights proclaimed in 1776, "Freedom of the Press is one of the greatest bulwarks of liberty, and can never be restrained but by despotick Governments."
When James Madison presented the proposed Bill of Rights to his fellow
congressmen in 1789, he echoed Mason's language, avowing that "the freedom of the press, as one of the great bulwarks of liberty, shall be inviolable."
Later, when the First Amendment was adopted, Congress was prohibited
from "abridging the freedom of speech, or of the press."[5] There were no
objections.

Yet determining the boundaries of free speech and press was not as
straightforward as declarations of rights suggested. Because republican principles elevated the role and importance of the people and "public opinion" in
sustaining government, the limits of free expression were often contested. It
was easy enough to assert that "the PEOPLE are the Basis on which all power
and authority rest" and that "the extent of their knowledge and information"
determines public security, but it was harder to agree on the proper "extent
of their knowledge and information" in practical terms.[6] Early in President
Washington's administration, his secretary of state, Thomas Jefferson, advised him that appropriate "knowledge and information" should include
criticism of the government, even the present government, because "no government ought to be without censors: & where the press is free, no one ever
will."[7] Within a few years, however, Jefferson qualified his support of a free
press with words that looked back to 1766 and forward to the Federalists'
Sedition Act of 1798. "Printing presses shall be free," Jefferson proclaimed,
"except as to false facts published maliciously."[8] The necessity of distinguish-
ing liberty from license, and protecting the one while prohibiting the other,
seemed inescapable.

At the most fundamental, abstract level, American leaders agreed with Jefferson concerning the necessity of a free press and an informed citizenry. But when it came to actual cases, their perspectives differed. Often the differences were partisan and depended on whether their own policies were being attacked. The inconsistent twists and turns in Jefferson's own attitudes toward the press—saluting press freedom and condemning its excesses—reveal the depth of the challenge posed by a free press in a republican context.

In 1799, when the Sedition Act was in force, Vice President Jefferson declared that he was "for freedom . . . of the press" in the broadest terms. It made no difference whether "the complaints or criticisms" against government officials were "just or unjust." It was, he said, a violation of the Constitution "to silence [critics] by force and not by reason." Jefferson maintained this position, at least rhetorically, as he entered the presidency, but by 1803 he was complaining to a French correspondent that "the abuses of the freedom of the press here have been carried to a length never before known or borne by any civilized nation." Still, the president believed "it better to trust the public judgment, rather than the magistrate, with the discrimination between truth and falsehood." This was the same view that Jefferson proclaimed in 1805 at his second inaugural. Although he applauded "the salutary coercions of the law . . . against false and defamatory publications" and deplored the "demoralizing licentiousness of the press," he urged the nation to rely not on prosecutions and courts but on "the censorship of public opinion."9

Two years later, however, Jefferson had difficulty extolling the press as "important to freedom and science." He was so disillusioned that in private he now claimed that "truth itself becomes suspicious by being put into that polluted vehicle." Because newspapers regularly published "fables" under pretense of fact, Jefferson argued, "the man who never looks into a newspaper is better informed than he who reads them. . . . He who reads nothing will still learn the great facts," whereas the details reported by the press "are all false." This was not the expression of a passing mood, the temporary petulance of a proud official under attack. Even after leaving office, when he enjoyed the serenity of Monticello, Jefferson wrote privately of "the lying and licentious character of our papers." Five years into his retirement, Jefferson was deploring "the putrid state into which our newspapers have passed." It was so bad that the major political purpose of free speech itself had been undermined since "as vehicles of information, and a curb on our functionaries, they have rendered themselves useless, by forfeiting all title to belief."10

In truth, Jefferson, like many others of his generation, was ambivalent about newspapers and the consequences of a free press. Thomas Paine, who made his career under the protections of a free press, agreed with Jefferson that "*error of opinion might be tolerated, when reason was left to combat it,*" but he emphasized that "there is a difference between error and licentiousness."[11] Jefferson, though he grew to be alienated from the press as it was, continued to proclaim that "where the press is free, and every man able to read, all is safe." Even at the age of eighty, he would assert that "freedom of the press" was not only a "formidable censor" of public officials but "also the best instrument for enlightening the mind of man, and improving him as a rational, moral, and social being." But because Jefferson ultimately gave up on newspapers, these fine pronouncements had a hollow, ritualized quality. He continued to read books, but as for newspapers, "I rarely think them worth reading," he wrote to President James Monroe. "I have ceased to read . . . the newspapers . . . in a great degree," he remarked to his former secretary of state, Albert Gallatin. By 1820, he admitted to another old colleague, "I read but one newspaper and that of my own State, and more for its advertisements than its news."[12] Committed republicans of Jefferson's generation could not help but feel equivocal about press freedom because of the fundamental paradox that lay at the core of its rationale: that to advance the true and the good, the false and the bad must also be permitted.

Even more fundamental beliefs were also at stake. As a 1790 debate between Vice President John Adams and his cousin Samuel Adams, the Massachusetts lieutenant governor, revealed, conflicts could also be based on different assessments of human nature and institutions. Both Adamses believed "that knowledge and benevolence ought to be promoted"; John declared, however, that these qualities would never be "sufficiently general for the security of the society." The problem was that "human appetites, passions, prejudices, and self-love" were so powerful that they could "never be conquered by benevolence and knowledge alone."[13] To this, Samuel Adams rejoined with historical example: "Wisdom, Knowledge, and Virtue have been generally diffused among the body of the people" in Massachusetts, enabling them to preserve "their rights and liberties." And if knowledge and virtue could be so effective in Massachusetts, they could work elsewhere as well. "The present age is more enlightened than former ones," he reminded the vice president, and he reeled off a litany of advances: "Freedom of enquiry is certainly more encouraged: The feelings of humanity have softned [*sic*] the heart. The true principles of civil, and religious liberty are better understood: Tyranny in all its shapes, is more detested, and bigotry . . . is despised." Now, with the victory of American liberty and the promise of a republican revolution in Catholic France, Samuel Adams clinched his point by declaring what most American leaders, including John Adams, believed —that "future Ages will probably be more enlightned [*sic*] than this."[14]

Whereas John Adams emphasized human "appetites, passions, prejudices," his cousin declared that "the Love of Liberty is interwoven in the Soul of Man."[15] This debate had its ironies, such as the fact that Samuel was an orthodox Calvinist and John was a rational Deist. Yet their views were alike on many political issues, and they agreed as well on the fundamental human potential for good and evil and on the necessity of promoting the former and discouraging the latter through human institutions like governments, churches, and schools. But even among leaders whose origins, beliefs, and constituencies were so similar, policies concerning free speech and an informed citizenry could provoke debate.

Much of the sensitivity surrounding the subject of freedom of the press grew out of a newfound appreciation of the importance of what James Madison called "public opinion." In a brief, unsigned newspaper commentary of December 1791, Madison declared that rules and constitutions notwithstanding, "public opinion sets bounds to every government, and is the real sovereign in every free one."[16] At the time, Madison's words did not evoke much discussion, but President Washington would declare in his Farewell Address that "it is essential that public opinion should be enlightened," and by the end of the 1790s, the control of public opinion became a leading theme of partisan politics.[17] The First Amendment to the Constitution prohibiting Congress from "abridging the freedom of speech, or of the press," which was drafted by Madison, was challenged by the Sedition Act, which President John Adams signed into law on July 14, 1798. This law and its denunciation by Jeffersonian partisans as a violation of the First Amendment illustrated just how hard it was to reach a consensus on the boundary between liberty and license where public opinion was concerned.

The Sedition Act forbade "writing, uttering or publishing any false, scandalous and malicious writing" with the intent to "defame" or excite "contempt" or "hatred" toward the government of the United States, the president, or Congress or to stir up opposition to laws. Contrary to English jurisprudence, the law followed the libertarian principles of New York's 1735 Zenger case: that defendants would present "the truth of the matter" as evidence, and juries would "determine the law," that is, whether the statement was or was not libelous.[18] Therefore, the authors of the Sedition Act could claim with some justification that their law preserved free speech by establishing its limits, as did Jefferson, at the "false, scandalous and malicious" boundary. Such restraints, it was said, were necessary to preserve "the purity of public opinion."[19] Public opinion must not only be informed; it must be rightly, truthfully informed. An informed citizenry must not be left to chance.

To realize this objective on a national scale, Congress early established the U.S. Post Office.[20] By setting low rates for the distribution of newspapers and providing for their free exchange among publishers, the national government promoted the circulation of information throughout the republic. As Madison had explained in 1791, "a general intercourse of sentiments . . . is equivalent to a contraction of territorial limits . . . where these may be too extensive."[21] For the United States, Congress recognized, it was especially important that "territorial limits" be reduced by the spread of information; indeed, some believed that in the state of Massachusetts poor communication had been partly responsible for the eruption of political disorders. In the "two western Counties, where . . . Boston papers never circulate generally . . . the good people have no direct means of speedy information. . . . In consequence," it was said, "they have been liable to misinformation."[22] During the climax of Shays's Rebellion, Jefferson claimed that the people would not engage in such irregular activities if they could receive "full information of their affairs thro' the channel of the public papers." Several months later, the Connecticut leader Roger Sherman noted that "the people . . . want information and are constantly liable to be misled."[23]

These immediate, palpable dangers made the creation of a national postal system crucial. Madison argued that postage on newspapers must be low since anything "above half a cent, amounted to a prohibition . . . of the distribution of knowledge and information" throughout the country. Referring to this policy, a North Carolina congressman told his constituents that "if the people hereafter remain uninform'd it must be their own fault."[24] Blaming the people, of course, would be small comfort if the republic collapsed due to demagoguery and civil strife. What was essential was that both public and private means be employed in order to assure that citizens of North Carolina and everywhere else were not "uninform'd" or, as Madison complained of Virginians, in a "state of darkness."[25]

In Massachusetts, where the Puritan desire to maintain a literate population was linked to the Radical Whig ideal of a politically informed citizenry, the state constitution of 1780, drafted by John Adams, emphasized the fundamental importance of the Whig ideal and supplied the institutional means for its support. By providing a religious establishment, as well as a state-sponsored educational system and protections for freedom of expression, the

Massachusetts constitution bound several traditions together—Puritan, enlightened, and Radical Whig. This union was convenient, even creative, but it would prove unstable when the diversity among Massachusetts's inhabitants generated conflicts over religious freedom and equality.

In Virginia, revolutionary reformers viewed the religious establishment not as an agency to promote an informed citizenry but as one of its chief impediments and thus made a sharp break with the colonial past. In place of an established church, in 1786 the legislature enacted a bill, drafted by Jefferson, "for establishing Religious Freedom." According to this law, established churches tainted the formation of public opinion and spoiled the climate of free inquiry by giving official sanction to a particular dogma and by making religious belief a criterion for citizenship. "Our civil rights," the legislators declared, "have no dependence on our religious opinions, any more than our opinions in physics or geometry." In words that echoed Milton in *Areopagitica,* the Virginia statute proclaimed "that the truth is great and will prevail if left to herself, that she is the proper and sufficient antagonist to error, and has nothing to fear from the conflict, unless by human interposition disarmed of her natural weapons, free argument and debate."[26] Freedom of religion, no less than free speech, was essential to the formation of an informed citizenry according to this Enlightenment formulation.

Paradoxically, the same legislature that enacted Jefferson's bill granting religious freedom rejected his plan for establishing a secular education system. Because of its expense, the difficulty of its implementation in sparsely settled counties, and western complaints about inequalities in the sizes of districts—all complaints with a parochial flavor—the much admired Bill for the More General Diffusion of Knowledge became a victim of the very political ills it aimed to remedy.[27] Existing county officials were unwilling to share power with new boards of aldermen, and the wealthy resisted financing schools for their neighbors' children. Anglicans disliked the generally secular character of the system at a time when state support for religion was being withdrawn; Presbyterians disliked giving support to the Anglican College of William and Mary; and Baptists and Methodists resented all tax-supported establishments. Consequently, the goal of achieving an informed citizenry would have to be primarily a private endeavor.[28]

The fate of Jefferson's plan, which James Madison had championed in the Virginia legislature, though disappointing to cosmopolitan republicans, was actually characteristic of state policies in the United States generally. Now that every free man was a citizen, the idea that every free man should be informed concerning public affairs was widely accepted. But, as in Virginia, there was no consensus as to who bore the responsibility for achieving such a goal. Except in Connecticut and Massachusetts, where an attenuated version of a religious establishment survived, legislatures had terminated the state's role in supporting religious instruction. Except in these two states, access to secular information and education had always been achieved chiefly through private and voluntary means. Parents paid for as much schooling for their children as they were willing or able to provide. Adults sought opportunities to enlarge their understanding of public affairs to the extent determined by their occupation, social standing, resources, and temperament. The English heritage concerning public policy focused on a free press and free public assembly: that is, it promoted restraints against government interference rather than a positive government role. With only a few significant exceptions, this negative conception of the state would prevail for generations in the United States. Schools and libraries, debating clubs and lyceums, political parties and religious sects, as well as the newspapers and periodicals that flourished in every region—all these expansive, innovative agencies of public instruction were private and voluntary.

It is ironic, then, that the leaders of the early republic who were most concerned with assuring that the United States would have an informed citizenry directed most of their attention to government policy rather than private initiatives. In the United States land ordinance of 1785, Congress set aside a one-square-mile lot in every new thirty-six-square-mile western township in order to endow "the maintenance of public schools within the said township." Two years later, Congress reinforced its intentions by enacting the northwest land ordinance, declaring that "religion, morality, and knowledge, being necessary to good government and the happiness of mankind, schools and the means of education shall forever be encouraged."[29] Evidently, national leaders viewed the defeat of Jefferson's bill in Virginia as only a temporary setback since they used his plan as a point of departure in their carefully designed programs to erect multitiered public school systems. The American Philosophical Society, whose members included many of the nation's leading thinkers, even sponsored a contest in 1795 aimed at determining the best "plan for instituting and conducting public schools in this country."[30]

Both Republicans such as Benjamin Rush and Federalists such as Noah Webster were deeply engaged in the attempt to design rational mechanisms that would create a perpetual supply of virtuous citizens to maintain the republic and raise it to ever-higher levels of production and civilization. Being informed was considered so critical to the proper exercise of the duties of citizenship that in Rush's 1786 plan for public schools in Pennsylvania, literacy was declared a voting requirement. Simultaneously, Rush asserted his belief in the public necessity of private virtue by requiring voters to prove their literacy by reading biblical passages. Twenty-four years later, the aging signer of the Declaration of Independence would argue that "in a republic no man should be a voter or a juror" without knowledge of "reading, writing, and arithmetic."[31] Thomas Jefferson sounded a similar note in 1816, when, in the midst of the nationwide movement to end property restrictions on suffrage, he praised the wisdom of "a principle entirely new to me" that was then being considered in Spain—"that no person, born after that day, should ever acquire the rights of citizenship until he could read and write."[32] From the perspective of the necessity of an informed citizenry, this scheme made perfect sense. But John Adams pointed out its antirevolutionary implications when he reminded Rush in 1811 that this doctrine, if applied to the republic of France, would immediately disenfranchise the majority and put their "lives, fortunes, character . . . at the absolute disposal of" a minority. In Adams's view, it was wiser and more just to promote "free schools, and all schools, colleges, academies and seminaries of learning" than to restrict suffrage or citizenship by imposing literacy tests.[33]

The prevailing orientation of such learned, cosmopolitan republicans in the 1780s, however, is suggested by the fact that one of the American Philosophical Society's prizewinning plans affirmed that "it is proper to remind parents that their children belong to the state" and that it was the duty of the nation "to superintend and even coerce the education of children," while the other prizewinner advocated a "uniform system of national education."[34] Romantic individualism, like Rousseau's assertion of the innate virtue and natural wisdom of noble savages, was misguided and would undermine the republican state. Rush argued that "our common people be compelled by law to give their children (what is commonly called) a good English education" rather than elite classical instruction. Eager to subordinate private to public interests, in his "Address to the people of the United States," Rush admonished his fellow citizens that "every man in a republic is public property."[35] So steeped were these learned men in classical models that they expressed a most un-British, indeed, positively Roman, confidence in the state, modeling their notions of citizenship on their readings of Cicero and the history of the Roman republic.[36]

They departed from tradition, British and Roman, however, in the attention they gave to women's education. To be sure, women would not be among those citizens who directly possessed political responsibilities. But the Roman matron, who raised her sons as virtuous citizens and managed a civilized and productive household, was indirectly vital to the well-being of the state. This was one of the reasons that the Virginia Bill for a More General Diffusion of Knowledge had provided for public education for girls, and it was why Benjamin Rush argued that in addition to their "usual training," women should be taught "the principles of liberty and government, and the obligations of patriotism." No less an authority than David Hume had recommended "the study of history for girls and women" because, he said, it "amuses the fancy, as it improves the understanding, and as it strengthens virtue."[37] Women would not serve in the Senate or lay down their lives on the battlefield, but as mothers and wives, they influenced men from the cradle to the grave. As one legal educator noted, women shaped not only the morality of their offspring but also their sons' character as public speakers. Mothers and wives were critical in the formation of "great and good men." John Adams went further, declaring that "it is by the female world, that the greatest and best characters among men are formed."[38] Moreover, Rush asserted, women's approval was often "the principal reward of the hero's dangers and the patriot's toils." Consequently, he maintained, women's education, like men's, must not be left to private discretion; it was a public responsibility.

At the head of the informed citizenry, a properly educated national elite should guide the United States, according to these leaders, and to assure the availability of such an elite, they proposed the creation of a national university. George Washington was one of its earliest advocates, promising his own financial support for such a university even before the drafting of the Constitution.[39] Wartime experience had convinced Washington that mixing together "young men from different parts of the United States" caused them to shed "those jealousies and prejudices which one part of the Union had imbibed against another part." During the war, he had seen this process work dramatically, and he was sure nothing would be as effective in forming a national leadership class as the creation of an institution that fostered "the intimate intercourse of characters in early life, who, in all probability, will be at the head of the councils of this country in a more advanced stage."[40] In Benjamin Rush's view, Congress should create a "federal university . . . where the youth of all states may be melted (as it were) together into one mass of citizens." Trained together in "the law of nature and nations" as well as comparative government and history, agriculture, manufactures, commerce, applied sciences, and modern languages, this republican elite would "render the American Revolution a blessing to mankind." Rush wanted to maintain an informed national leadership and to guard against "quacks in government" by legally requiring that thirty years after the national university was created, each person "chosen or appointed into power or office" must hold "a degree in the federal university."[41] Advocates of an informed citizenry who were themselves leading men often favored some form of elite nationalism.

But the national university scheme, like Jefferson's plan for public education in Virginia, could never quite muster the necessary political support. From the president's first annual message to Congress in January 1790 to his last will and testament, George Washington remained an advocate of a national university.[42] During the early 1790s, both John Adams and Thomas Jefferson seriously considered bringing the entire faculty of the University of Geneva to the United States as the foundation for such an institution, but by the time Adams and Jefferson succeeded to the presidency, they no longer viewed the creation of a national university as an urgent matter.[43] Not until James Madison became president was the idea pressed forward again. Three times, in 1810, 1815, and 1816, Madison used his annual address to call upon Congress to establish "a national seminary." His 1815 speech reworked the themes that Washington had articulated a generation earlier:

> Such an institution claims the patronage of Congress as a monument of their solicitude for the advancement of knowledge, without which the blessings of liberty can not be fully enjoyed or long preserved; as a model instructive in the formation of other seminaries; as a nursery of enlightened preceptors, and as a central resort of youth and genius from every part of the country, diffusing on their return examples of those national feelings, those liberal sentiments, and those congenial manners which contribute cement to our Union and strength to the great political fabric of which that is the foundation.[44]

Although no one in Congress disputed President Madison's ideas, like earlier proposals, they were blocked by congressmen protective of states' rights, wary of elitism, and averse to expanding the role of the national government. Drawn from a wide array of backgrounds, and representing various educational institutions in their home districts, delegates refused to create a university.

By Madison's era—indeed, from its beginnings in the Washington administration—the national university proposal had major sectional implications. Washington himself had wanted to place the university in the District of Columbia not only because it was to be the permanent seat of government and enjoyed a central location but also because, as he explained to Jefferson, "one half (or near it) of the district of Columbia, is within the Common-wealth of Virginia; and the whole of the State is not inconvenient thereto."[45] Thus Virginians' access to and influence on the national university would magnify their role in shaping the culture of the nation's elite.

But a generation later, because the old, established northern universities had emerged as quasinational centers for the education of leaders, political considerations led Virginians to seek their own university rather than sup-port a rival national institution. Thomas Jefferson, for example, who had ear-lier supported Washington's efforts, made no attempt to advance Madison's proposal. His goal was to create a first-class Virginia university that could compete as a regional and national training ground for American leaders. As Jefferson explained to a fellow Virginia Republican: "We are now trusting to those who are against us in position and principle, to fashion to their own form the minds and affections of our youth. . . . We must have there [at northern seminaries] five hundred of our own sons, imbibing opinions and principles in discord with their own country." The sectional conflict over Missouri statehood was, according to Jefferson, "the speck in our horizon which is to burst over us as a tornado sooner or later." Consequently, north-ern colleges were "no longer proper for Southern or Western students. The signs of the times admonish us to call them home. If knowledge is power, we should look to its advancement at home." A "real University" at home, one that could compete with Harvard, Princeton, Columbia, and the University of Pennsylvania, would become "the rallying centre of the South and the West."[46]

Jefferson was so anxious to create a politically correct university that a few years later he went on to declare that although faculty members should oth-erwise be free to select textbooks for their students, an exception should be made for political subjects. Politics was, uniquely, "a field in which heresies may be taught, of so interesting a character to our own State and the United States, as to make it a duty in us [the trustees] to lay down the principles which are to be taught."[47] In the context of religion, Jefferson would have condemned such a doctrine as a popish restriction on free inquiry. Almost forty years earlier, he had written in the Statute of Religious Freedom that "to suffer the civil magistrate to intrude his powers into the field of opinion, and to restrain the profession or propagation of principles on supposition of their ill tendency, is a dangerous fallacy, which at once destroys all religious lib-erty."[48] But Jefferson's political anxieties were so acute in 1825, and his sense of the particular mission of the University of Virginia so strong, that he was ready to make his university a center for his own political orthodoxy.

This shift from the plane of high principle to that of power politics was unusual in the discussion of an informed citizenry among spokesmen of secular enlightenment. But it resembled the hardheaded reasoning that had long been expressed by New England Calvinists seeking to maintain their church establishment and their control over religion and education. Rejecting liberal pluralism as "that blind catholicism, which is at present, with many so popular," one Massachusetts cleric preached a sermon entitled *The Diffusion of Correct Knowledge of the True God, A Leading Object of the Christian Ministry.*[49] "Let us," said another clergyman in a secular Independence Day oration in 1802, "revere the Christian Religion, as being above every thing else adapted to the preservation of our freedom and systems of policy."[50] These men were worlds apart from Jefferson in their beliefs about religion and its proper role in public life, but like him, they were convinced that it was urgent that government should take a positive role in assuring that the American citizenry was truthfully informed. Deeply committed to their beliefs, no one could persuade Jefferson or the Yankee clergymen that their truth was not the truth.

Moreover, the belief in extensive government-supported public education, whether at the national or state level and whether articulated by members of the American Philosophical Society and other elite cosmopolitans up and down the Atlantic seaboard or by the Calvinist clergy of New England, was rarely challenged in public manifestos. In fact, judging by public discussion, one could almost suppose that these cosmopolitan republicans and New England clergymen were merely expressing a broad, nonpartisan consensus. But the history of education bills in the state legislatures indicates that even though the idea of public education commanded support and won some victories—sometimes at the primary level and sometimes at higher levels—that support was always limited and qualified so that the overall results were inconsistent and piecemeal. States readily accepted the congressional subsidies that were financed through western land sales to set up "literary funds" used to support elementary and/or higher education. Taxation, however, was a different matter and generated opposition rooted in both expediency and ideology. Enthusiasm for a national education system was narrowly confined to a fraction of the most cosmopolitan leaders, and no legislature adopted the idea that children belonged to the state rather than their parents.[51]

The precise character of resistance to a multitiered national system varied from one state to another, but the overall pattern of responses displayed common themes and operated at all levels of government from New England to the South. Jealousies among the propertied classes and between them and the poor influenced every discussion of public measures, especially when taxation or public spending was at stake. Voluntary, private alternatives for promoting an informed citizenry operated as barriers to wholehearted support of public programs. In spite of their unanimous rhetorical commitment to the principle of an informed citizenry, in practice Americans did not agree on precisely what the principle meant or what sacrifices should be made, and by whom, to achieve such a goal.

As had been true in England, one of the first concerns was the education of the poor. Operating on the assumption that "affluent and independent" citizens could send their own children to private "colleges and academies," the plan that Benjamin Rush proposed in 1787 for Philadelphia was aimed at "the humble and indigent classes of the people." It proposed that "FREE SCHOOLS" be subsidized by public funds. Anticipating resistance to taxation from "the affluent and independent," Rush pointed out that "the children of poor people" were powerful social actors both in the present and over the long run. Echoing arguments that had been expressed three generations earlier on behalf of London charity schools, Rush asserted that "their ignorance and vice when neglected are not confined to themselves; they associate with and contaminate the children of persons in the higher ranks."[52]

In the United States, however, Rush claimed, the situation was more urgent than it had ever been in London. In America, when these poor children grew up, they would help select "rulers who govern the whole community." The outcome could be disastrous. "If the common people are ignorant and vicious," Rush warned, "a republican nation can never be long free." Clinching the argument with an explicit appeal to self-interest and patriotism, he concluded that "as we love our offspring and value . . . our country," we must "provide for the education of the poor children."[53]

Rush's poor children's curriculum, however, did not so much prepare them for active political roles as assure that they would grow into productive, orderly, virtuous adults. "Above all," he advised, "let both sexes be carefully instructed in . . . the Christian religion." This training would make them "good husbands, good wives, honest mechanics, industrious farmers, peaceable sailors, and . . . good citizens." For this reason, Rush urged that individual churches be given public funds to set up free schools under clerical supervision.[54]

This plan addressed several common political obstacles. In the first place, the drain on public revenues would be comparatively modest since taxes would pay for only the poor. In addition, although no one church would be given preference, every Christian denomination in Philadelphia would have the opportunity to train its own poor with the support of public subsidies. By joining secular and religious self-interest with community spirit, Rush's plan drew on deep, broadly shared values. Yet the proposal for tax-supported free schools could also be seen as a kind of compulsory charity that violated the voluntary principle. Whereas taxation to support military defense and the administration of law and justice had always been mandatory, support for education had long been optional.

Only in New England had a different tradition reigned, but popular representative government did nothing to strengthen this tradition. In 1775 Samuel Adams bemoaned the fact that "some of our towns have dismissed their School masters, alledging that the extraordinary Expence of defending the Country renders them unable to support them." Adams urged that "the leading Gentlemen" counteract this movement "by impressing upon the Minds of the People, the Necessity and Importance of encouraging that System of Education."[55] As the war dragged on, the problem that Adams had identified at the outset became so acute that in the 1782 Massachusetts election sermon, his cousin the Reverend Zabdiel Adams warned the state's leaders that "the promotion of learning demands the attention of the civil authority." Certainly no one "expected that all should be philosophers," the clergyman explained, but everyone "ought to be taught the rudiments of science." Reverend Adams applauded the formation of new private academies and the continuing support for Harvard, but that was not enough. "The infinite necessity of diffusing intelligence among the body of the people," Adams declared, required that "schools should be maintained at the public expense, for this purpose."[56] This appeal for public schools at a time when New England clergymen were suffering cruelly from wartime inflation and importuning their towns for payment of arrears in their salaries was especially telling. The Revolution was eroding tax support for education even in the region where it seemed most secure.

When John Adams reflected on the problem of an informed citizenry during the mid-1780s from the vantage point of his diplomatic post in London, he, too, was convinced that tax-based public education was absolutely essential, notwithstanding the fundamental political obstacles blocking its realization. "The whole people must take upon themselves the education of the whole people," he believed, "and must be willing to bear the expenses of it" as a matter of principle. Adams believed that charitable endowments had a place but that in a republic they were not the proper way to support education. "There should not be a district of one mile square, without a school in it," he declared, "not founded by a charitable individual, but maintained at the expense of the people themselves."[57] The curriculum should supply instruction not only for the people's "moral duties" but also for "their political and civil duties." This education was not just for "the rich and noble," or just for the poor, but for "every rank and class of people, down to the lowest and the poorest." To end tyranny, Adams believed, nations must commit themselves to the policy that "no human being shall grow up in ignorance."[58]

But John Adams, like his cousins Samuel and Zabdiel, knew that such a policy was easier to proclaim than to implement. As one who had been intimately acquainted with local politics in the decades before independence, as a selectman and the son of a selectman in Braintree, Massachusetts, and as a Boston delegate to the legislature, Adams knew all about education and tax resistance. In contradiction to enlightened political wisdom, "such is the miserable blindness of mankind," he admitted, that "it is very doubtful whether the pitiful motive of saving the expense would not wholly extinguish public education." Reflecting upon his own reading in political history and his personal experience with democracy in the town and in the legislature, John Adams believed that if "the people in one assembly ruled all," without the leadership of an enlightened upper house, it was unlikely that any people anywhere would be "so generous and intelligent, as to maintain schools and universities at the public expense." Adams feared that "the stinginess, the envy, and the malignity of the base and ignorant, would be flattered by the artful and designing, and the education of every family left to its own expense, that the rich only might have their children educated."[59] Experience had taught Adams that "too large a portion of the People and their Representatives, had rather starve their Souls than draw upon their purses to pay for nourishment of them."[60] As caustic as his analysis was, with respect to public expenditures, it was remarkably prophetic. Not surprisingly, those who had the most real-life experience with popular government anticipated its limitations.

In Virginia, where the tradition of a tax-supported church was repudiated in the 1780s, the movement toward a tax-supported education system was halting at best. The general situation that Adams had predicted, that "the education of every family [would be] left to its own expense," prevailed in a state where suspicion toward government and belief in the voluntary principle was stronger than in New England. In 1786 Jefferson preached "a crusade against ignorance" through his "law for educating the common people," proclaiming that "the tax which will be paid for this purpose is not more than the thousandth part of what will be paid to [the] kings, priests and nobles who will rise up among us if we leave the people in ignorance." But neither a majority in the House of Burgesses nor a majority of their constituents hastened to act. Years later, when he was president of the United States, Jefferson more accurately expressed Virginians' thinking when he stated that although "education is . . . among the articles of public care," he would not "take its ordinary branches out of the hands of private enterprise, which manages so much better all the concerns to which it is equal."[61] With such ambivalent support from their most prominent advocate, tax-supported public schools did not move forward.

At this time, however, Jefferson reported the multiplication of "petty *academies*," which to his scorn were "springing up in every neighborhood." As late as 1813, Jefferson claimed he was still hopeful that the public school plan in his Bill for the More General Diffusion of Knowledge—now thirty-five years old—would be enacted as "the key-stone of the arch of our government."[62] But this never happened. As Jefferson explained in his 1821 "Autobiography," his bill was revised in the legislature so that his plan would fail. Each county was empowered to decide for itself whether to implement the plan and, if so, to finance it with local taxes. This made public education a matter of local option and thus "would throw on wealth the education of the poor." Since the men who ran the counties "were generally of the more wealthy class, [they] were unwilling to incur that burden." Regretfully, Jefferson reported that "it was not suffered to commence in a single county." What another Virginian called "a most deplorable destitution of public spirit" was evident in a society where few were willing to look "beyond the confines of their own private affairs."[63]

James Madison, who had originally shepherded Jefferson's plan in the House of Burgesses, believed these actions resulted from "a hasty and superficial view of the subject." The "people at large" believed they had no interest in higher education since their sons would not enjoy the benefits directly, while the rich regarded the education of the poor and middling as no concern of theirs. This analysis of the politics of education echoed, in some respects, that of John Adams. But Madison offered an argument that he hoped would encourage men of all classes to recognize that by their measures they were providing "not merely for the existing generation, but for succeeding ones as well." In Virginia and throughout the United States, there was "a constant rotation of property." Anticipating the common maxim that in America social and economic mobility moved men "from shirtsleeves to shirtsleeves in three generations," Madison argued that "the rich man, when contributing to a permanent plan for the education of the poor, ought to reflect that he is providing for that of his own descendants;

and the poor man who concurs in a provision for those who are not poor that at no distant day it may be enjoyed by descendants from himself." Madison, who was himself in his early seventies, observed that "it does not require a long life to witness these vicissitudes of fortune."[64]

Madison's defense of public expenditures for education, whether justified by the promise of broad advantages—political, moral, economic—in the here and now or across the generations, appealed chiefly to those who were already sympathetic. Throughout much of the nation, as in the South, tax resistance, sectarian jealousies over who would control the system and for whose benefit, as well as a multitude of regional and jurisdictional differences all combined to make education mostly a local and voluntary affair operating within flexible state guidelines.[65] Indeed, some believed that this was the best solution. They opposed public school establishments just as they resisted church establishments. Both, it was asserted, were founded on the unduly gloomy belief that common people were naturally vicious and thus required compulsory indoctrination. Just as New Lights believed that men and women could find religious truth freely, so it was said that humanity's natural, inquisitive spirit would lead Americans to inform themselves through voluntary means.[66]

As it turned out, during the two generations from 1776 through 1826, the idea of a nationally defined and generated program for the formation of an informed citizenry never flourished in the United States. True, elements of positive government support existed nationally. The 1785 United States land ordinance required that land be set aside for schools in every new township, and later Congresses furnished subsidies to the states to further their educational efforts.[67] The U.S. government also sponsored the creation of an extensive postal system to enable newspapers to circulate nationally and subsidized their distribution to make them widely available. State governments, too, made provisions for public education. But at the national level, the ruling principle was usually a policy of empowerment of states and localities rather than direct government support. Although early national leaders were sometimes reluctant to accept it, releasing the energies of groups and individuals and encouraging their initiatives to engage in all sorts of political, economic, and cultural activities were more popular politically than any national, centralized, tax-supported program.[68]

In New York, the anti-Federalist governor, George Clinton, urged the 1792 legislature to promote "seminaries of learning" because "the diffusion of knowledge is essential to the promotion of virtue and the preservation of liberty." Ten years later, he sought "encouragement of common schools" inasmuch as "the advantages to morals, religion, liberty and good government arising from the general diffusion of knowledge" were "universally admitted."[69] What was not universally accepted, Clinton had learned, was any particular scheme to supply the state with common schools. Only in 1812, after another decade's worth of political maneuvering, did the New York legislature adopt a durable arrangement. Significantly, this plan drew on programs that had been set up in the 1790s, whereby the state supplied up to one-half of local school costs. New York required all local communities to take the initiative in 1812 and thereafter. The community would supply a school building within which a state-reimbursed teacher would instruct children in "reading, writing, arithmetic, and the principles of morality," preferably including the reading of chapters from the Bible at the opening and closing of the school day.[70]

Except for Bible-reading, the public consensus regarding the curriculum was confined narrowly to a focus on skills rather than substance. As the legislative report of 1812 explained:

> Reading, writing, arithmetic, and the principles of morality, are essential to every person, however humble his situation in life. Without the first, it is impossible to receive those lessons of morality, which are inculcated in the writings of the learned and pious; nor is it possible to become acquainted with our political constitutions and laws; nor to decide those great political questions, which ultimately are referred to the intelligence of the people. Writing and arithmetic are indispensable in the management of one's private affairs, and to facilitate one's commerce with the world. Morality and religion are the foundation of all that is truly great and good, and are consequently of primary importance. A person provided with these acquisitions, is enabled to pass through the world respectably and successfully.[71]

In the North, at least, providing the basic means for citizens to educate themselves was politically appealing because it was relatively inexpensive and did not demand that a divided, heterogeneous electorate reach agreement as to the specific information the public ought to command. Within states such as New York and Virginia, as in the nation as a whole, representative politics precluded the adoption of uniform, centralized, European-style systems to inform or indoctrinate the citizenry with some particular body of knowledge. Even within communities as small and homogeneous as a Connecticut school district (of which there were often eight to twelve in a single township), each family selected the textbooks its own children would read; nothing of substance was centrally prescribed. Broadly speaking, responsibility for shaping the specific characteristics of America's informed citizenry was left to families, individuals, and the cultural marketplace.

This is why the most dramatic, far-reaching developments in the elaboration of ideas concerning an informed citizenry occurred in the private sector. Here decentralized, private, voluntary movements sprang up and multiplied on an unprecedented scale. The great statesmen, such as John Adams, Thomas Jefferson, and James Madison, who advocated the idea of an informed citizenry primarily for defensive reasons—to safeguard liberty from tyrants and demagogues—never saw all of their favorite public information schemes enacted into law. Still, they witnessed the emergence of a great voluntary movement to make it possible for citizens to acquire information in order to become empowered socially, culturally, and politically—to become informed in order to enrich and improve their lives.

The foundation of this movement—which was carried forward in the press, in public speaking, and in a wide array of voluntary associations—was the ideal that these statesmen had articulated and promoted so assiduously. It was true that people were reluctant to employ state power to require people to be informed; but it was also true, as the response to *Common Sense* had suggested in 1776, that many Americans believed that being informed was a necessary part of their citizenship. As long as being informed did not require deference and as long as it was voluntary, they exhibited a huge appetite for information. Moreover, because Americans were a diverse people without centralized institutions, with no one prescribed orthodoxy in religion or politics, their hunger for information promoted a self-intensifying competition among messages and media for public attention.[72]

No clearly defined consensus as to the body of knowledge citizens should possess, no canon for an informed citizenry, ever emerged. Even among such enlightened reformers as John Adams, Thomas Jefferson, James Madison, Benjamin Rush, and Noah Webster, men who broadly concurred in their belief in an informed citizenry, major differences existed in their views on the aims and the content of the citizen's ideal curriculum. Some favored information that would assist directly in the defense of political liberty. Others believed that Christianity must have priority. Advocates of practical education argued that the public good was best served by promoting individual material prosperity and happiness. The self-sacrificing classical republican commitment to the public over the private good that was prominent in 1780s rhetoric waned with each passing decade.

As early as 1776, John Adams was arguing that the study of geography was "absolutely necessary" not only for "every Person of public character" but also for "Merchants."[73] Almost fifty years later, James Madison argued that beyond "Reading, Writing, & Arithmetic," the usual curriculum for "the poor," geography was essential, including the study of "the Solar System," which would "expand the mind and gratify curiosity." Information of this sort, Madison said, was a substitute for travel and would "weaken local prejudices and enlarge the sphere of benevolent feelings." It also fostered "a general taste for History, an inexhaustible fund of entertainment & instruction."[74]

Political knowledge could be gained from newspapers after the framework for interpreting its significance had been established through acquiring knowledge of geography and history. In addition, Noah Webster, the educator and lexicographer, recommended that in the United States "every class of people should *know* and *love* the laws . . . by means of schools and newspapers."[75] From this perspective, the chief reason to foster an informed citizenry was political.

To others, however, the most critical objective of public education was religious knowledge. For many Evangelicals, no other type of knowledge was nearly as important, but they believed that the best role for the state in this process was to get out of the way. In contrast, orthodox Anglicans and Congregationalists who supported religious establishments and Presbyterians like Benjamin Rush believed public education should be synonymous with Christian education. Nondenominational Protestant instruction, they argued, was essential to social morality. Indeed, Rush asserted that "without religion," by which he meant Protestantism, "learning does real mischief to the morals and principles of mankind."[76] John Adams, who had written provisions for a religious establishment into the Massachusetts constitution, also believed that "no other Institution for Education, no kind of political Discipline, could diffuse this kind of necessary [moral] Information, so universally among all Ranks and Descriptions of Citizens . . . [as] the Christian Religion."[77] Rush even went so far as to claim that Satan "never invented a more effectual means of extirpating Christianity from the world than by persuading mankind that it was improper to read the Bible at schools."[78]

Rush exaggerated. In the United States, at least, Bible reading was one of the few elements in the elementary curriculum—other than basic literacy and numeracy—that enjoyed general support. So ordinary, indeed, was the practice that the orthodox Congregationalist Noah Webster claimed that the Bible was "as common as a newspaper and in schools is read with nearly the same degree of respect." As Webster saw it, religious instruction belonged in the home and family, not in the school. Biblical passages dealing with history and morality could make valuable school texts, but using the Scriptures profanely for literacy training, Webster argued, diminished the power of the sacred text.[79]

Noah Webster certainly shared the view that religion inculcated necessary private virtues like honesty, orderliness, and industry, but in advocating an informed citizenry, his ambitions were much broader and included practical as well as political objectives. "When I speak of a diffusion of knowledge . . . necessary for the yeomanry in a republican state," Webster declared, "I do not mean merely a knowledge of spelling books and the New Testament." This, after all, was no more than what a charity school in Old England might provide. In contrast, Webster advocated a school curriculum that would furnish "an acquaintance with ethics and with the general principles of law, commerce, money, and government." Textbooks and newspapers, he believed, could be vehicles for supplying these kinds of information.[80]

Another approach to practical education was more explicitly utilitarian. According to the English-born Delaware journalist Robert Coram, the purpose of universal, state-supplied education should be to enable inhabitants "to provide for subsistence in civil society," in other words, to earn a living. This meant instruction "in arts as well as sciences," including arithmetic, bookkeeping, natural history, mechanics, and husbandry. Believing that "a becoming [economic] independency" for all should be the objective in a republic, he insisted that instruction in religion, manners, and foreign or dead languages should be specifically excluded.[81] Subjects like these were essentially private matters of parental discretion, not public responsibilities.

Antipathy to training in languages was partly based on the conviction that foreign and classical languages were merely ornamental elements of an aristocratic education and hence impractical. Benjamin Franklin, who favored education in modern languages, believed that time spent on ancient languages was inefficient. But there were also those who opposed the moral impurities they believed French novels and classical literature could convey. Benjamin Rush consistently opposed reading the classics because, he told John Adams, "human intellects are brutalized by being stuffed in early life with such offal learning." As far as the Philadelphia physician was concerned, "were every Greek and Latin book (the New Testament excepted) consumed in a bonfire, the world would be the wiser and the better for it." Rush classed such books "with Negro slavery and spirituous liquors, . . . as, though in a less degree, unfriendly to the progress of morals, knowledge, and religion in the United States." John Adams, Rush's fellow signer of the Declaration of Independence and fellow advocate of a citizenry informed by Christian principles, dismissed Rush's position as nonsense. "I should as soon think of closing all my window shutters, to enable me to see, as of banishing the Classicks, to improve Republican ideas," he replied to Rush.[82] Clearly, when those who advocated public measures to assure an informed citizenry could not agree on whether a subject as fundamental as classical learning should be included in the educational diet of republican citizens, no single canon could be said to prevail.

The meaning of "practical education" could also be quite broad. Whereas, on the one hand, Benjamin Rush's interpretation could be narrowly utilitarian—the public must be informed of the dangerous effects of "drinking cold water" in summer when they "were heated by labor"—the Jeffersonian journalist Samuel Harrison Smith pursued a comprehensive vision. In one of the American Philosophical Society's prize-winning essays, Smith argued that natural philosophy—the sciences—should be taught in order to promote individual happiness as well as national wealth. Farmers and mechanics, Smith explained, would be more productive if they were introduced to basic chemistry and physics. Instruction in history, moreover, would not only inform all classes of citizens about power, politics, and war but also teach ethics by providing examples, both good and bad. Thus trained, citizens would be virtuous republicans and possess an individual "happiness" that, Smith asserted, "will greatly depend upon the general diffusion of knowledge and a capacity to think and speak correctly."[83] This sort of practical education reached beyond mere productivity to a secular kind of personal and private fulfillment, an objective that would enjoy great popularity in the middle decades of the nineteenth century.

The contention over what, exactly, "practical" knowledge meant, or what subjects and topics should be taught, was part of a larger struggle to identify and establish a cultural orthodoxy for the new republic. Among the difficulties in resolving this conflict, however, was the fact that a major, universally accepted principle of republican ideology was that truth should be established in the context of free and open inquiry and debate. Consequently, no one was required to defer to the cultural judgments of others. Truth should vanquish error by persuasion, and thus contention was widespread.

Competition even within particular types of printed materials in addition to competition between such information mediums as print, oratory, and voluntary organizations was widespread.[84] Almanacs, for example, had been fairly standard in the eighteenth century. Designed to sell within a particular regional market as defined by latitude and commercial networks, they varied mostly because of the personal tastes or idiosyncrasies of their publishers.

But in the early republic, and especially after 1800, they lost their generic identity. Almanacs carrying the neutral name of their printers were widely supplanted by almanacs identified as Christian, temperance, farmers, mechanics, or antislavery, among others. Information as seemingly innocuous as that contained in an almanac was packaged according to the cultural preferences of a segmented market.[85]

The same kind of development was characteristic of periodicals, which were increasingly tailored to specific audiences. By 1830, every movement and every denomination, and almost every trade and occupation, seemed to have its own monthly journal. Technical and scientific information, sometimes called "useful knowledge," was also conveyed to various audiences in specialized magazines. A process of specialization was under way that simultaneously served the needs of efficiency and personal identity. In fact, the contents of many publications with specialized labels, such as the *Christian Herald and Seaman's Magazine,* which was published in New York City from 1816 to 1824, overlapped with more general publications. At the same time, however, they possessed a distinct character and appeal.[86]

American culture exhibited some unexpected paradoxes. Many of the same citizens who adamantly rejected compulsory deference voluntarily embraced a kind of cultural deference. Although they felt that no Adams, Jefferson, or Madison should prescribe their behavior, many common men aspiring to higher ranks hastened to emulate the cultural preferences of the upper classes. This "democratization of gentility" affected a wide range of tastes in personal fashion, furniture, architecture, and manners.[87] It also influenced notions about learning and the idea of being politically informed. Books, newspapers, reading, and education generally became fashionable. Tax support for public secondary schools was rare, but private academies and social libraries flourished. The informed citizen was in vogue in republican America.

The public goal of universal education was extensively and variously pursued as a private, voluntary enterprise. In 1789, for example, a New Jersey printer founded the *Christian's, Scholar's, and Farmer's Magazine,* which he hoped would sell widely by providing instruction in the liberal arts to traders and shopkeepers as well as farmers and mechanics. Believing that all kinds of citizens "should possess considerable degrees of Literature," the publisher aimed to provide his subscribers with college training at home, without demanding that they know Latin.[88] To judge by the polite magazines of the early republic, all sorts of information, from the culture of turnips and the management of bees to the meanings of Hebrew and Anglo-Saxon words, should be mastered.[89]

Newspapers, too, became repositories for information about the natural world, history, politics, and culture. The Reverend William Bentley, a celebrated Massachusetts polymath, spent much of his career preparing news digests that provided the public with a comprehensive stream of information on public affairs, natural and ecclesiastical history, and scientific advances. Enlightenment-bred optimism led Bentley, like other Jeffersonian intellectuals, to hope that the challenge of creating the informed citizenry the republic needed could be fulfilled by making knowledge broadly available. If people were given access to the refreshing streams of information, they would drink.[90]

Although this optimism was not universal, in the half century following the War for Independence, the expansion of American printing and publishing, the rise of American learned societies, and the spread of voluntary associations rendered it plausible. It was, after all, a matter of established fact that private initiatives for promoting an informed citizenry were flourishing as never before and on a comprehensive scale that overshadowed government-sponsored schooling. One emblem of the realization of this vision was the lyceum movement that began in the late 1820s. Initiated in Boston by the immigrant mechanic Timothy Claxton, who joined with the Yale-educated Yankee Josiah Holbrook, the lyceum movement had roots in the British campaign to spread useful technical information via mechanics' institutes. At first, the lyceums emphasized popular scientific subjects, including physics, chemistry, and geology. But after Holbrook redirected the orientation of the lyceum movement toward families in the 1830s, their content became more eclectic. General adult education, including geography, history, and literature in addition to science, broadened the movement to include clerks and farmers as well as women and youth of both sexes. In the 1830s and 1840s, as lyceums sought and achieved ever greater popularity across the nation, the uncertain balance between useful and entertaining knowledge shifted toward the latter. Judgments about which topics were useful and which were merely entertaining, such as the hugely popular subject of phrenology, were bound to be subjective.[91]

The concept of "useful knowledge," which from the time of Francis Bacon had joined the material and practical to the speculative and cultural, came to be all-encompassing. Care of the body as well as the soul could be served by advances in information, as could care of the farm, the shop, and the store. Attention to the practical advantages to be gained from the circulation of information was not new—Benjamin Franklin had published a "Proposal for Promoting Useful Knowledge among the British Plantations in America" in 1743—but now, in contrast to 1743, Americans responded through their reading preferences and their associational activity.[92] The enlightenment of practical improvements that Franklin championed, as well as the cultural enrichment and social elevation his own career embodied, possessed a broad appeal in a society where both the means of production and the ambition to advance were widely distributed.

The predominant concerns of the cosmopolitan leaders who most assiduously promoted an informed citizenry—Adams, Jefferson, Madison, and Franklin—were secular. Such republican leaders recognized the importance of religious information only to the degree that it secured social and political benefits in this world, as the Massachusetts constitution stated. But there were other voices in the early republic for whom an informed citizenry meant being informed regarding the vital facts of damnation and salvation. Largely separated from the Radical Whig preoccupation with political liberty or from any social aspiration toward republican gentility, tens of thousands of people who viewed republican civic culture with a skeptical eye expressed a powerful demand for information focused on the next world.[93] As the Second Great Awakening unfolded, those who were engaged in this movement seldom contributed directly to public discussions of the idea of an informed citizen, but their interest in freely developing evangelical information and production and distribution networks worked to buttress the entire private and voluntary information marketplace politically as well as economically. And like their secular counterparts, Evangelicals were ready to innovate and to employ the whole panoply of publications and associational activities. Consequently, the American Tract Society, organized by Evangelicals in the 1820s, became the great pioneer in the use of stereotype printing plates for mass printing in the United States in addition to forming the first nationwide distribution network.[94] The same enabling legislation and preferential postal rates that fostered the spread of secular information applied equally to the efforts of religious groups.

These several kinds of commitment to an informed citizenry—political, social, practical, and religious—supplied the impetus that led Americans to make print, which had long been a scarce commodity, into one of the ubiquitous necessities of life.[95] They led Americans to merge their drive for information with their sociability, a characteristic Alexis de Tocqueville called the "natural social principle," by forming and patronizing thousands of voluntary associations in the decades between 1780 and 1830.[96] To be sure, regional variations existed. In the North, where a more densely settled, egalitarian social system operated and where economic development and transportation networks stimulated each other, the movement for an informed citizenry was more pronounced and reached a greater portion of the free population than in the South. But in the South, too, the same interest in reading and the same penchant for voluntary associations were growing.[97]

One evocative manifestation of the several cultural tendencies that were converging was a resolution published in 1833 by the Petersburg, Virginia, chapter of the American Bible Society. Quoting an injunction in the book of Isaiah that "the earth shall be full of the knowledge of the Lord," the Virginians resolved "that the world shall be supplied with the Holy Scriptures in twenty years." Recognizing a "responsibility resting upon Christians for the universal diffusion of the sacred Scriptures," the national organization formulated a plan to furnish Bibles "to all the inhabitants of the earth accessible to Bible agents, and who may be willing to receive, and able to read, that sacred book."[98] Such a resolution could never have passed a state legislature or won tax support; also, originating in a region where one-third of the inhabitants were slaves who were widely forbidden literacy by statute, it expressed a peculiar irony. Still, the goals stated in the American Bible Society resolution illustrate one of the many variant forms that the ideal of an informed citizenry took in the early republic. Enlightened and romantic at the same time, and blending the Christian idealism of encompassing all the peoples of the world with the practical recognition that Bibles were only useful to those who could read, the project indicates the kinds of motives that were operating freely in the competitive environment of early republican political culture.

Education promoted both secular and religious objectives. Good Christians would be good citizens. As a Massachusetts Unitarian clergyman explained in an 1806 Independence Day oration, "The elementary plan of education, which is extended to the rich and the poor, which embraces the whole mass of our citizens," would promote "the ability to understand our religion, in its evidence, its spirit and design; by which men are guarded against . . . superstition, . . . the delusions of enthusiasm, and are enabled to direct their religious observances to real attainments in moral life."[99] Christianity itself was "above everything else adapted to the preservation of our freedom."[100] Now its advocates proclaimed that the idea of an informed citizenry, which had first been shaped by the political needs of Renaissance gentlemen, should be extended to include virtually every living soul on earth and need have nothing whatever to do with the state. Whereas the primary objective for Adams, Jefferson, Rush, and their generation of political leaders had been to secure the American republic by means of creating an informed citizenry, other voices were shifting the emphasis to an informed humanity.

The universalism of the American Bible Society scheme to place the Holy Scriptures in every hand represents the almost boundless reach of the idea of an informed citizenry in the early republic. In practice, however, the idea's reach was far more restricted. The slave system, for example, barred the realization of a universal ideal because slave preaching was carefully monitored and literacy was often forbidden to slaves by state statutes and informal prohibitions among masters that were extended and strengthened in the 1830s and 1840s. The core tradition, after all, had never been universal; it was national, secular, and political, and it focused on enfranchised citizens. Liberty and just government combined with enlightened inquiry and progress were the ideals that were emphasized as connected to an informed citizenry in thousands of Independence Day orations, political speeches, and newspaper commentaries as well as in the charters of schools, colleges, libraries, debating societies, and lyceums. The political benefits of a broad diffusion of knowledge among citizens, regarded as critical for repelling the greedy march of ambition and tyranny, remained central to American beliefs.

Nevertheless, the ideal of an informed citizenry shifted significantly during the early decades of the nineteenth century. The acute anxiety that the Revolutionary War generation of leaders had expressed over tyranny and the survival of the United States led Adams and Jefferson to advocate a major role for the state in education. To them, it appeared that the republican state must require its citizens to be informed in order to assure its own permanency. In the wake of the French Revolution and the election of Thomas Jefferson, Federalists, especially, were worried about the direction education would take. "By education the tender youth may be fitted for treason, stratagem, and death," a Federalist orator warned in 1802, "or they may be trained up for order, peace, and happiness. Much depends on the systems of education." Such dangers were not merely hypothetical since "the disorganizers of the present day" were indeed "infusing into the minds of the young the principles of disorder, and training them up for anarchists." Early in the century, such frenzied reactions—including anathemas against atheism, skepticism, and "sending abroad the fairer part of creation in the attire of a female Greek"—were voiced even by advocates of public education.[101]

John Adams, who expressed the most profound and durable commitment to public education, was not hysterical but merely skeptical due to his belief that the problems of creating an informed citizenry involved more than partisanship. Some were structural. Although he believed ultimately in the judgments of public opinion, in every society, monarchical or republican, that opinion "is not always right, until it is too late," since "public information cannot keep pace with facts." Moreover, as eager as Adams was for information to be "spread . . . even to the lowest dregs of the people," even among slaves, and to let "every human being,—man, woman, and child,—be as well informed as possible," he recognized that dangers would persist. The essential problem was not the canon of information or how it was taught, though these matters were important. Rather, it was that there was no "good without an evil, in this mingled world," which meant that "knowledge is applied to bad purposes as well as good ones."[102] In reality, there was "no necessary connection between knowledge and virtue." One had only to "read the history of all the universities, academies, monasteries of the world, and see whether learning extinguishes human passions or corrects human vices. You will find in them as many parties and factions, as much jealousy and envy, hatred and malice, revenge and intrigue, as you will in any legislative assembly or executive council, [or] the most ignorant city or village."[103] Human beings and human societies, regardless of forms, displayed certain characteristics that led Adams and many others who believed in the American republic to be concerned over its future.

By the 1820s, these anxieties were being eclipsed by the optimism of the rising generation. Elite American leaders had witnessed several decades of dramatic improvements in the dissemination of information, wherein private, commercial, and voluntary efforts were paramount and the state had played only an enabling role. Moreover, in contrast to Adams and Jefferson's generation, the leaders of the 1820s had been touched by romanticism. Although they paid an almost obsequious homage to the Revolutionary War generation, they confidently extended the ideal of the informed citizen to encompass a comprehensive vision of knowledge broadly diffused and ever expanding. Among aging Federalists and Whigs especially, the old worries persisted and acted as a continuing spur to action. But publicly, at least, the glass was decidedly half full, not half empty, and the new generation of leaders confronted the dire fears of the Revolutionary War leaders optimistically in the celebratory eulogies of 1825 and 1826.

Daniel Webster's nationally celebrated speech at Bunker Hill on the fiftieth anniversary of the battle was so widely reprinted in the next generation that it became, quite literally, a textbook example of American oratory.[104] In it, Webster sang the praises of the heroism of the revolutionary soldiers and the glories of American liberty. It is significant, therefore, that his patriotic exhortation included a panegyric to the expansion and diffusion of knowledge that reached toward infinity. Webster did, of course, affirm the basic political point that "the popular form of government is practicable, and that, with wisdom and knowledge, men may govern themselves."[105] But he elaborated it on a truly transcendental scale with the declaration that "knowledge, in truth, is the great sun in the firmament," giving life and power to men.[106] As a demonstration of this assertion, Webster proclaimed that "knowledge has, in our time, triumphed, and is triumphing, over distance, over differences of languages, over diversity of habits, over prejudice, and over bigotry." What was emerging around the globe was a "vast commerce of ideas" that made "innumerable minds, variously gifted by nature, competent to be competitors, or fellow-workers, on the theatre of intellectual operation."[107] From this historic development, he was sure, political and material progress would flow, giving to mankind a genuine hope of peace and prosperity. The concern for the purity of public opinion that had animated Webster's Federalist forebears was supplanted by confidence in commerce and the competition of a free marketplace of ideas. As Webster painted the scene, ignorance, not purity, was the issue. To remain ignorant deliberately in such an era was worse than unpatriotic, it was atavistic. To be informed, he implied, was not just a duty of citizens, it was the duty of everyone who was not forcibly restrained by tyranny or bondage.

According to U.S. Supreme Court Justice Joseph Story, the foundation for such bold declarations lay in the growing realization that, notwithstanding the shortcomings of popular politics and the inadequacies of public education policies, the United States was enjoying a "general diffusion of knowledge" among all social classes, including "the peasant and the artisan." In another classic oration of the period, Story, the one-time Federalist turned republican whom Jefferson had appointed to the high court, underlined Webster's arguments and elaborated on them. Owing to the freedom of the press and its "cheapness," the "universal love and power of reading" had come to fruition in the present era, which Story called "the age of reading." As Story viewed it, the republic was secure because "wherever knowledge circulates unrestrained, it is no longer safe to oppress; wherever public opinion is enlightened, it nourishes an independent, masculine and healthful spirit."[108]

Story's confident tone, like Webster's, was new. The connections between ignorance and dependence, knowledge and independence, were embedded in the revolutionary tradition. Usually, however, these ideas had been expressed as warnings, admonitions against a chronic peril. "Ignorance and slavery, knowledge and freedom are inseparably connected," a clergyman had proclaimed at the Massachusetts ratifying convention nearly forty years

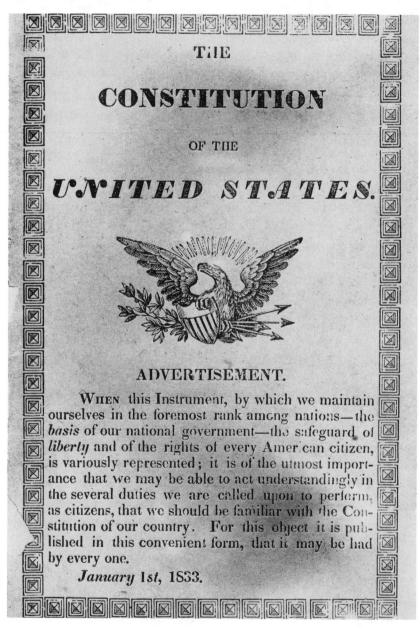

This cover of an 1833 sixteen-page pamphlet edition of the U.S. Constitution emphasizes the core concept of the early republican idea of an informed citizenry: "That we may be able to act understandingly . . . as citizens, . . . we should be familiar with the Constitution." The pamphlet sold for only a few cents. Courtesy American Antiquarian Society.

before Webster's and Story's orations, and twenty years earlier, a Vermont Jeffersonian had tersely explained that "knowledge is the standing army of Republics."[109] But now the tone was celebratory. A literate public with access to a free market of ideas and information was secure; the public good would be realized through the private pursuit of individual aspirations in a free, competitive society. Clearly, the ideal of an informed citizenry had attained fulfillment.

The richness and scope of this fulfillment were much broader and more comprehensive than leaders of the revolutionary generation had anticipated. Their own ideas had been drawn from secular British and Enlightenment traditions that linked free speech and a vigilant, politically informed citizenry with free scientific inquiry and the conquest of tyranny and superstition. Now, however, Jefferson's former protégé, Story, in the same speech in which he extolled knowledge as the bulwark of liberty, went on to declare that it was "the peculiar pride of our age, [that] the Bible may now circulate its consolations and instructions among the poor and forlorn of every land in their native dialect."[110] Although this Christian universalism overlooked American slavery, it gave the idea of an informed citizenry an almost unlimited appeal. The American Philosophical Society and the American Bible Society, like political, religious, and reform movements of all stripes, were invited to take shelter under the capacious tent of the informed citizenry.

The triumphant spirit of orators in the 1820s and later was based largely on their perceptions of actual improvement. Statistics on the spread of post offices, newspapers, books, schools, lyceums, and the like revealed that public information, once scarce, was now circulating extensively and that institutions to promote learning in all of its branches were more and more part of the cultural landscape. Orators' own experience and their hopeful intuition encouraged the belief that with the demise of practical impediments to the circulation of information, in time enlightened knowledge would vanquish superstition. Paradoxically, Americans had adopted a policy that relied primarily on private, voluntary means to achieve the public goal of creating an informed citizenry.

Owing to their diversity and their widespread resistance to tax-supported public institutions, Americans embraced a system that was driven by competing, voluntary efforts to inform the public. What was overlooked, however, was the sheer multiplicity of popular concerns and interests, among which civic consciousness was not necessarily a high priority. Every white man might be a citizen, but partly because that status no longer conferred prestige, citizenship did not determine the primary conscious identity of many men. Identifying themselves in terms of family, occupation, sect, and community, they often displayed only haphazard or superficial interest in acquiring information connected to citizenship. It was important, of course, that public information be available, but being informed required time, energy, and, most important, motivation. During the Jacksonian era, recognition of the importance of motivation would drive politics. During that time, a principal objective of everyone concerned with promoting an informed citizenry became persuading men that attending partisan rallies and parades was not enough; they should take the time and trouble to be correctly informed.

Chapter 5 🌰 The Idea of an Informed Citizenry and the Mobilization of Institutions, 1820–1850

The celebrations that marked the fiftieth anniversary of American independence represented a zenith for the nation's canonical ideal of an informed citizenry. As expressed by political and cultural leaders like Daniel Webster and Joseph Story, the republican standard of a politically informed electorate within a generally educated, moral citizenry had become a national mandate. All that remained, it seemed, was to implement the idea fully through the mechanisms of printing and public speech, newspapers and periodicals, the book trade, libraries, lyceums, and above all, schools, especially public common schools and Sunday schools. Although, as Webster and Story proclaimed, much had already been achieved, the tasks that lay ahead in a dramatically expanding, changing United States were formidable. Rhetorically, the opposition to the doctrine of an informed citizenry was puny; indeed, alternative viewpoints seldom found their way into print or onto the platforms of public discussion. But as a matter of practical politics, the idea faced major, persistent, and complex impediments. Old ways of thinking and acting and entrenched inertia combined with tax resistance and democratic individualism—the belief in personal autonomy and responsibility rather than public or communal control—to make actual implementation of the lofty vision of an informed citizenry a difficult challenge.

These kinds of practical and theoretical obstacles were compounded by the fact that almost from the moment the republican ideal of an informed citizenry achieved hegemony in public discourse, it was subject to revision and outright criticism. Ironically, the success of the idea of an informed citizenry was so complete and overwhelming that virtually all groups claimed it as their own, investing the concept with meanings that suited their own objectives and values but were not always mutually consistent. Like representative government itself, the idea of an informed citizenry enjoyed nearly universal support, but various constituencies understood the idea differently.

For example, the purpose of being informed might be public and political—the original revolutionary formulation—or it could be Christian and evangelical. Increasingly, being informed was said to be desirable in order to achieve personal fulfillment, to rise economically and socially, or to enhance the productivity, morality, and good order of society. At the same time, the substantive meaning of being informed varied just as widely and might include knowledge of the English language, arithmetic, history, and geography—the common school curriculum—or an array of other subjects, embracing such topics as practical science, the Bible, and American laws and constitutions. Lacking any official agency authorized to prescribe the orthodox subject matter of a properly informed citizenry, Americans engaged in a cultural free-for-all.

Most controversial of all was the meaning of citizenship. Individual states set their own standards of inclusion, and U.S. citizenship was something entirely different. Whether nonpropertied, female, and immigrant whites or blacks, mulattoes, Native Americans, and Asians could be citizens varied at different times and in different jurisdictions. Nor was there any consensus regarding the rights and privileges inherent in citizenship status. Citizenship might include public rights, such as the right to petition and to vote as well as to serve on juries and to hold public office. Citizenship might also convey private rights regarding property holding and equal treatment before the law. In addition to racial and ethnic considerations, questions of gender, wealth, and age all figured prominently in these considerations. Although it may have been easy to talk and write about the American citizenry in the decades after 1820, defining that citizenry with precision was another matter.[1]

As a result, the triumph of the idea of an informed citizenry, which orators such as Daniel Webster, Joseph Story, and Edward Everett proclaimed in the 1820s, did not mean that the meaning of citizenship became fixed, but it did place the creation of an informed citizenry at the head of the nation's cultural agenda. For decades, even generations, this idea would serve as the focus for debates that reflected contests over the definition of American identity—whether America was essentially a white or a multiracial society and whether it was patriarchal or egalitarian regarding women and men. The shape of these debates and their direction reached far beyond the initial visions that Thomas Jefferson, James Madison, or even John Adams had propounded. This chapter will explore the efforts of officeholders and public figures to mobilize institutions in order to develop a politically informed electorate within a society of educated, moral citizens. The next chapter will take up the challenges presented by various "outsiders"—workingmen, African Americans, Native

Americans, and women—who were officially excluded from the electoral arena by the old republican understanding of the boundaries of citizenship, the political community, and the meaning of being informed.

During the first half of the nineteenth century, the movement to educate and elevate common people, especially common men, embraced not only republican America but also the British and Continental monarchies. Because their cultural and religious connections to the United Kingdom were reinforced by trade, investment, and immigration, Americans were especially conscious of British approaches to the subject. When, for example, New England Evangelicals created the American Tract Society in 1814, they followed English tract society models, distributing millions of copies of short, accessible essays that taught lessons of piety and morality to common people scattered across America's urban and agricultural landscape.[2] The characteristically American movement to found lyceums was also connected originally to earlier English mechanics' institutes.[3] Similarly, when a nonpartisan assortment of prominent national leaders drawn from twenty-six states and territories joined together in 1836 to form the American Society for the Diffusion of Useful Knowledge, they were following the lead of a similarly styled 1827 British society. The British organization sought "to impart useful information to all classes of the community, particularly to such as were unable to avail themselves of experienced teachers, or who might prefer learning by themselves."[4] The American society took a passage from Washington's Farewell Address as its motto, declaring that it would "promote, as objects of primary importance, institutions for the general diffusion of KNOWLEDGE."[5]

When these American leaders formed the society in 1836, they were actually trailing behind public demand. Already a number of books first sponsored by the British society, as well as other similar works, had been published commercially in the United States. In Boston and twenty-one other cities from Portland, Maine, to Mobile, Alabama, a little book called *The Pursuit of Knowledge Under Difficulties; Illustrated by Anecdotes* had appeared in 1831 as the eighth volume in the Library of Entertaining Knowledge—a series launched by the British society.[6] This collection of biographies sifted from European and classical history told inspiring stories of both noble and poor men who, like the inventor Richard Arkwright, were placed in difficult personal and financial situations but achieved knowledge chiefly through their own efforts. Teaching by example, such a work encouraged aspirations to upward social and cultural mobility through self-help.

In New York, Philadelphia, and Springfield, Massachusetts, a Scotsman, Thomas Dick, brought out a popular work two years later that carried a rational and utilitarian message, *On the Improvement of Society by the Diffusion of Knowledge: . . . The advantages which would result from a more general diffusion of rational and scientific information among all ranks.*[7] Dick aimed to use "Knowledge in Dissipating Superstitious Notions and Vain Fears" as well as to demonstrate the "Absurdity of astrology." He went on to offer practical arguments for "the Utility of Knowledge in Preventing Diseases and Fatal Accidents" as well as the advantages of knowledge for the progress of science and general comfort. Dick also advocated rational Christianity, asserting that ignorance sustained "grovelling conceptions of the Deity both in heathen and Christian countries." In contrast, he pointed to the "Beneficial Effects of Knowledge on Moral Principle and Conduct" and its "Utility . . . in Relation to a Future World" and "the Study of Divine Revelation." To summarize what he called the "Ignorance of the dark ages," Dick pointed to "the scarcity and high price of books" in that era, a circumstance very different from his own enlightened age. In part, Dick's message was a thinly veiled attack on the British establishment, whose "bigotry" he contrasted with the "Liberality of Religious Sectaries in America."[8] More broadly, it was an argument for improving society by informing and elevating the people. Since literacy was widespread and printing was cheap, there should be no impediments to realizing this goal.

In these British-influenced publications, the motives that sustained the idea of an informed population had little to do with republican ideology. The linking of the terms "useful" and "entertaining," which went back at least as far as 1711 in the *Spectator* essays of Joseph Addison, did not point to the defense of liberty.[9] The subjects these works presented—natural science, mechanics, poetry, and belles lettres—included political content only indirectly through articles on ancient and modern history and biographies of such famous Americans as Benjamin Franklin and George Washington. The motto of the pocket-sized *Monthly Repository and Library of Entertaining Knowledge,* "Knowledge is power—is wealth—is honor," spoke less to readers' political empowerment than to their ability to advance upward in society by accumulating property and social respect.

The republican standard of public virtue, in which an alert citizenry was ever watchful against abuses of power, was being overshadowed by attention to private virtue and personal advancement. Just as liberal political economy was founded on the idea that collective prosperity derived from the individual pursuit of wealth, so the advocates of popular information—who dwelled in an environment where many of the assumptions of evangelical Christianity prevailed—declared that the morality of society was the sum of individuals' morality. Consequently, instead of promoting public consciousness, these writings explained that the acquisition of knowledge fostered virtuous personal conduct. Admittedly, one might find scholars who were "bad men" on occasion, but in general the "intellectual enjoyments" and "the habit of assiduous study" of the devotee of learning were inconsistent with "a life of vicious pleasure."[10] As a Moral Reform Society speaker in Philadelphia explained: "A man having within himself an opulent fund of intellectual enjoyment, will not be so much inclined as others to seek happiness in the gratification of his appetites and passions. The attractions of the gambling table and the ale house are not, in his view, to be compared with those found in his own domicil[e]—in the rich volumes of a well selected library. . . . Instead of this seeking happiness in the lowest depths of ignominy and disgrace, you will find him in the hall of science, the moral lyceum, or in some useful institution . . . increasing his own intellectual enjoyments."[11] Being informed, it was said, brought moral "happiness, as well as power and virtue."[12]

Most important of all, acquiring knowledge was "the cheapest of all amusements, and consequently the most universally accessible," available to "all, in all circumstances," male and female, young and old, in city or in country, and it could be pursued during short snatches of time or extended periods of solitude.[13] In contrast to former ages, when access to knowledge was a privilege denied to the poor, now it could be said that "a book is emphatically the poor man's luxury; for it is of all luxuries that which can be obtained at the least cost," whether by purchase or through cheap rental libraries. Through reading, "almost every individual" could obtain "an inexhaustible store of intellectual amusement and instruction." Until recently, it was true, "these advantages have been chiefly in the possession of the middle classes, to which they have been a source . . . of enjoyment . . . of intelligence and influence."[14] But now in both Britain and the United States, ordinary people of small means were said to enjoy similar opportunities.

Advocates of popular education based their appeals to common people on the grounds of personal enjoyment, fulfillment, and individual advancement—a package of enlightened self-interest. To judge from the rising commercial popularity of publications reflecting these values, they struck a responsive chord. At the same time, however, the Americans who formed the organizations promoting an informed citizenry and who articulated its goals—for the sake of both individual advancement and a republican defense of liberty—had other social and political agendas, among which social control and the formation of an orderly, progressive, morally respectable republic were prominent.

Among American Calvinists, the necessity for social control was seen as a fact of life. As Frederick A. Packard, the secretary of the Philadelphia-based American Sunday School Union, put it in 1836, "Ever since the world began, the depraved passions of men have required some kind of restraint." In a free republic, "if education and religion do not provide [such restraint]," then the violent coercion of "bayonets and halters must take their place." Making his argument by means of a qualified Miltonic statement concerning free speech, Packard asserted that if "error may be safely tolerated where reason is left free to combat it," then that reason "must be enlightened and sanctified reason," not the reason of slavish or heathen peoples. Sounding a theme that echoed seventeenth-century Puritan thought, the American Sunday School Union leader expressed concern that "our liberty [could be] used as a cloak for licentiousness."[15] This anxiety, though articulated in its most stark, explicit terms by Calvinist clergymen like Packard, was actually widespread among leaders of various orientations, both secular and religious; it also found a political home in the national Whig Party.[16] In a nation where social tensions were fueled by internal migration, the growth of cities and factories, the arrival of immigrants, and fluctuations in the business cycle—in addition to such explosive public issues as the abolition of slavery—the optimistic self-assurance of previous decades seemed naive.

The social analysis presented by the American Society for the Diffusion of Useful Knowledge, though not quite hysterical, was anything but complacent. At the society's founding meeting, held in August 1836 in the resort town of Saratoga Springs, New York, Professor John Proudfit of New York University pointed to "the moving, heaving surface of our American population." He portrayed "the elements of Society" in the United States as being "in a state of perpetual excitement. They need," he said, "but a touch to kindle them into a flame." As a result, the duty of the society was "to control and direct into right channels, the mighty, irrepressible, ungovernable activity of such a mass of mind."[17] By using the printing press to distribute useful, informative, moral reading matter, the society could reach people of all denominations and viewpoints.

Ultimately, of course, it was imperative to reach "the rising generation." As a Moral Reform Society orator explained, the education of youth was critical for a comprehensive array of cultural reasons. "Good education" would fill the nation with "useful citizens and enlightened Christians" whose refinement would spread "happiness" throughout society. This would "ban-

10. LITERATURE AND EDUCATION. Comprising a collection of standard works, in English Classics, with which every family should be acquainted. Works on education, giving its history, its progress and prospects, the philosophy of its principles, in a way calculated to extend and deepen the interest in universal education.

It will be the object of the Society to embrace in the range of the publications all subjects of general interest and utility, and their greatest care that the whole be pervaded and characterized by such a spirit of Christian morality as shall fit it to refine and elevate the moral character of our nation.

The volumes are designed to be of about 250 pp. 12mo. ; to be bound in a uniform and very thorough manner, and boxed in sets, so as to be bought, sold and transported with the convenience and safety of bales of merchandise ; and the box to be so constructed as to answer the purposes of a case, when it reaches its final resting place in the school room.

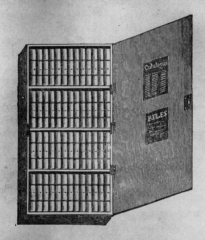

It is, as will be perceived, a flat box, two feet long, one foot wide, and six inches deep, divided by partitions which become shelves when the box is placed upright, into four compartments. The cover is to be attached by hinges so as to become a door when the box is opened.

This illustration was published by the American Society for the Diffusion of Useful Knowledge of New York City in its 1837 Prospectus for the American Library *to help market its "American Library" to families and schools. Shipped in wooden crates that could later serve as bookcases, this set of books made knowledge a commodity that could be manufactured efficiently and shipped anywhere. Courtesy American Antiquarian Society.*

ish from their religion that superstition, and from their devotional exercises that wild, ranting fanaticism, which are the legitimate fruits of ignorance."[18] As a result, a moral and respectable order would prevail. The idea of information as a mechanism of social control was made explicit by the American Society for the Diffusion of Useful Knowledge when it asserted that "an entertaining book is one of the strongest keepers a child can have. Its chain is invisible, and it neither chafes nor annoys the wearer. But it is more effectual than almost any other restraint." Reading could end idleness, dissipation, brawls, and "wicked conversation."[19] Although the objectives of this viewpoint were benevolent since books would restrain vice and liberate virtue, the idea that books could actually operate as invisible chains represented a departure from the revolutionary republican notion that books and the knowledge they supplied broke the chains of ignorance. But even as early as 1820, Daniel Webster, speaking in the Massachusetts constitutional convention, had lauded popular education as a "wise and liberal system of police."[20] Even within the republican tradition, tension between restraint and liberation recalled the Calvinist distinction between liberty and license.

One of the most common ways of addressing this concern was to advocate the dissemination of "useful knowledge," which by definition could not be frivolous and, unlike "entertaining knowledge," never encouraged misbehavior. Noah Webster, whose spellers, readers, and dictionaries were widely used, had brought out a multivolume textbook series between 1806 and 1812 called *Elements of Useful Knowledge,* in which he promised to combine "the attractions of delight, with the labor of study, to allure the minds of youth along the difficult road to Knowledge."[21] The book's contents, political and natural history and geography, were more useful than entertaining. Webster's competition, works such as William Mavor's *Catechism of Universal History* and *Catechism of General Knowledge,* were also intended for family use as well as for schools and shared his emphasis on usefulness rather than amusement.[22]

Since the question of whether information was useful or entertaining was often subjective—and it could certainly be both—the way information was presented reflected the values approved by the intended audience or market. Museums, which gained widespread popularity as educational and commercial ventures during the first half of the century, stood precisely at the intersection of the useful and the entertaining. Initially, under the guidance of such gentlemen as Charles Wilson Peale, the museum was a collection of natural history objects that provided scientific instruction through direct observation and lectures. When Peale sought a subsidy from the city of Philadelphia in 1816, he called his museum "a school of useful knowledge" that would "amuse and in the same moment instruct the adult, as well as the youth," of both sexes in addition to reinforcing the deferential social order by leading "all classes of society . . . [to] feel the charms of gratitude to their pastors, to their parents, to their compatriots." Peale even went so far as to appeal to the city's commercial interests, asserting that his emporium of knowledge would boost the city's retail businesses since his visitors "must spend money at places of entertainment" and "could scarcely pass our shops and stores without stopping to purchase something."[23] In this context, the usefulness of knowledge extended from the improvement of the individual and society to the enrichment of local businessmen.

Over time, the museum balance shifted away from useful and improving knowledge to entertainment. Starting in 1828, a Cincinnati promoter opened a museum that invited the public to visit Hell, made lifelike with transparencies, sound effects, and automated wax figures. At this time, all of the New York City museums competed for the public's attention by featuring musical bands, dog acts, ventriloquists, and freaks of nature. By 1843, when P. T. Barnum purchased Peale's once-scientific museum, the management had already turned to sideshow spectacles to bring in customers.[24] Useful knowledge, though it offered "the attractions of delight" as Noah Webster had put it, could not compete commercially in the marketplace as popular entertainment. To succeed financially, the movement for the diffusion of knowledge needed to be connected to the popular ambition for self-improvement, and even then it would generally require subsidies from private and public sources.

As a result, America's learned elite began to create a new kind of scientific collection aimed—like Philadelphia's Academy of Natural Sciences—primarily at the increase and advancement of knowledge rather than its diffusion among the masses. Even so, however, starting in the 1840s, the nonprofit Philadelphia academy invited the public to view its collections gratis twice a week. And when Congress acted in 1846 to fulfill the bequest of James Smithson, the Englishman who in 1829 had willed his fortune to the United States for "the increase and diffusion of knowledge among men," the legislation emphasized the diffusion of existing knowledge more than its increase and called for a museum, a library, an art gallery, and a lecture room—all open to the public.[25]

By this time, the lyceum and public lecture movements were flourishing all across the North and West and in a number of southern cities. These communal instructional events made the diffusion of information from the speaker's platform a kind of performance art.[26] In the amateur-operated lyceums, debating and library societies, and mechanics' institutes of the 1830s and 1840s, self-education flourished as members delivered lectures to each other on subjects they had studied in books. In addition, they used the debate format to discuss controversial issues of the day as well as to improve participants' skills in reasoning, argument, and social self-assurance. This kind of active self-development, which was especially common among the armies of young men who were pursuing nonfarm occupations as clerks and apprentices in law, commerce, medicine, and the manual trades, embodied a fulfillment of the idea of the informed citizen. The fact that women, too, participated in this movement, sometimes in separate societies, sometimes with men, illustrates how pervasive—and ultimately inclusive—the idea could be.

The public lecture movement, which built on the interests and audiences that the amateur associations cultivated, was even more inclusive. Relying on famous speakers like Ralph Waldo Emerson, Louis Agassiz, and Wendell Phillips, who were known for their oratorical skills and their publications and who attracted large paying audiences, these lectures encouraged people of different ages, sexes, occupations, and religions to share a common culture by becoming informed together on the same subjects. General cultural knowledge—philosophy, science, history—was presented, never the divisive or partisan sectarian and public issues that might endanger the broad-based patronage such a lecture series required.[27] For controversial subjects, Americans went to hear touring reformers and evangelists or attended the political rallies of electoral candidates. By participating in this wide range of informative activities, Americans displayed their commitment to their ideas of an informed, knowledgeable citizenry.

Indeed, so often repeated were the appeals for an informed citizenry and so pervasive was the movement for the diffusion of useful knowledge, that there was a discernible public reaction against it. The secretary of the Massachusetts state board of education, Horace Mann, commented in 1848 that "the necessity of general intelligence under a republican form of government . . . is so trite . . . as to have lost much of its force by its familiarity."[28] Ten years earlier in Massachusetts, an anonymous satire was printed purporting to present the annual proceedings at the "Asineum" of the "Society for the Diffusion of Useless Knowledge and the General Confusion of the Human Understanding." Filled with pretentious, multisyllabic pronouncements and beginning with an "introductory discourse on the usefulness of useless knowledge," the satire concluded that "useless knowledge was never more highly prized."[29] In the minds of some, at least, the earnest labors of information promoters needed to be deflated.

Several years later, a humorous critique of "Popular Lectures" called attention to their changing character. Although originally "considered the *luxuries*, they are now the *necessaries* of life"; they had become the cultural and intellectual counterparts of factory-made consumer goods.[30] Indeed, lectures were described as "a perfect system of patent instruction for adults, on every subject." At first, the lecture system had been seen as a secular counterpart to churchgoing in which adults and children could be instructed simultaneously on topics that were "scientific" and "useful." As with church attendance, women were said to have been especially supportive, and in addition, "fathers of families deemed it incumbent on them to lay in tickets . . . for general and constant use."[31]

The style of lectures, too, had followed the traditional method of the orthodox pulpit. First, the "famous man" placed "his manuscript before him," and then, in a "voice as thin as small beer," he proceeded to explain his subject—typically, to "strew the path which leads to comparative anatomy, with more flowers than bones." Earnest, at least, if not especially intellectual, the lecturer emphasized information and instruction; he neither pretended to be extemporaneous in his delivery nor embellished it with "fanciful gestures." The lecturer did not electrify his crowd anymore than did the common parish parson. But for an entire week following a lecture, it was said that "nothing is heard of, but 'mental power;' 'dignity of man;' 'cultivation of the mind,'" and other themes from the lecture.[32] As ridiculous as it seemed to the humorist who made these observations, the process he described represented one of the ways that a "culturally informed" citizenry, such as it was, developed.

In the 1840s, the critic noted, the lecture system was changing so as to emphasize "fashionable" performance. Now the lecturer presented a memorized text and roamed the platform with a display of "posturing" and "gymnastics" before an audience that was less likely to include families than it was to include unattached young people of both sexes, courting couples, and middle-aged and elderly men and women. Lectures had become a respectable form of educational theater, in which certain clichés functioned as predictable applause lines, such as "extension of commerce," "convenience of rail-roads," and the "utility of steamships"; "the fine arts," "the worth of woman," and "the magnificence of the firmament"; "the power of the press," "the intelligence of the people," and "democracy."[33] When audiences departed the lecture hall, they were said to be slightly more knowledgeable than when they entered. More important, however, as with museums a few years earlier, the mixture of "useful and entertaining knowledge" enabled audiences to feel as-

This 1844 image of a lecture shows a well-dressed audience of respectable men and women attracted to such improving entertainment. The speaker's dramatic gestures and extemporaneous delivery set him off from ordinary clergymen. The organ visible in the background suggests that the auditorium is a church. From Pills for the People (Boston, 1844). Courtesy American Antiquarian Society.

sured of their own inclusion in the society of the informed. The original idea of the politically informed citizen who jealously defended his rights and public liberty had not been lost, but it had been overlaid by the immediate, personal desire to achieve and maintain social standing in a land where rank was often said to depend on personal qualities more than accidents of birth and wealth.[34]

This combination of impulses was evident in the history of libraries. Whereas before the Revolution most substantial libraries had been the personal possessions of learned gentlemen and professionals, now the emphasis had turned to collective libraries of many kinds, catering to particular, self-defined communities of men and women. The library, by promoting efficient, inexpensive access to a multitude of publications, gave participants the heady feeling that they not only commanded a wide array of choices but also possessed a measure of control in a publishing marketplace of books, periodicals, and newspapers that was growing exponentially. Because many libraries were originally voluntary associations formed by like-minded people, they also fostered the sense of inclusion characteristic of membership organizations. Significantly, the public library movement that emerged in the 1840s and 1850s grew upon a base of local and private social libraries that, with antecedents stretching back to the 1730s, had been formed mostly in the decades after 1790.[35]

These social libraries, which in northern and especially New England villages and towns drew together the most prosperous farmers with merchants, lawyers, doctors, and clergymen, were complemented by the libraries, usually linked to a church, that their wives and daughters formed in order to share books and periodicals, which they purchased with their membership fees. By the 1820s and 1830s, such libraries often held debate and discussion activities attended by both sexes. In addition, local lyceums, which in the 1830s and 1840s also included men, women, and youths, formed libraries. By this time, privately financed libraries for merchants, mechanics and apprentices, and clerks and workingmen generally were operating in cities, sometimes as quasipublic institutions.[36]

All of these libraries emphasized morally correct, improving and useful knowledge, not entertainment. Horace Mann, who once said, "Had I the power, I would scatter libraries over the whole land, as the sower sows his wheat-field," was adamant on this point.[37] It might be appropriate to mix some amusement with instruction, he believed, but fictional romances supplied miseducation. In Mann's 1839 report to the Massachusetts legislature, he called attention to the fact that the "ignominious life" of the confidence man, "the notorious Stephen Burroughs . . . commenced when he was reading a pernicious book." Burroughs himself had reported this "fact" deliberately in order to elicit just such a response from authorities like Mann, who railed against "that contaminating and pestilential class of works which is now hawked around the country, creating moral diseases."[38] Clergymen, many of whom headed academies and colleges, were especially outspoken in denouncing the rise "of fiction and other light and ephemeral trash" that issued from a "licentious press."[39] Whereas good books could help to mold a virtuous, informed public, bad books contributed to the creation of a vicious, misinformed citizenry.

If all libraries had been controlled by "responsible" community leaders who were concerned, like Mann, with morality, Mann would have been more hopeful. But ever since American independence, circulating libraries, from which borrowers could rent reading matter by the day, had been growing in commercial centers. These libraries often included well-stocked reading rooms supplied with newspapers and magazines and offered a wide range of titles, but it was the rise in the popularity of novels that spurred their growth, especially in the decades after 1800. By the time Mann registered his complaint against the "contaminating and pestilential class of works" that threatened to supplant "useful knowledge," circulating libraries were common in all regions. Run by various types of people, male and female, and out of venues ranging from riverboats and taverns to milliners' shops, they operated beyond the reach of the monitors of social control. Ultimately, however, the influence of circulating libraries was restricted, both by the emergence of paperbound books sold so cheaply they were considered disposable and by the competition of subsidized libraries—public and semipublic and in schools.[40]

The recognized stature that the principle of free access to information had gained is manifest in an appeal to "the Authors, Editors and Publishers of the United States" issued in 1850 on behalf of the fledgling library of the Utah territory. The U.S. Congress had appropriated $5,000 to start the library, and now Utah settlers solicited the generosity of the information industry on the grounds that "a LIBRARY . . . is vital to our existence." More than just the settlers' ability to fulfill their duties as republican citizens was at stake. The press was the "Fountain" of light in the darkness, for "without it neither the Christian nor the Philosopher could hope to transmit his faith in God, or his discoveries in science, or to improve the condition of those who are living in the depths of superstition and bodily degradation."[41] In short, libraries stood between Christian civilization and pagan savagery.

Although libraries came to be regarded as essential to the moral and political stamina of American society and lyceums, lectures, and museums were considered important as well, nearly everyone agreed that, apart from churches, the single most influential agency for developing a virtuous and informed citizenry was the school. The Revolution had elevated schools to a priority status that was expressly articulated in the constitutions of many states and in a host of statutes. Yet in the early decades of the nineteenth century, after the republican ardor of newly won independence faded, actual commitments to education were fitful and sufficient to realize only a fraction of states' constitutional and statutory objectives. Even in Virginia and Massachusetts, where Thomas Jefferson and John Adams had taken the lead, established customs and tax resistance combined with new appeals to democratic individualism to obstruct the expansion of schooling. Parents, opponents of public education often claimed, not the state, bore responsibility for their children's training. Or if the public did have an obligation to educate children, then local autonomy in the actual control and direction of schools should be preserved. As a result, even in Connecticut and Massachusetts, which were often held up as models for the nation, the operation of publicly financed schools required incessant justification.

Over the years, these justifications changed, and with them, the idea of an informed citizenry changed as well. By 1847, a decade after Horace Mann had begun his crusade to elevate the schools of Massachusetts to a uniformly respectable standard, he was merging narrow appeals to self-interest with the lofty though familiar republican and Christian arguments for an informed citizenry. If Massachusetts would only adopt his school reform proposals, Mann claimed, "the great body of vices and crimes which now sadden and torment the community may be dislodged and driven out." To taxpaying voters whose tight fists remained clenched in opposition, Mann warned that "an ignorant people not only is, but must be, a poor people."[42] An educated citizenry, Mann seemed to promise, would be prosperous as well as moral and law-abiding.

The appearance in the 1840s of this kind of practical appeal to voters' immediate self-interest resulted from a two-generations-long struggle to achieve a broadly based, inclusive school system that could fulfill at least the minimum conditions that reformers like Jefferson and Rush had advocated several decades earlier. During these years, as American politics evolved in a democratic direction, the early republican concept of an informed citizenry was modified, often in ways that members of the federal era ruling elite had feared. In a polity where new state constitutions were being written in every decade and reflected changes in politics and the principles that informed them, the idea of an informed citizenry was inherently unstable. After common people themselves came to use politics and the information marketplace to express their preferences regarding the purposes of information and education, lofty abstractions about the long-term vitality and virtue of the republic yielded precedence to "useful knowledge" and low-cost education designed to enhance common citizens' material prosperity and accelerate their own social and political empowerment. Examining the way in which this process unfolded is instructive for understanding the multiple meanings that were being assigned to the idea of an informed citizenry as those meanings were shaped in the decades before 1860.

As had been evident from the time of the Revolution, concern for the creation of an informed citizenry originated at the top of society, among elite public figures and clergymen who were worried that their revolution, their Christian republic, would be undermined even before it could be securely established. Filled with a sense of urgency, they rallied to the proposition that education should be pressed forward and expanded by every available means. In 1795–97, when the American Philosophical Society was running its competition "for the best system of liberal education and literary instruction, adapted to the genius of the government of the United States; comprehending also a plan for instituting and conducting public schools in this country, on principles of the most extensive utility," its members understood that the purpose of such a plan would be to serve as a model for reformers to employ in arguing the case for education in the several states and perhaps in Congress.[43] No single blueprint would be applicable or acceptable everywhere.

The priority of parents' responsibility to educate their own children was a starting assumption, but reformers also believed that since the public and its agent, the state, had an interest in forming good citizens, government, too, had a duty to promote education. Parents should, as in the past, pay for their children's schooling, but government should assist and encourage education by subsidizing the capital and operating expenses of schools. Few people saw any need for a comprehensive, compulsory school system or believed one could be sustained.

The immediate advantages connected to this noncoercive, voluntary approach were substantial. Generally speaking, existing institutions could be accommodated. The laws were drawn loosely enough to allow for adaptations that suited the wishes of various communities and constituencies. And the approach was easy on taxpayers, whose tolerance for educational reform was always sensitive to taxation. At the beginning of the nineteenth century, there was a general understanding that these modest constitutional and legislative efforts would not yield a fully informed citizenry, but the expectation of progressive improvement helped to offset fears that Americans would become a degenerate citizenry.

But in urban areas like New York City and Philadelphia, the growing numbers of poor children—native and immigrant—caused city fathers alarm. Church schools had room for only a few pupils who could not pay tuition; as a result, some of the poor were receiving no training at all in letters or numbers. Traditionally, no public provision was made for the education of children who worked, children from one-parent families of laborers or laundresses, or unattached orphans. One response, recalling the eighteenth-century British charity school movement, was to create new institutions dedicated to serving this population. In 1805, for example, New Yorkers formed a society to operate "a free school for the education of poor children who do not belong to, or are not provided for by any religious society."[44] This privately financed school supplied only a basic education, not a curriculum aimed at informed citizenship or upward mobility.

It was no wonder, then, that when Joseph Lancaster's London system for cheaply educating massive numbers of poor children was introduced around 1798, urban elites were interested. Lancaster's approach offered the pedagogic analogue of the factory system. In his schools, one adult instructor supervised the teaching of as many as 500 children simultaneously by means of a graded system consisting of small groups, each taught by a trained "monitor." "Youths of fourteen or fifteen years of age," Lancaster proclaimed in 1810, were "conducting with almost the regularity of a machine, schools containing several hundreds of children, and imparting to them, with unexampled rapidity, the elements of education."[45] Those elements included reading, writing, arithmetic, and "habits of Cleanliness, Subordination, and Order." Expressly nondenominational, the schools offered limited religious instruction in "the Ten Commandments and the Lord's Prayer, . . . Lessons selected from the *Scriptures,* or . . . the Reading of the Scriptures themselves." Parents, Lancaster advised, should bring their children to church on Sundays, and he directed that pupils report the sermon's text to the schoolmaster on Mondays.[46]

Although parents generally paid the small tuition Lancaster charged, the schools' objectives were far from republican; indeed, their aims were virtually identical to the Anglican charity schools of a century earlier. And, as with the charity schools, when Lancaster addressed British audiences, he offered assurances against Mandevillean objections that had revived in the

" On a miserable bedstead, without any covering but
a heap of rags, lay the almost dying parent."

See page 21.

"The Tawny Girl," the 1823 true story of Margaret Russel, the London-born daughter of a black West Indian father and an Irish servant mother, appealed to the compassion of Christians on both sides of the Atlantic. As a poor, illegitimate mulatto girl, Russel epitomized social degra-

THE TAWNY GIRL ;

OR THE

HISTORY

OF

MARGARET RUSSEL,

ILLUSTRATING

THE BENEFITS OF EDUCATION

ON THE

Most Degraded Classes of Society.

———◆———

" Nor hear with a disdainful smile,
The short and simple annals of the Poor."—GRAY.

———✳———

NEW-YORK:

PUBLISHED BY SAMUEL WOOD & SONS,
NO. 261, PEARL-STREET ;
And Samuel S. Wood & Co. No. 212, Market-street,
Baltimore.
1823.

dation, but her innate spirit nurtured by the kindness of Christians made her an exemplar of
the effects of benevolence. Arthur Anderson's woodcut supplied sentimental appeal for the movement to maintain free schools in port cities. Courtesy American Antiquarian Society.

ROYAL BRITISH SYSTEM of EDUCATION

" It is my Wish that every poor CHILD should be taught to read the BIBLE."

Spoken by His Majesty George the 3.ᵈ to Josʰ Lancaster at Weymouth 1805.

This 1813 broadside was used to promote Lancasterian schools in Britain. It expresses the traditional approach to the education of the poor dating from the eighteenth-century charity schools onward. King George's condescension is complemented by the submissive posture of the child who receives the royal gift of learning. Courtesy American Antiquarian Society.

era of working-class protest following the French Revolution. "The general diffusion of knowledge will by no means be found unfavorable to industry," he asserted. Instead, education would "soften and civilize . . . the lower orders of Society . . . [and] inure them to habits of subordination and controul." The record in Scotland, where the "peasantry and other labouring classes" were recognized as the "best informed and the most industrious and sober in Europe," should convince skeptics that "the diffusion of knowledge" would not lead common people to shirk labor or to challenge the existing social order. If a handful of poor individuals did climb up a rung or two on the social ladder as a result of their education, Lancaster, himself the son of a common redcoat who had fought for the king in the Revolution, saw no reason "why [they should] not."[47]

Lancaster's nonrepublican justification for informing common people included a blunt appeal to the self-interests of "the superior and middling classes" in an era when working-class radicalism was beginning to mount political challenges. Lancaster reminded propertied people that "the poor are our inmates, and our guardians. They surround our tables, they surround our beds, they inhabit our nurseries. Our lives, our properties; the minds, and the health of our children, are . . . dependent upon their good or evil." Responding directly to Mandevillean fears of disorder in a postrevolutionary era, he claimed that if "our subordinate brethren" were educated, they would also be "more trust-worthy," whether "as domestics, as artisans, as manufacturers, as persons entrusted with . . . our property in a thousand ways."[48]

DeWitt Clinton and his New York associates may not have endorsed precisely these antirepublican elements in Lancaster's overall appeal, but they did regard Lancaster's pedagogical scheme as heaven-sent. The order, the scope, the efficiency of the Lancasterian school was, in Clinton's eyes, magnificent. Rhapsodically, the future governor and canal builder exclaimed: "When I perceive one great assembly of a thousand children, under the eye of a single teacher, marching, . . . with perfect discipline to the goal of knowledge, . . . I recognize in Lancaster the benefactor of the human race." More concretely, Clinton and the other leaders of early nineteenth-century education reform in New York admired the "economy, facility, and expedition" of Lancaster's monitorial approach, which provided them with nothing less than "a system . . . in education, what the neat finished machines for abridging labor and expense are in the mechanic arts."[49] This economical method of mass education for poor children was, for a time, a republican panacea for realizing the ideal of an informed citizenry in Baltimore, Philadelphia, New York City, and a handful of other American towns.

Although American political leaders liked the emphasis on order and discipline in Lancaster's system, its most appealing characteristic was its economy. Many of the states, starting with Pennsylvania and North Carolina in 1776, Georgia and Vermont in 1777, and Massachusetts in 1780, had made some broad provision for public education in their constitutions; however, the idea of general tax support for schools, rather than parent-paid tuition, enjoyed little support anywhere.[50] Significantly, the most widely used source of public funding was not taxation but revenue from the sale of public lands as in the United States land ordinance of 1786.

Nevertheless, the great advantage of Lancasterian schools—low cost— was not enough to make them thrive in America much beyond 1820. Although they could teach basic literacy and numeracy to poor children, they were quickly recognized as unsuitable for the education of republican citizens and poorly adapted to the yeoman farming population that was spreading over the American interior. Indiana's 1816 constitution, for example, in provisions later copied by Arkansas, recognized "knowledge and learning generally diffused through a community" as not only "essential to

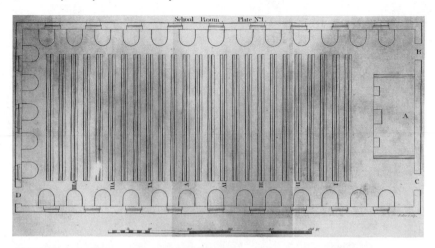

Monitor's Seat and Desk.

These illustrations are from the Manual of the Lancasterian System, *published in 1820 by the Free School Society of New-York.*

Plate no. 1 shows a classroom floor plan providing for 225 pupils in 8 grades, 25 monitors, 2 assistant teachers, and 1 teacher. The beginning students sit in front, the advanced in the rear. The half-circles at the perimeter designate areas to be used by small groups of pupils for recitations and arithmetic. The teacher and his assistants are to be seated on the raised platform at the front of the room.

Plate no. 4 shows a young monitor and his charges, each holding a slate on which letters and numbers will be formed. Each classroom was to contain twenty-five such benches. Courtesy American Antiquarian Society.

the preservation of a free government" but also vital for "spreading the opportunities and advantages of education." The objective was primarily individual and social advancement, not social control. By calling for "a general system of education, ascending in a regular gradation from township schools to a State university, wherein tuition shall be gratis, and equally open to all," and by including provisions for public libraries in every county, Indiana's constitution expressed democratic, egalitarian values that were alien to Lancasterianism.[51]

By the 1830s, the idea of a separate and inferior system of education for the poor and common people was entirely outmoded. Nor could Lancaster's scheme for the efficient training of the poor be remodeled to suit the temperament of American society. As a New England critic explained, the Lancaster plan was useful for Britain, perhaps, insofar as some education was better than none, but "to throw *our* children into a sort of intellectual hopper, where they must be ground in a mill . . . and the whole body taught to march on like a platoon of soldiers, as if they were moved by one spring and were parts of a single machine," was wholly unsuitable. "For republicans, for freemen, for self-controlling, and elevated masters of their own destiny" something better was required. Significantly, the elite advocates of Lancasterian schools like DeWitt Clinton never enrolled their own children in those schools, whereas, as an 1837 article in the *Common School Advocate* of Cincinnati noted, the son of a sawyer was enrolled in a Boston public school in the same class as the son of John Quincy Adams and outstripped his highborn classmate by winning a prize. "The narrow notion, that there is to be an education for the poor as such" had been played out and repudiated by 1840.[52]

In North Carolina, the complex process of actually establishing common schools reveals variations in the ways that the idea of an informed citizenry was articulated and justified in the dynamic cultural and political environment of the first half of the nineteenth century. In 1776, when North Carolina's first constitution was written, enlightened republican ideology had led to the adoption of article 41, which provided "that a school or schools shall be established by the legislature, for the convenient instruction of youth, with such salaries to the masters, paid by the public, as may enable them to instruct at low prices; and, all usefull learning shall be duly encouraged and promoted in one or more universities."[53] The assumption, clearly, was that parents and the public shared responsibility for educating children. The concern for "usefull" learning at the university level signaled public mistrust of the world of higher learning, which, from the North Carolina gentry's viewpoint, might be merely speculative, metaphysical, ornamental, and frivolous. Here, manifest in the constitution itself, were some of the enduring tensions connected to public policy aimed at the realization of an informed citizenry in a state where as late as 1831 the lower house voted against the purchase of a clock, the emblem of rational time management, for the wall of its chamber.[54]

In this one particular, perhaps, North Carolina was unusual, but the route it followed toward the creation of a common school system reflected general American patterns, especially in heavily rural states. In the revolutionary era, the passionate concern for liberty and the people's ability to defend their rights had led to the constitutional mandate for schools. But a generation or two later, the majority of white citizens no longer viewed the government as a threat to their freedom—after all, they controlled the government. Instead, they worried about special privileges for the few and about taxation in general. In this context, advocates for an informed citizenry supplemented the old republican defense-of-liberty arguments with assertions of economic and cultural advantages. Ultimately, they invoked the central values of the Second Great Awakening—morality and Christianity.

During the first three decades of the nineteenth century, elite cosmopolitan leadership, usually represented by the governor, articulated the arguments for an informed North Carolina citizenry. "Where the people are everything," Governor Nathaniel Alexander admonished in 1806, "it becomes infinitely important that they be sufficiently enlightened to realize their interests." Otherwise, Alexander predicted, "their enemies will seduce them from the pursuit of their true interests, or their own prejudices [will] lead them into fatal dangers."[55] For poor white North Carolinians, "a portion of instruction" was said to be especially important to "enable them satisfactorily to discharge the most important duties of society."[56] Insofar as the need to be informed was concerned, the North Carolina elite saw a real distinction between the prosperous and the poor. "A certain degree of education should be placed within the reach of every child in the state," Governor Benjamin Smith argued in 1811. He was sure it could be done cheaply, so that "the poor of every neighborhood . . . might be brought up in the true principles of the Christian Religion." Basic education would have the added benefit of preventing "the multiplicity of crime."[57] The fact that at this time less than half the free men and even fewer free women in some North Carolina counties could write their names led to a decade-long interest in Lancasterian schools.[58] From 1814 to 1823, monitorial schools were set up in several counties, but the same democratic objections that closed them else-where in the United States also doomed them in North Carolina. An educa-tional system that operated to solidify privilege and hierarchy held little appeal, even though it promoted obedience and morality at low cost.

In contrast, state leaders advocated an informed citizenry in order to fos-ter the upward social and political mobility characteristic of meritocracy, an important element of Jefferson's plan for Virginia. In 1817 the state senate Committee on Education, which was headed by Archibald DeBow Mur-phey, a Presbyterian reformer and 1799 graduate of the University of North Carolina, issued a report proposing a systematic plan to implement the edu-cational provisions of the 1776 constitution. In the report, Murphey's com-mittee particularly emphasized the viewpoint that bright children of the poor should be set on the path "to wealth and honors." Because "Providence has generally bestowed upon [the poor] the blessing of intelligent children," the committee declared that the state should act to nurture and harvest this valuable resource. Far from being a handicap, the self-made Murphey as-serted, "poverty is the school of genius . . . in which the active powers of man are developed and disciplined." Turning the Mandevillean analysis on its head, the North Carolinians declared that poverty was not the nursery of rude passions and menial service but a school for "moral courage." The humble dwellings of the poor, not the mansions of the gentry, the report stated, produced "those men who act the principal parts upon the theatre of life." Calling upon a classical Roman model just as another Presbyterian, Benjamin Rush, had done a generation earlier, Murphey closed the report with the declaration: "Poor children are the peculiar property of the State, and by proper cultivation they will constitute a fund of intellectual and moral worth which will greatly subserve the public interest." The North Carolina Senate Committee on Education completed its inversion of Lancasterian doctrine by asserting that instead of forming a class of good ser-vants, educating the poor would prepare a class of good rulers. When this re-port was presented by the committee to the lower house, it concurred unanimously.[59]

Murphey's bill proposed an integrated, three-tiered public education sys-tem modeled on systems in Virginia and several New England states and the French national scheme. It subsidized the education of tuition-paying stu-dents as well as providing need-based support to those who could not afford tuition. Like Jefferson's Bill for the More General Diffusion of Knowledge, it aimed to include all free children. In principle, it seems, the legislature ap-proved of the plan since the proposal passed both houses on its first reading.

But thereafter the plan died, never reaching the floor of either house for the necessary second vote. The scheme was too novel in 1817, too expensive— perhaps even too radical—for legislators to go beyond symbolic approval to actual implementation. The following year, when Governor John Branch pressed the legislature to create an education system, imploring members to fulfill article 41 of the 1776 constitution, a much more modest plan was proposed that would have provided free tuition and textbooks at schools for the poor. Its fate, however, was much the same as Murphey's bill; after passing two readings in the senate and one in the house, it sank into oblivion.[60]

Comprehensive schemes for creating an informed citizenry were distinctly associated with cosmopolitan culture and concentrations of poor people; thus, in a state as thoroughly rural as North Carolina—no town had as many as 2,000 white inhabitants in 1820—the tendency toward localism sustained a wholly voluntaristic approach to creating an informed citizenry.[61] The gentry and yeoman farmers founded dozens of tuition-based schools and academies around the state in the first half of the nineteenth century—not in every county, to be sure, but in most. They even created more than two dozen schools for girls from 1800 through the 1830s. The major educational ideas, from Lancaster and Johann Pestalozzi to military academies and Philipp Fellenberg's manual labor approach, all found favor among some prominent North Carolinians.[62] But support for a uniform, tax-supported public system languished. As one leader noted at the end of 1817, the spread of private academies was extinguishing country schools by depleting them of students whose parents could pay and leaving the remnant, whose parents could not support a teacher's salary, on their own. The problem was further compounded by the chronic shortage of able teachers.[63]

When the next substantial reform effort was mounted in the 1820s, senators acknowledged that "already has the State afforded to the affluent and wealthy the happy opportunity of educating their sons" at the university. But nothing had been done for poor youths, who were largely "doomed" to a "wretched state of ignorance." The resulting waste of talent among "persons of low estate and obscure birth" continued to trouble senate leaders.[64] But persuading the legislature to lay taxes to pay for the education of poor children remained an obstacle even when, as Governor Gabriel Holmes pointed out in 1824, the treasury was "flourishing." In that year, a bill was offered to create a fund to educate "destitute" children with taxes raised from luxuries including billiard tables, the gates erected at the entrances of the driveways of the gentry, and their natural and artificial curiosities as well as duties on peddlers and slave traders. But even these slight, narrowly based taxes were deemed onerous when their objective was educating other people's children. To Governor Holmes's dismay, the bill failed. The cause of an informed citizenry in North Carolina, he said, was "almost hopeless" when he saw "our sister states boasting of millions appropriated" for education, whereas "not one cent" had been approved by his own state legislature.[65]

The repeated defeats that governors and education committees suffered revealed a significant conflict between the state's most elite, cosmopolitan leaders and the majority of rural backbenchers, who could not be convinced that the voluntary, localistic arrangements already in place were so inadequate that new taxes were justified. Majorities rejected arguments supporting free elementary schools that taught reading, writing, arithmetic, and other useful knowledge based on the New England model. Assertions that even the wealthy had a real interest in the education of poor and middling farmers because some of their own children and grandchildren would probably be among them—the same arguments that James Madison was making to Kentucky leaders in the 1820s—were brushed aside.[66]

Finally, in 1826 the North Carolina General Assembly acted to fulfill, at least in part, the fifty-year-old education provision of its constitution. The law enacted that year creating a state "literary fund" represented a true compromise. To satisfy localists as well as the advocates of state support for the creation of an informed citizenry, the state would apportion money to counties according to their white population for the purpose of subsidizing schools in whatever manner county leaders saw fit. Resistance to new taxes to finance the state literary fund was addressed by using a statewide lottery instead of taxation. As a result, in those counties where voters were willing to create public schools supported by local taxes and tuitions, the state literary fund would help to lighten the burden.[67] But in counties where wealthy planters provided private schooling for their children and the remaining inhabitants were so poor and so scattered that local support for education was absent, the state subsidy—which was designed to help those who were helping themselves—would change nothing. One critic complained in 1827 that in some places "the people are left to rust in primeval ignorance"; another argued that North Carolina's weakness in national councils could never be remedied "until the people are redeemed by education from the state of ignorance to which they have been doomed by our penny-saving Legislators."[68] The literary fund law was simply inadequate to address the fundamental problem—"want of general knowledge."

Later in 1827, when "penny-saving" legislators tried to abolish the literary fund even before it was fully implemented, the House Committee on

Education defended it on cultural and political grounds, contrasting "the sullen discontent of an ignorant people, brooding over evils which do not exist, and wrongs never sustained, with the happy condition of a well-informed people, whose sound judgments discriminate between the declamatory froth of a demagogue, and the sound doctrines of political philosophy."[69] The North Carolina Literary Board vowed that "the establishment of schools" was "a moral duty imposed upon all government." This duty was especially vital in a democratic republic in order to ensure that "the citizen may read and think for himself." Above all, such education was essential to teach men their Christian duty now and for the hereafter.[70] In North Carolina, as everywhere else across the United States, republicanism and awakened Christianity complemented each other.[71]

For opponents of state action, tax resistance was their most effective common denominator, but it would be a mistake to view their resistance to cosmopolitan efforts to establish the institutions of an informed citizenry as merely "penny-saving." Their opposition carried cultural messages that only occasionally appeared in print. A crusty letter to the *Raleigh Register* in 1829, for example, merged opposition to schools, roads, canals, and the university. Existing transportation networks had made "our fathers . . . rich" and would serve the needs of the present generation as well. "Innovations and alterations" were simply unnecessary, no matter how they might be described as "improvements." Similarly, this critic found "our good old-field schools are . . . sufficient" to provide whatever literacy was needed. But his criticism went beyond such particulars to express a broad, down-to-earth, practical conservatism that was indifferent if not actually skeptical about the idea of an informed citizenry.

Since money was scarce, the writer claimed, and existing schools had vacancies, there was no sense in starting more of them. Rhetorically, this skeptic asked: "Would it not redound as much to the advantage of young persons, and to the honour of the State, if they should pass their days in the cotton patch, or at the plow, or in the cornfield, instead of being mewed up in a school house, where they are earning nothing?" It was wrong, he asserted, to think "that *everybody* should be able to read, write and cipher." Such skills might be needed "if one is to keep a store or a school, or . . . be a lawyer or physician . . . ; but if he is to be a plain farmer, or a mechanic, they are of no manner of use, but rather a detriment."[72] Working hard and keeping taxes low were the route to general prosperity, according to the *Raleigh Register*'s homespun, latter-day Mandeville.

Furthermore, the university was an expensive institution that did more harm than good. "College learned persons," he wrote, "give themselves great airs, are proud, and the fewer of them we have amongst us the better." Universities were intrinsically "aristocratical" and "opposed to the plain, simple, honest matter-of-fact republicanism." As for university studies, they were mostly "arrogant and useless." "Who," he asked, "wants Latin and Greek and abstruse mathematics . . . in a country like this?" According to this populist conservative republican, taxpayers might just as well "patronize alchymy [*sic*], astrology, heraldry and the black art." To cosmopolitans who complained that North Carolina's educational system was weak compared to those of other states, he delivered an insular rejoinder: if those states wished to follow other paths, that was their business; North Carolinians would pay lower taxes and be "perfectly independent."[73]

Moreover, the champions of similar views were not necessarily back-woods populists. John Randolph, the Virginia patrician, told his colleagues at Virginia's 1829 constitutional convention that if the government paid to educate children in common schools, then parents could spend their earn-ings on liquor and the hardworking, deserving poor would end up paying for the lazy. Honest farmers' sons would have to stay out of school and labor all summer in order to pay for the education of the children of drunkards. According to Randolph, "The education of their children is the first and most obvious, as it is the most interesting duty of every parent; and one which the most worthless alone are ever known to neglect."[74]

These were precisely the views of Thomas Cooper, the president of the University of South Carolina, who argued that if the state paid children's tu-itions, the bonds of reciprocal obligation between parents and children would be destroyed. "There is no man so poor," Cooper claimed, "that he cannot afford half a day's wages per week for the education of his child." Such men, Cooper insisted, "would rather pay a small sum to a good school, frequented also by the children of more opulent parents, than to send their children to a charity school." By paying tuition, fathers would see education as a "right" and would "take an interest in the management and the success of the school."[75] According to Cooper, "only the children of deserving pau-pers should have their way paid before being bound out to some industrious calling" at twelve or fourteen years of age. The college president favored a basic education for all free boys but nothing more. Too much education among common men would lead them to "roam abroad, and endeavour, like the pretenders who swarm as schoolmasters throughout our country, to live by head-work; because they have been rendered too idle by the very superfi-cial knowledge they possess, to live by the labour of their hands."[76] Although it is impossible to determine just how widespread such views were, the long struggle to establish comprehensive systems of state-supported schools in large, populous states like Virginia and Pennsylvania, not just North Carolina and Georgia, suggests that this kind of conservative populism, often represented in the Democratic Party, enjoyed a following in parts of both the North and the South.[77]

Yet a decade later, in 1839, during a period when the Whig Party controlled the state capital, North Carolina enacted a public school law. Notwithstanding their southern sectional allegiance, school advocates claimed that "in the North, the system of Public Schools has been adopted, and their people are now prospering." In addition, the old republican and meritocracy appeals for an informed citizenry—"popular intelligence is the mighty lever of a free government," the antidote to "demagogues," and "merit constitutes the passport to honor and office; the road to promotion is open to all"—provided justifications for the law.[78] The establishment of fully tax-supported free schools was still optional in each county, but whereas Virginia's school law required a two-thirds vote to create common public schools, North Carolina now called for only a simple majority.[79] Viewed from the perspective of earlier decades, this law represented a landmark in state sponsorship of an informed citizenry.

Both rhetorically and as a matter of actual policy, the connection between public schools and an informed citizenry was securely established by the 1840s. But as common school reformers continued to insist, only a beginning had been achieved. In the South, some legislatures still refused to fund common schools. Even in "model" states like Connecticut and Massachusetts, the quality and extent of public education fell far short of any uniform standard of merit. The voluntary principle embodied in lectures, lyceums, libraries, political parties, and the use of oratory and print remained fundamental and applied to schools as well. No state compelled school attendance any more than it compelled citizens to go to lectures, libraries, political rallies, or the polls. Although there was a broad consensus sustaining the idea that institutions should promote an informed citizenry and enable individuals to advance in knowledge, ultimately the whole structure rested on voluntary choice.

For this reason, exhortation remained as fundamental to the idea of an informed citizenry as institutions. Because, like Christian conversion, being informed could be neither compelled nor inherited, every segment of each generation had to be persuaded of its importance. "America is a great lyceum," one reformer exclaimed, "a grand debating society, a mass convention sitting permanently, and courting the utmost freedom of expression."[80] As a result, public life generated a profusion of rhetoric to support every measure that promoted an informed citizenry and oppose all obstacles that stood in its way.

The arguments of the Sunday school leader, Frederick A. Packard, reveal the ways in which many mainstream Christians were prepared to go beyond the old republican ideal without rejecting it. Common schools were "emphatically a *failure*," Packard claimed, since fewer than 5 percent of pupils were educated in the manner that "the public good" and "*public safety*" as well as their personal well-being required. Because pupils left school not fully literate, they could not "think, read, nor observe, profitably," and they were so narrowly informed that they were subject to "violent prejudices" and liable to become "the dupes of the wicked." As of 1840, Packard surmised, more than a quarter of the free inhabitants of the United States over the age of ten years could not read well enough to fulfill their public and private responsibilities. Education, he declared, should teach Americans what "our country [is] bound to do for us, and what are we bound to do for her." He was alarmed by the increase in the number of ignorant adults since "an ignorant man is incapable of bringing up his family."[81]

Like many people who addressed the question of an informed citizenry, the Presbyterian Packard adamantly supported moral training because he believed that "education, without religious instruction, could not control the strong passions of the human race." The poor were better left "in ignorance" than to be educated in a purely secular way. Declaring himself a foe of "bigotry, sectarianism, and fanaticism," he nevertheless argued that all teachers should instruct children "in the fear of God" through Bible-based lessons. The specifics of salvation should be left to others, but schools should counteract the "destructive influence of a heartless, intolerant infidelity." Because so many parents seemed unable or unwilling to fulfill their responsibilities, Packard believed no dependence should be placed on "the voluntary action of the people." School attendance should be compulsory. The wise and the good should unite to support state initiatives.[82]

A few years later, the Whig congressman Henry A. Wise delivered a farewell address to his Virginia constituents in which he pointed to the failures of his own district and state. Unlike Packard, whose concerns were primarily moral, Wise was troubled by the same issues of inequality that Murphey had addressed in North Carolina nearly thirty years before. Wise lamented the accuracy of his opponents' contemptuous charge that many of

This Arthur Anderson woodcut of a sabbath school in which a male instructor teaches boys and girls suggests a traditional classroom that was more refined and orderly than most common schools. From Publications of the American Tract Society, *vol. 4 (New York, [1825–27]). Courtesy American Antiquarian Society.*

his voters "cannot read or write." By his own calculations, more than a quarter of his constituents were illiterate, and voters in his district supported less than half the necessary number of schools. As a result, statistics showed that the majority of poor and near-poor children were growing up in ignorance. Virginia's policy of requiring everyone but the poor to pay tuition promoted feelings of inequality that were counterproductive: "The child of charity is humbled by the comparison of itself with those who pay." In addition, the policy discouraged the enrollment of most poor children since "the pride of the parents so often revolts at the dependence and inequality in the school, that they often refuse to allow their children to enter." Current policy deterred the very families who most needed schools from using them. Wise declared that the answer was to raise taxes in order to fund free schools for all white children, regardless of wealth; all should "be regarded as the sons and daughters of the commonwealth." Poor men, after all, were citizens who paid taxes, served on juries, and took up arms to defend the state. Therefore, it was only right that a poor man should be guaranteed the "ordinary privileges of citizenship" such as voting and, Wise asserted, "should have his children educated as of right free of charge." Only then could Virginia achieve an informed citizenry. Wise, who would serve as the state's governor during the Civil War, told his constituents in 1844 that he wished to be remembered by the next generation as the man "who told our parents that *the state was bound to teach us all as its own children, and persuaded them to bear taxes for our education.*"[83] Ironically, this ideal, which reached back to Thomas Jefferson, could not win support as public policy until Confederate Virginia was defeated and a Reconstruction government took power.

Wise's vision of the school as an agency of equality in a republican meritocracy expressed a national ideal. Five years after Wise admonished his Virginia constituents, the Boston Unitarian minister Theodore Parker declared in a lecture in Syracuse, New York, that "to educate the people is one of the functions of the State. . . . The community owes each child born into it a chance for education, intellectual, moral, and religious . . . not as a charity, but as a right."[84] In the North, such views were easier to translate into policy than in the South, but tax resistance reinforced by democratic individualism was an obstacle everywhere.

Even in the largely urban, industrial, progressive state of Massachusetts, the secretary of education, Horace Mann, faced opposition similar to that in the rural South. Patriarchy endured in New England and farmers relied on their children for labor, so Mann had to give up any thought of compulsory attendance at rural schools.[85] The conduct of industrial workers, even in the Bay State, where public schools charged no tuition, was often distressingly similar to that of rural people. In 1839 Mann railed at the "many parents, not only of our immigrant, but of our native population, so lost to the sacred nature of the relation they sustain to the[ir] children . . . , that they go from town to town, seeking to consign them to unbroken, bodily toil, although it involves the deprivation of all the means of intellectual and moral growth."[86] A decade later, Mann would press unsuccessfully to require such children's schooling.

By this time, Mann was warning of a polarization between rich and poor in which the latter were degraded and exploited, much like the polarization that troubled Wise in Virginia. Wise had argued that in any state where "one man is to be cultivated in his mind, whilst the other is permitted to grow up in ignorance . . . the rich [become] richer, and the poor poorer—the strong stronger, and the weak weaker."[87] Mann's language was different, but his perception was the same—"nothing but universal education," he said, "can counter-work this tendency to the domination of capital and the servility of labor."[88] Midcentury reformers like Mann, Parker, and Wise justified the movement for an informed citizenry by cautioning against a contemporary variant of the

European-style crisis of corruption envisioned by early republican reformers. Already, Wise believed he could see "the foundation of despotism."[89]

By midcentury, the movement to create an informed citizenry, which had once implied a kind of elite republican social control through the indoctrination of the common people, was being complicated by the voluntary principle and a democratic individualism that undermined the authority of all political and cultural prescriptions. In the revolutionary and early national eras, advocates of an informed citizenry had assumed that heads of families would hold an enlightened view of their self-interest and therefore act rationally when provided with opportunities to pursue it. Education would be embraced eagerly because it empowered adults politically and helped to assure the preservation of citizens' liberties. The cultivation of personal virtues and abilities that education promoted also enhanced one's social and career opportunities. To reformers, it was unthinkable that some parents would deliberately reject such advantages when supplied freely by the state. But by 1850, advocates of an informed citizenry had learned otherwise, and their response was to attempt to implement more public paternalism. Although children were not said to "belong to the state" in the neoclassical terms that Rush had proclaimed in the 1790s, reformers believed that "good men in society" could use the powers of government to "send redeeming influences to those children who suffer under the calamity of vicious parentage."[90] The problem for such reformers in the political arena was that not everyone agreed on who "the good men in society" were. Reformers like Mann, Wise, Parker, Packard, and the founders of the American Society for the Diffusion of Useful Knowledge, among hundreds of others, were prepared to identify themselves as "good men," but no parents came forward to disqualify themselves as "vicious" and resign willingly their parental authority to the state. The idea of forcing citizens and their children to become informed had a self-contradictory flavor, and it violated widely shared cultural and political assumptions. Exhortation and policies to encourage the institutions that enabled citizens to become informed, rather than coercion, best suited American political and cultural traditions and expectations.

Exhortation, however, produced some unexpected outcomes. As elite advocates of an informed citizenry strove to bring learning into the households of every white farmer and militiaman, their messages also reached into the ranks of workingmen, African Americans, and women. Ironically, their arguments helped to mobilize disenfranchised groups to assert their claims for inclusion in the nation's informed citizenry. And for such disenfranchised groups, becoming informed had the further attraction of lending legitimacy to their assertions of citizenship, whereas for those men who already possessed the rights and privileges of citizenship, becoming informed was purely a matter of personal preference.

The pursuit of an informed citizenry combined the impulses of elites to achieve some measure of social and cultural control with a much broader, more popular appetite for social and cultural opportunity in a complex, dynamic political and cultural marketplace. Reform spokesmen were chronically frustrated because their reach always exceeded their grasp, and commercial purveyors of information were challenged by an ever-changing competition with each other and with the private and public agencies that generated various forms of subsidized information. In this environment, the idea of an informed citizenry itself continued to evolve in an open-ended process of mutation in which the core idea of responsible citizenship was overlaid with concerns for occupation, personal fulfillment, and privilege and status that were as various as the American people themselves.

Chapter 6 Testing the Meaning of an Informed Citizenry, 1820–1870

In the 1840s and 1850s, when reformers like Congressman Henry Wise and the educator Horace Mann asserted that access to schooling and becoming informed were the birthright of every citizen, not a matter of private privilege, they were carrying the argument for an informed citizenry toward its logical limits. Their unspoken assumption, of course, was that this birthright applied only to free boys—in the Virginian Wise's case, to free *white* boys—since they would grow up to exercise political power as voters. But others who stood outside the political mainstream held no such exclusive assumptions. African American reformers and women's rights advocates believed that African Americans and women shared this birthright of citizens. Labor reformers noted with outrage that the terms of factory employment often precluded schooling and participation in civic culture so that the capacity of workers to function as informed citizens was being endangered by the spread of European-style ignorance. Ironically, the rhetorical triumph of the informed citizenry ideal and its expanding institutional foundations in public culture were accompanied by a polyphony of criticism directed at the remnants of the "freeholder" concept of citizenship, which continued to exclude substantial numbers—indeed, a majority of American-born adults—from the civil rights that were routinely proclaimed as quintessentially American.

During the half century from 1820 to 1870, the notion that voting was a privilege strictly connected to freeholder status collapsed under a barrage of criticisms. Landowning requirements yielded early—in 1776 in Pennsylvania —and were erased under pressure from common revolutionary soldiers and their sons. By the 1820s, these restrictions, as well as religious tests, had nearly all been eliminated by state constitutional conventions, but barriers based on race and sex remained secure, justified by the surviving image of the self-governing (if not actually landowning) citizen as well as prevailing prejudices and ideologies of racial and gender hierarchy.[1] For Native Americans, who were generally viewed as foreign peoples—outsiders to the American polity—additional complexities blocked inclusion.

Ultimately, the successful drive for the abolition of slavery, which culminated in the ratification of the Thirteenth Amendment in 1865, undermined the exclusion of African Americans from full citizenship rights, and in 1870 black men were granted the franchise via the Fifteenth Amendment. Women, white and black, were simultaneously excluded from this constitutional provision by omission and by subsequent Supreme Court rulings. Moreover, although revision of the laws of coverture extended the rights of women to hold property independently in the 1840s and 1850s in a dozen states, the limited, second-class character of their citizenship was formalized by the U.S. Supreme Court in 1875.

By this time, however, the idea that women could not and should not be voters did not mean that keeping them ignorant and uninformed was acceptable. There were echoes of Lancasterian and older charity school ideas about appropriate limits on the education of women and African Americans, limits that would suit them for subordinate social roles, but no Mandeville spoke up to defend a prescription of pure ignorance. By now, the justification for an informed citizenry had moved so far beyond its original argument—that it was necessary to ensure the defense of liberty by voters in the political arena—that the doctrines of universal education and universal suffrage could be separated. The purposes of an informed citizenry, once essentially political, had shifted to encompass such personal goals as individual fulfillment and career advancement as well as social objectives like honesty and industriousness or, in the case of women, domestic productivity and exemplary wifehood and motherhood. The core principles of political liberty, including freedom of speech and of religion and the whole array of rights that had been so prominent in seventeenth- and eighteenth-century struggles, no longer supplied the paramount rationale for an informed citizenry. Instead, these principles were buttressed by a legion of other justifications.

If the meaning of being informed varied and became especially fluid during the decades after 1820, so too did the criteria for American citizenship. When the American lexicographer Noah Webster composed the entry for "citizen" in his *American Dictionary of the English Language* in 1828, he presented five distinct definitions, several of which were in current use.[2] Neither common understanding nor contemporary law was clear and unequivocal, and where ambiguity reigned, controversy flourished. Since the meaning of citizenship was freighted with profound political consequences, reformers and defenders of the status quo understood that control of the concept, both in law and in rhetoric, was crucial.

Free African Americans and their white abolitionist associates were especially eager to establish a definition of citizenship that would provide civil equality for free persons of color. But in a test case in the Connecticut Supreme Court in 1833, they ran headlong into Chief Justice David Daggett. This aging Federalist anticipated the spirit of Jacksonian Roger B. Taney's ruling a generation later in the Dred Scott case by asserting definite racial criteria for citizenship. Concerning Native Americans and African Americans, free or slave, he claimed that according to the U.S. Constitution, as well as every state constitution, "they are not citizens."[3] Rejecting Noah Webster's fourth definition of a citizen as "a native or permanent resident of a city or a country," he quoted from Webster's more restricted and political fifth definition. This version defined a citizen in the United States as a man who possessed "the privilege of exercising the elective franchise, or the qualifications which enabled him to vote for rulers, and to purchase and hold real estate."[4] Although this definition clearly limited citizenship to men, it was Daggett who interpreted Webster's words to mean *white* men. The Connecticut jurist chose to ignore the fact that, in reality, some African Americans could and did actually vote as well as "purchase and hold real estate" in such powerful and prominent states as New York, Pennsylvania, and Virginia—as well as in his own state of Connecticut.

Indeed, there was some irony in the fact that as late as the 1830s a Yankee judge would enunciate a view of citizenship more in keeping with southern than northern doctrines. The common source was an increasingly anachronistic neoclassical republicanism that defined citizens as an aristocratic elite. In an 1835 address to the South Carolina Society for the Advancement of Learning, a local jurist and politician, William Harper, expounded this vision of citizenship, which, he was quick to admit, contradicted the Declaration of Independence's egalitarian precepts. "Natural equality and universal freedom," Harper asserted, "never did and never can exist." The lesson of history was unmistakable: "All the great and successful republics of the world have been aristocracies."[5]

Harper explained that the policies of states "in which universal suffrage exists and domestic slavery is excluded" could only lead to public disaster. Inevitably, despite "schemes of universal education at public expense," control of government would "pass into the hands of men without property, without the means of education, and consequently with defective intelligence and morality." Sounding a Mandevillean note, he exulted that in South Carolina "the menial and laborious offices of society—are occupied by those who have no political power." By contrast, "every citizen is raised to the rank of patrician," and among citizens, Harper boasted, "we shall certainly have a larger proportion than any people ever had, of education, intelligence and character." Blending arguments in favor of plutocracy and natural aristocracy, Harper declared that the man who gained wealth "by his own exertions . . . has given presumptive evidence of intelligence, industry, and orderly habits," and the man who "inherited it . . . has had an opportunity of acquiring liberal ideas and a cultivated intellect."[6] This vision of an informed citizenry revived the model of enlightened, Augustan England and the freeholder republic.

Such exclusive proclamations of citizenship would have been unnecessary, whether in Connecticut or South Carolina, if other voices had not been calling for the realization of the Declaration of Independence's natural rights philosophy. Even though there was a broad consensus that every white person, regardless of age, sex, or national origin, was a citizen in the sense of being a "permanent resident," Webster's fourth definition, there was disagreement as to whether merely being a white person justified having a political voice. And if a person had no right to vote, then being informed was not necessarily a matter of public interest.

African Americans and their allies challenged these restrictions on citizenship with arguments based on natural rights doctrine. They noted that African Americans had enlisted in the fight for American independence and that in the first years of the new republic none of the states had applied a color test for voting. When racial restrictions were added to the voting laws of South Carolina in 1778 and Delaware in 1787, most states did not choose to follow suit. Free blacks, they said, were generally allowed to vote in the 1780s and much later—in Virginia as late as 1850. U.S. naturalization law in 1790 did proscribe foreign blacks as well as Native Americans and Asians from becoming citizens, but except for American Indians, these restrictions had no bearing on persons born in the United States. The U.S. Constitution itself made no racial distinctions as such.[7]

Advocates of women's rights could not lay claim to the franchise based on women's military service in the Revolution—although a few women did participate in the war—but they could argue that the U.S. Constitution made no distinctions based on sex. Of course, no one claimed that white women were not citizens, but if married, as most of them were, women were generally barred from exercising the key rights of citizens, such as the right to hold and alienate property freely; to make wills independently; to serve on juries and be tried by a jury of peers; and, except briefly in New Jersey, to vote in local, state, and national elections.[8] As the reformer Ernestine L. Rose argued at a New York City women's rights convention in 1853, the law permitted "all persons, *except* idiots, persons of unsound mind, married women, and infants" from making wills, even though women were recognized as mentally competent to manage property, whether married or not, and were allowed to make marriage contracts even before the age of twenty-one.[9] No one even hinted that married women, America's mothers, were not citizens, yet like African Americans and Native Americans, in a political sense they were classed with children and people who were mentally handicapped.

Even white men did not always enjoy citizenship to its fullest extent. In a literal sense, the freeholder concept of citizenship had lost its grip by 1830— except in Rhode Island, where an uprising in the 1840s led to its demise— but its biases persisted. Thomas Cooper, the president of the University of South Carolina and the author of an important textbook in political science, was ready to drop landowning requirements for voters, but he still sharply criticized "UNIVERSAL SUFFRAGE . . . the root of the evil." Reacting against the writings of English and American reformers of the 1820s, he focused his objections on the "unmarried operative, whose whole property is upon his back or in his bundle; who has no local permanent attachments, who is a mere sojourner among us, a passenger, here to-day and gone to-morrow." Such men, Cooper argued, had "no stake in the community," whereas, he insisted, "the right of voting, . . . is a right to be earned" and thus ought to be "restricted to *householders who have paid taxes for a year*."[10] It was imperative that such voters be qualified as informed by their literacy, and each voter should "be bound to declare . . . that the ticket by him delivered in, is in his own handwriting."[11] Such men were responsible for educating their children at their own expense. In contrast to Europe, Cooper maintained, in the United States "there is no man so poor . . . that he cannot afford half a day's wages per week for the education of his child."[12]

Cooper's recipe for full citizenship rights expressed a somewhat old-fashioned flavor to northern tastes. He was, after all, like Harper, a spokesman for the most frankly elitist of the American states. Yet the contemporary protests of factory workers who dwelled in the very New England states that were held up nationally as model republics of informed citizens indicate that the issues Cooper was addressing were national. The actual experiences of some Yankees who worked in textile mills, however, flatly contradicted Cooper's assertions about their ability to inform themselves and educate their children. The factory workers' movement to ameliorate their own circumstances and those of their children by reducing the workday to ten hours appealed to the mainstream ideology of an informed citizenry of freemen, white men who could join in what one scholar calls "Herrenvolk egalitarianism."[13]

The most plaintive of the workingmen's appeals to the ideology of an informed citizenry were not truly radical but backward looking, even nostalgic. In 1832 an open letter addressed to all New England factory owners expressly declared that the existing system "foster[ed] ignorance" and would ultimately so degrade a large mass of the people that they would either "become fit instruments to establish domestic slavery" or else become so demoralized that they would "tamely surrender it [the country] to a foreign despot." Two-thirds of the men who worked in factories put in 78 to 96 hours weekly and thus could not begin to "store their minds with useful information, to become acquainted with the principles of our government . . . and be prepared as good citizens."[14] Such men could not help but be ignorant, the potential tools of despots and demagogues. The 80,000 women and children who worked in cotton factories, who would later become "mothers of families" or "fathers and citizens," were also "deprived of the means of that mental culture, necessary to prepare them to fill with honor, those stations designed for them . . . by the American Constitution."[15] Striking an elegiac note, this admonition to factory owners concluded with the warning that "the last remains of a more favored generation now surround you. . . . But the period is rapidly approaching, when those remains shall have passed away." Then the United States would face a republican apocalypse "in all its horrors," with its citizenry reduced to "a race of ignorant, unenlightened beings," and all would "hear the expiring groans of American Freedom!" Before it was too late, factory owners should recognize the evil tendencies of their policies and embrace both the ten-hour workday and provisions allowing factory children to attend common schools.[16]

In one sense, Yankee workers' struggles to maintain their self-respecting "freeman" citizenship set them apart from African Americans and others who were widely excluded from voting. But the connections across racial lines were drawn explicitly in an 1833 workingmen's appeal arguing that it was primarily the condition of being informed that separated these two classes of inhabitants. "The inferiority of our colored population," the argument stated, "arises chiefly from their ignorance; and were the whites deprived of their present opportunities of knowledge, they would soon relapse into the degradation and barbarism of the enslaved African and the savage Indian."[17] From this perspective, being informed was not only vital to republican liberty but also crucial in establishing identity itself.

This issue of identity, as suggested in the preceding chapter, was bound up tightly with education and knowledge, or the sense of being informed. This is revealed in the workingmen's press, which treated subjects associated with

selfhood extensively. Because the boundaries as well as the definitions of social class were fluid, the entire subject of class was contested, and the fact that
many workers began their lives in yeoman or artisanal families gave the question of identity a special immediacy. As the above suggestion that whites
might suffer the degradation of blacks and Native Americans demonstrates,
white workingmen felt beleaguered in the new world of competitive capital-
ism because it challenged their ability to maintain a respectable station.

Workingmen's ideas about an informed citizenry were affected in several
ways by the increasingly competitive society. They sought public, egalitarian
schools and advocated manual labor schools because these institutions
promised to enable the children of workingmen to achieve respectable stations in life. Conversely, anything that smacked of exploitation or class privilege, including excessive child labor for the poor and the higher education of
men of means, created a gulf of ignorance that would debase and humiliate
workingmen and their children. Like others, workingmen valued self-education and self-culture highly, not only as a means of economic advancement
and political empowerment but also as sources of self-esteem. Generally,
workingmen's specific views were close to those of the mainstream spokesmen who lectured publicly throughout the country, but sometimes workingmen expressed opinions that were at variance with prevailing conventions.

The sentiments of Edward Everett, one of America's great popular orators
from the 1820s through the 1860s, supply a revealing counterpoint to workingmen's views. Everett repeatedly celebrated the importance and freedom of
"each individual." American institutions, he said, provided the level playing
field on which "our system of free schools has opened a straight way from the
threshold of every abode, however humble . . . to the high places of usefulness, influence, and honor." In this free, competitive environment, everything rested on personal responsibility: "It is left for each, by the cultivation
of every talent; by watching . . . for every chance of improvement, by
bounding forward . . . at the most distant glimpse of honorable opportunity; . . . by redeeming time, defying temptation, and scorning sensual pleasure; to make himself useful, honored, and happy."[18] Ignoring the
advantages that wealth and class provided, the Harvard man Everett declared
that there was "no important difference in the situation of individuals, but
that which they themselves cause or permit to exist." To him, inequalities of
wealth were merely "another excitement to that industry, by which . . .
wealth is acquired."[19] Workingmen shared Everett's belief in individual exer-
tion, but their view of reality was not as rosy.

For one thing, a committee of the New England Association of Farmers,

Mechanics, and Other Workingmen declared in 1832, most factory owners only permitted children "to obtain an education . . . on the Sabbath, and after half past eight o'clock, of the evening of other days."[20] Such obstacles barred any "straight way . . . to the high places of usefulness, influence, and honor." Moreover, it was not just children who worked in factories who were at a disadvantage. In 1833 a writer complained in a Boston workingmen's newspaper that "the aristocracy . . . seem determined violently to oppose a system of education free for all, at the expense of all—a system which will place side by side the children of the rich and the poor."[21] According to the workingman John B. Eldredge, there was simply no legitimate reason "why knowledge should not be equal among the poor as well as the rich." Without a suitable republican education for all, "the bonds of mental slavery" would subvert the principles of 1776. Edward Everett was describing a mythological world, Eldredge declared, whereas in reality for over fifty years "many free born citizens of this Republic have been compelled by poverty to grovel in the darkness of ignorance." The fact that America was not, as Thomas Cooper had said, as bad as Europe did not mean that all was well since for years parents had been forced to anticipate "their children's future hardships and degradation—of seeing their offspring bandied about as the sculions [*sic*] of every man that will afford them a shelter."[22]

According to the analyses of writers in the workingmen's press, the United States had a class problem created by the disparities between the rich and the poor. The wealthy were trained to see themselves as thinkers and rulers, whereas the poor were raised to see themselves as laborers and followers. Tax-supported public schools could change these perceptions by educating all children together, both to think and to do manual labor. After their minds had been shaped in this republican setting, they could go their various ways.[23] John Eldredge argued further that "a democratic form of government . . . is incomplete and insufficient" without a state-run education system "which shall afford to every citizen the scientific and political knowledge necessary to qualify him as an independent voter and equal member of a popular government."[24]

But public schools were only part of the solution to the problems of class inequalities and a republican citizenry. Self-education provided a sure foundation for the development of self-respect among people of all ages and conditions, according to Edward Everett as well as workingmen's writers. It was true, of course, that "there is a little time, and a *very little* it is, in which mechanics may improve their minds." But "Othman" argued that they could still "obtain much useful knowledge." He recommended that "when we retire from our work in the evening, an hour or two, devoted to reading, or discussing some question, is worth double that time thrown away in a dram shop or a tavern." Workingmen possessed the ability "to become useful" in a larger sense, for among them were "young men who would not disgrace the legislature of any state" if they engaged in proper self-education. It was time, "Othman" said, "we aroused ourselves in pursuit of knowledge." The task of bosses was to shorten hours and increase pay in order to encourage working-men's education.[25]

Because arguments for the informed workingman were connected to the movement for a ten-hour workday, one might be tempted to discount them as mere political propaganda. After all, in the political battle to limit the power of bosses to dictate working conditions, arguments that focused on the creation of informed citizens were linked to mainstream Democratic and Whig republicanism and made the bosses look like Mandevillean tories who were willing to sacrifice the republic's future on the altar of greed. Yet because the arguments were chiefly presented to an audience of workingmen in their own press and did not circulate widely in mainstream commercial papers, there is reason to believe that they truly expressed some workingmen's views. At a Utica, New York, "Mechanics and Laboring Men's" meeting, for example, one complaint the participants registered was that toiling twelve to fifteen hours daily "shuts out all opportunity for the improvement of the mind." The members went on to pledge that if they could secure a ten-hour workday, they would use their time as much "as may be practicable for the purposes of acquiring useful and practical intelligence, and of disseminating the same to those around us." Moreover, they would create their own reading room and stock it with books, newspapers, and periodicals so that they could become informed on current events.[26]

Another telling example was a satire of an Edward Everett–style address to mechanics extolling "the great engine of knowledge, the Press, [which] is free, unshackled—shedding upon all the brightest beams of literature, science and arts." In the satire the orator, using Everett-like platitudes, advises mechanics that "by books we can draw around us the vast fields of knowledge which have been sown and cultivated by the great and learned of all ages and nations, and there we can gather a plentiful harvest of knowledge." But the mechanic replies that he knows of the importance of reading; the problem is that mechanics "see 'the streams of information flow' by them while they are not permitted to drink. Because . . . time will not permit." Employers, he says, were either indifferent to their workers' cultural needs or actively hostile; for laborers "to leave their task is sure to merit a snarl, and often times a dismissal." What mechanics needed from their "avaricious employers" was "time to read."[27] One cannot say how many workingmen shared this view, but the laborer's voice expressed in this satire was not the rhetoric of mainstream propaganda, and its central complaint—that little time was available for self-education—was commonplace in workingmen's publications of the 1830s. As the editor of the *New England Artisan and Laboring Men's Repository* put it, no matter how much Connecticut might boast of its universal literacy, the ability to read was useless "if a person be debarred the privilege of *reading, study,* and *reflection.*"[28] From the perspective of employees, it was clear that the factory system was squeezing their time for the cultural activities essential to informed citizens.

Although workingmen saw long hours and greedy bosses as major barriers to elevating their social standing and becoming empowered through being informed, they also recognized—as the Utica resolutions attest—that using their time constructively was their own problem. According to labor reformers, the two temptations that most often diverted workingmen from the culture of self-improvement were frequent tavern-going and the unrelieved pursuit of the last dollar by working as much as possible. Visiting taverns sometimes led to excessive drinking and always involved what was criticized as idle sociability, in which hours slipped by in gossip and storytelling. Overwork was said to be founded on a single-minded, practical materialism and the belief that books and lectures consisted of airy speculations and imaginings, which were of little use in the much-to-be-preferred concrete world of the here and now.[29] Both of these behaviors presented obstacles to developing the social self-respect and self-assertion that political empowerment demanded.

The problem of gaining self-respect operated on two levels. First, and most obvious, was the fact that workingmen lacked book-learning and public-speaking skills. As a New Bedford, Massachusetts, spokesman put it: "We are at present deficient of those mental acquirements which to a society are indispensably necessary."[30] But underlying this limitation was a deeper deferential attitude that held workingmen back—"their unfounded self-distrust." The workingman "must disabuse himself of his fear and trembling at the power and bluster of men, no wiser nor better than himself." Instead of accepting the top-down leadership criteria that had long been employed in politics, religion, and education, workers should elect men who were qualified for office because of their "honest poverty and humility, simplicity of manners, frugality in living, and patient industry." Calloused hands, apron, and smock should no longer be regarded as "unfitting" for a man aspiring to public service.[31]

Calls like these resonated among workingmen and helped to promote their participation in self-improvement culture. But regardless of how accessible print became in the 1830s and 1840s, self-improvement required more than closeting oneself with books. Some considered the lyceum movement a panacea because it was cheap, entertaining, social, and informative. In 1832 the New England Association of Farmers, Mechanics, and Other Workingmen resolved that "whereas *Ignorance* is believed to be the principal cause of the evils connected with the condition of the working classes . . . the formation of Lyceums and other Associations for mutual improvement, are among the best measures . . . to improve the minds of the working classes; and to increase their power, augment their wealth, and extend their influence in the Republic."[32] Accordingly, these workingmen recommended that their "brethren throughout the country" form lyceums and "extend the benefits of them to both sexes and all ages of their families, friends, and neighbors."[33] These workingmen's lyceums would pursue subjects in the liberal arts and natural sciences and, by including exercises in declamation, would "increase the confidence of speakers in debate."[34]

Improving their skills at public speaking was especially important to workingmen because such skills were central to their political enfranchisement. As long as they could be out-talked by gentlemen and professional men, their autonomy as citizens—informed or not—was compromised. Since self-culture, including public speaking, was crucial for their political advancement, the lyceum appeared to be a promising institution. Yet within months of the prolyceum resolutions of the Farmers, Mechanics, and Other Workingmen's Association, a caustic critique of lyceums was printed in the workingmen's press arguing that, especially in cities and large towns, lyceums were not only failing to diffuse information among all classes but actually reinforcing class boundaries. "They too frequently kill the sparks of ambition . . . of the young laborer or mechanic," the critic observed, "while they kindle and invigorate that, which spurs on the son of the lordling." The problem lay in the social dynamics of such gatherings, which put down workingmen:

> Let him whose hard hand is the *insignia* of his calling, rise in one of our modern Lyceums to express his honest views on a question under debate, and how is he received by a *fashionable* audience. If not frowned down by any impudent young pettifogger—the sarcastic smiles of the pedlars of ribbons, or indirect manifestation of displeasure from gentlemen of leisure, palsies his confidence, cherishes his credulity, and renders him in

their hands, like clay in the hands of the potter. . . . [Lyceums] therefore, benefit the affluent, the learned—and them alone—instead of demolishing the partition walls which divide class from class, lay them broader and more formidable than before. . . . *Lyceums* conducted on the present plan—we believe them to be aristocratic establishments, gotten up by the rich and the influential to perpetuate their power and consequence . . . where the people are required to meet at set times to hear a flippant lawyer or some other candidate for popular favor display his college learning in the use of hard words and unmeaning phrases, which are of no sort of consequence to those who get their bread by the sweat of their brow.[35]

Lyceums based on this model would not inform as much as they would indoctrinate workingmen, disempowering them by convincing them to accept the hegemony of the ruling classes.

But lyceums open to all—which quickly became agents of elite dominance—though widespread in the North, were not the only lyceums available. The New Bedford, Massachusetts, *Workingmen's Press* praised "Associations for Mutual Improvement" that limited membership to "common people" as "an efficient method of diffusing rational knowledge among the young men, and especially among young mechanics."[36] In Boston, too, the "Mechanics' Lyceum" worked effectively, and it was reported that "the members acquire a habit of doing their own studying and speaking, . . . calling into exercise the faculties of their own minds, and . . . improving their own manner of delivery."[37] In theory, the ideal of mixing all ages and classes in one community of self-improvement might be appealing, but it could never work properly because "the few" would always pursue "their diabolical purposes." Since the producing classes had less time for study, it was said, they were less learned and therefore unable to compete successfully with the "non-producers," who used "satire to destroy their confidence and kill their ambition." If workingmen were to pursue the self-culture necessary to become informed citizens, a kind of self-imposed class segregation was necessary.[38]

One additional limitation on workingmen's efforts to acquire learning was a current of anti-intellectualism that ran through their rhetoric. Writers, scholars, and professors were all "non-producers," and the fact that higher education was seen as an agency that supplied "non-producers" with the tools to keep "producers" down tainted the entire concept of advanced and theoretical learning. When Seth Luther, the Yankee labor reformer who was imprisoned during Rhode Island's Dorr Rebellion, considered higher learning, he emphasized class issues: "We have been paying taxes, to build colleges, to educate rich men's sons to be doctors, and lawyers, &c. &c., to enable them to grind our own faces on the grindstone of monopolies and monied corporations."[39] Taxes, Luther argued, should be used to "establish Manual Labor Schools . . . for the benefit of all, at the expense of all." Workingmen were not opposed to learning per se, but they were wary of any institution or policy that strengthened their adversaries. Ultimately, Luther and his reform brethren argued, "we must make labor respectable."[40]

The ultimate irony of American policy from the workingman's perspective was that it was easier to become an informed subject of the "despotic" Prussian monarchy than it was to become an informed citizen of "free America" because the Prussian state supplied a comprehensive, truly public education system.[41] According to the Unitarian reformer Theodore Parker, Prussia's king "has yet done more for the education of all classes of his people, than all the politicians of the twenty-six States have done with the wealth of the public lands and the surplus revenue before them and the banner of freedom over their heads."[42]

The problem had many origins, including individualism, greed, sectarian and partisan concerns, and suspicion of government, among others. What Parker chose to emphasize, however, was a pragmatic anti-intellectualism that cut across all class and regional boundaries and encompassed the cultural mainstream. Parker argued that when Americans sought learning and information, they wanted "a result which they can see and handle; and since wisdom and manly excellence are not visible commodities, they say they have no time for mental culture." Consequently, workers became "hands, and hands only . . . who can eat, drink, and vote." Too many workers, Parker complained, "were content to do nothing but work" and left serious reading and thinking to others.[43] Reformers like Parker and Luther and the various workingmen's associations believed that even though workingmen possessed all the rights and privileges of citizenship, from property ownership to jury duty to the franchise, they were poorly informed and might even slide back into old-fashioned, European-style ignorance and depravity. No Mandevilles came forward to argue that laboring men should not be informed, but in Rhode Island, the nation's most fully industrialized state, not even the Dorr Rebellion of the early 1840s could completely erase taxpaying and property requirements for voting. Rhode Island Whigs preferred to limit suffrage for Catholics, foreigners, and factory workers rather than pay to educate them.[44] Moreover, although the people of Connecticut and Massachusetts prided themselves on their states' high literacy rates as America's "capitals" of informed citizenry, it was only after a decade or so of reformers' protests that their legislatures enacted child labor restrictions and common school provisions to assure that children who worked in factories would have access to public schools.

Whereas the case of propertyless workingmen required some adjustment of common understandings of citizenship and suffrage, the circumstances of Native Americans were truly anomalous. They were, of course, free native residents of the United States and often of particular states as well and thus were nominally qualified for full citizenship. Yet as long as they lived in "tribes," rather than as assimilated individuals, they were historically understood to be members of foreign nations. They and their lands were exempt from taxation, they entered into treaties with the U.S. government, and their administration was supervised as a branch of foreign relations by the secretary of state until the 1840s. The Constitution, which referred explicitly to Native Americans twice, excluded them from congressional apportionment calculations and empowered Congress to regulate trade with "Indian tribes" just as it regulated trade with foreign nations.[45]

Because Native Americans retained their group identity rather than assimilating as individuals among other citizens, they were not recognized legally as citizens or as participants in the American polity. Therefore, within the framework of American political ideology, the question of whether or not they were informed was irrelevant. But because missionaries persisted in trying to bring Native Americans to Christianity and to assimilate them into yeoman culture, the issue of whether or not they were informed was always important to some Americans. Indeed, what was most significant for the development of the idea of an informed citizenry was the way in which experiences with the Native Americans perpetuated the English charity school idea of education for piety, not politics. This conception of schooling was discarded in white society when the Lancasterian idea collapsed in the 1830s, but its persistence among missionaries to Native Americans and African Americans, both slave and free, had powerful consequences. For African Americans, especially, it complicated the movement for the recognition of full citizenship because the charity school idea separated education from political empowerment.

Native Americans' own ideas at that time about the nature of citizenship are not known except for those of the Cherokees, whose adoption of European customs in the 1820s included the formation of a constitutional government, a legislature, a written language, and a newspaper. Cherokee law, at least from the 1820s to the 1870s, made citizenship a matter of descent and included property and political rights for men. Non-Cherokees might be admitted to citizenship by the governing council but only on a case-by-case basis. As with many contemporary state governments, Cherokee law excluded "all free negroes" from "coming into the Cherokee nation" and prohibited both Native Americans and whites from marrying "Negro slaves."[46] The form of the Cherokee government, which was aimed at securing congressional recognition and protection, was broadly republican, and its principles included the declaration that "Religion[,] morality and knowledge being necessary to good Government, the preservation of liberty, and the happiness of mankind, Schools and the means of education shall forever be encouraged in this Nation."[47] However, nine of the twenty-one delegates who approved this constitutional provision could not sign their names, and the degree of actual commitment to schools was even more tenuous than in the southern states whose constitutions made similar proclamations. Judging from articles, editorials, and letters in the Cherokee press, the idea of an informed citizenry was developed almost entirely by missionaries and then only to a limited extent.

The most ambitious plan for creating an informed Native American citizenry was an abortive project launched by the American Society for Promoting the Civilization and General Improvement of the Indian Tribes in the United States, whose corresponding secretary and principal agent was the evangelical Calvinist and geographer Jedidiah Morse. Organized in 1822 in Washington, D.C., and sponsored by secular and religious leaders from throughout the nation, this society aimed "to secure for these tribes instruction in all branches of knowledge, suited to their capacities and condition; and for this purpose to ascertain the character and strength of their moral and intellectual powers." Ultimately, the society hoped to raise Native Americans "from a state of ignorance, heathenism and wretchedness" to "Civilization and Christianity" as yeoman farmers.[48] One of the society's most optimistic members, the Reverend William Jenks, had worked among Native Americans in Maine, and his goal was to link education with citizenship. In a letter to Morse that was published in the first (and only) annual report of the society, Jenks declared his belief that American Indians could "be educated . . . for the duties of freemen and citizens" and that "the United States could not be dishonored by citizenship awarded to such."[49]

The idea that Native Americans could become informed citizens through the Christian model and thereby be integrated into civic culture was echoed periodically in the late 1820s and early 1830s, at the same time that Cherokee removal beyond the Mississippi River was becoming fixed as U.S. policy. In

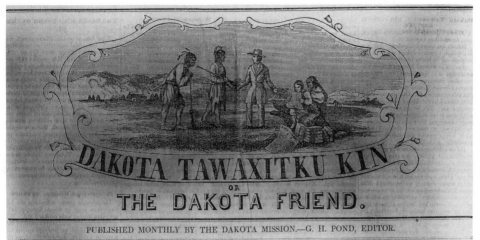

The idea that missionaries could lead Indians into Christian civilization persisted long after Cherokee removal. This 1852 St. Paul, Minnesota, periodical presents, among other texts, a translation from the Bible in the Dakota language. The masthead shows a missionary distributing books and the periodical to Indian men, a child, and a woman. At the left in the background is the mission, a gabled frame house surrounded by tepees. Courtesy American Antiquarian Society.

1828, during its first year of publication, the weekly *Cherokee Phoenix* referred to "the diffusion of political knowledge" as one of its purposes, together with promoting "a taste for literature and knowledge in general."[50] The next year, an academy was organized at the Cherokee capital of New Echota, justified in part because "it becomes every citizen . . . , particularly every ruler, as a guardian of the nation's welfare, to do his utmost to forward education" as the chief bulwark against "the common burial place of Indians—oblivion."[51] Five years later, a clergyman reviewed Thomas Dick's *On the Improvement of Society by the Diffusion of Knowledge* favorably in the *Cherokee Phoenix and Indians' Advocate,* underlining Dick's arguments against "superstition" and in favor of "the diffusion of *knowledge among the people.*"[52]

Indeed, the most powerful, consistent stream of rhetoric came from missionaries who believed that education for piety, morality, and salvation need not include civic or political information. After his arrival in the United

States, Joseph Lancaster recommended "manual, agricultural and mechanical arts" training for Native American boys and "every domestic art" for girls; in fact, a Lancasterian school operated briefly in Kentucky in 1828, serving Choctaw, Creek, Chickasaw, and other Native American children.[53] Training for useful, productive piety on the charity school model, not political or civic education, usually represented the most generous, progressive thinking of the era. In contrast, secular policymakers had no such agenda. P. B. Porter, the secretary of war in John Quincy Adams's administration, argued against any kind of education for Native Americans because it tended to create a permanent missionary infrastructure that might actively oppose removal of Native Americans to the West. In Porter's view—one that was widely held outside of missionary circles—education did Indians more harm than good and, in the end, ruined them by undermining their culture, making them good-for-nothing.[54] With voices like Porter's influencing national policy, arguments for fully informed and enfranchised Native Americans were not heeded. The strongest supporters of Native American education in the United States were missionaries, and their primary goals were Christian conversion and salvation, not political empowerment.

In some important ways, the discussion of an informed Native American citizenry overlapped consideration of an informed African American citizenry. In both cases, citizenship was widely denied, regardless of birthplace, at least partly on racial grounds. And in both cases, education was frequently promoted for apolitical evangelical reasons. But for African Americans, the issues were more vexed and controversial both because there were many more African Americans and because their populations—divided between the millions held in slavery and the hundreds of thousands who were free and living in northern and southern states—did not live apart from white America but were thoroughly enmeshed in American society. Unlike the Native Americans, no one thought of African Americans as separate nations only marginally involved in American life. From the moment David Daggett pronounced his 1833 courtroom assertion of black noncitizenship, it was doubtful and disputed. By the 1840s, it was deemed patently wrong in a number of states and vigorously challenged in others. Like workingmen, and in contrast to Native Americans, many African Americans actively pursued the fullest enfranchisement under the banner of the principles of 1776.

The complications of citizenship for African Americans were starkly illustrated by debates over their voting rights in New York, Connecticut, and Pennsylvania in the generation following the War of 1812. In all of these states, as in New Jersey, Virginia, and a few others, no racial restrictions on voting had been specified in their Revolution era laws. Therefore, if blacks fulfilled the general suffrage requirements of property, residence, and citizenship, they were allowed to vote, and they did so in small numbers. But when the numbers of free blacks grew in the early decades of the nineteenth century as a result of northern states' abolition of slavery and the enactment of liberal manumission laws in the upper South, white sentiment to keep blacks subordinate by excluding them from civic culture also grew. First in Connecticut and New York, then in other eastern states with significant black populations, efforts were made to rewrite state suffrage laws to end black voting. The implications of this restrictive movement to limit the boundaries of American citizenship affected the idea of an informed citizenry directly and suggested that perhaps the real issue for the United States had become whether it would possess an informed *white* citizenry.

In New York these issues were addressed at the 1821 state constitutional convention. At this gathering, a concerted attempt was launched to end the state's freeholders-only voting requirement. To do so, however, would instantly enfranchise a few thousand black men, many of whom dwelled in New York City. Therefore, the convention committee that recommended lifting the property restriction on voting substituted a new barrier of race. Native Americans were also affected by the substitution of the race restriction for the property restriction, but since scarcely any of them had ever met the old property restriction, their voting status changed little.[55] African Americans were the main target, as was evident from the intensely racist sentiments explicit in public discussion.

The committee chairman, John Z. Ross of Genesee County in the western part of the state, explained that, notwithstanding the principles of the Declaration of Independence, in civil society it was necessary to abridge natural equality for the sake of the general good. Employing an argument that would be used for generations to justify depriving blacks and women of equal rights, Ross asserted that the public good required their exclusion from voting. Since blacks were usually barred from militia service, Ross claimed that their disfranchisement was fair because, although they paid taxes like everyone else, they were seldom required to share the common burden of defense. In the end, however, these arguments were merely rationalizations for the racist judgment that African Americans were "a *peculiar* people, incapable . . . of exercising that [voting] privilege with any sort of discretion, prudence, or independence. . . . It is not thought adviseable to permit aliens to vote; neither would it be safe to extend it to blacks." Ross concluded by asserting erroneously that in almost every western and southern state and even Connecticut they were excluded from voting.[56] Later on in the debate, the racist core of the disfranchisement movement was displayed when one of its advocates attacked the notion that the possession of voting rights could elevate blacks anymore than "it would elevate a monkey, or a baboon, to allow them to vote!"[57]

Some representatives, however, voiced powerful counterarguments based on precedent and principle for maintaining full black citizenship. Robert Clarke of Delaware County pointed out that the U.S. Constitution apportioned representation and taxes according to the number of "free persons" without distinction of color and that the argument of militia exclusion was absurd because, not counting black Revolutionary War veterans, as recently as 1814 the New York legislature had accepted the services of "a corps of 2000 free people of color." Clarke admitted that many blacks may be "incapable of exercising that right of suffrage judiciously," but he and several others noted that the same was true of many whites.[58] Abraham Van Vechten of Albany stated that the convention could not possibly "prescribe the moral and intellectual qualifications" of voters and pointed out that "colored people" had been citizens for forty years, which was why it was necessary for restrictionists to use the expression "white citizens."[59] Correcting committee chairman John Ross, Van Vechten noted that although Connecticut did introduce racial restrictions in its 1818 constitution, it had refused to withdraw suffrage from the colored citizens who already possessed the right to vote.[60]

Opposition to the racial restriction on voting also came from conservatives such as jurist Jonas Platt, who confessed that if New York had many newly freed blacks, he, too, would want to exclude them from voting, but not by this "unjust and *odious* distinction of color." Instead, he would establish restrictions that "would not only exclude the great body of free men of color, but also a large portion of ignorant and depraved white men, who are as unfit to exercise the power of voting as the men of color."[61] The point, however, was academic since, as Peter Jay (the son of Federalist leader John Jay) pointed out, proportionately the New York black population—which was less than 3 percent—was decreasing, and even in New York City, blacks constituted fewer than 10 percent of the residents.[62] Chancellor James Kent, the state's most distinguished jurist, added the further argument that with so many races represented in and entering the United States, restricting suffrage to "white" persons would lead to a hopeless tangle of controversies over who was and was not "white."[63] Ultimately, it was another judge, Jesse Buel, who asserted the mainstream republican argument that universal suffrage was sound policy in New York because "the establishment of common schools, will in a few years extend the benefit of education to all our citizens." Republicanism would be safe because "the universal diffusion of information will forever distinguish our population from that of Europe."[64]

Notwithstanding all of these arguments, the vote on inserting a racial qualification was almost evenly divided—59 voted in favor and 63 voted against.[65] Later on, the convention settled for a provision that removed property restrictions on whites but retained property restrictions on blacks. Martin Van Buren, who voted with the majority on both measures, justified this compromise by pointing out that it linked taxation and representation. Blacks would only be taxed when they possessed enough property to qualify to vote.[66] Presumably, African Americans were citizens in any case, regardless of the extent of their property.

The struggle over voting—which had been a privilege in the days of freeholder qualifications but became a right in the era of universal manhood suffrage—led to explicit assertions of citizenship by African Americans in every state where they were free to organize. In New York, from the 1820s onward, blacks attacked the legitimacy of the new racial restriction in their state's constitution, as they did in Pennsylvania, New Jersey, Connecticut, and other states where legal disabilities were imposed. As the Reverend Samuel T. Cornish, editor of the *Colored American,* stated in an editorial protesting a New Jersey law that required every "free negro or mulatto" to possess freedom papers and carry them while traveling, such laws were all "unconstitutional." To his fellow African Americans, Cornish declared: "You are citizens of the State, in the strictest sense of the word, and just as much right has your State Legislature, to pass an act, requiring every red haired citizen, to carry his freepapers . . . as they have to require your compliance."[67] This kind of "*complexional standard,*" the black convention of Pennsylvania proclaimed in 1848, was analogous to the religious discrimination that had been practiced wrongfully in the past against Protestants, Catholics, Quakers, and Jews.[68] Prejudice was leading majorities to circumscribe and even deny African American citizenship in many states, but blacks challenged these policies, repeatedly asserting that their rights were founded in the Declaration of Independence and that the Constitution "guarantees in letter and spirit to every freeman born in this country, all the rights and immunities of citizenship."[69] Blacks should be allowed to vote on the same terms as whites, and whether they were presently barred from the ballot box or not, African American spokesmen argued that as citizens they should be informed.

The nongovernmental approaches that free blacks employed to achieve an informed African American citizenry were much the same as those used by whites—voluntary associations and schools. Their efforts to become informed, which they pursued without much help from whites and sometimes in the face of furious opposition, testify powerfully to their commitment to the ideology of informed citizenship and their belief that self-improvement could advance personal and collective goals. Lacking the financial resources and leisure time that whites possessed, excluded from public office as a scorned minority, and so scattered physically that the critical masses necessary for concerted action were scarce among the free black population, they nevertheless developed a state convention movement to advocate their political agendas. In addition, they formed secular and church-related cultural improvement societies. Although the David Daggetts and Roger Taneys of the legal and political world denied their citizenship, free blacks acted like citizens and worked to convince the political system to accept them.

State conventions, called intermittently by the "colored people" and "people of color" of nearly all the free states as well as the slave state of Maryland, created public forums for African Americans to express their views, exchange ideas, and achieve a public hearing. These meetings brought scores of self-selected delegates together to elect officers, hear addresses, debate policy, examine committee reports, and vote on resolutions. Covered extensively in the black press and given attention in some white newspapers, they almost always called for the recognition of free blacks' rights and for specific state legislative or constitutional measures. They might also include statements in support of abolition as well as self-improvement and education projects.[70]

One such project, launched by the 1831 Pennsylvania Convention of the People of Colour, which met in Philadelphia, called for the creation of a manual labor "College for Colored Youth," much like those education reformers were recommending for whites. Proposed for the college town of New Haven, Connecticut, where there was already a concentration of scholars as well as a "respectable" free black community, the scheme was backed financially by an incentive pledge from Arthur Tappan, the New York merchant and later abolitionist. As planned, the college was intended to promote the advancement and integration—economic and cultural—of African Americans in northern society. But to the surprise of the college's advocates, who were led by James Forten, the wealthy patriarch of Philadelphia's free black community, the citizens of New Haven found a hundred reasons to oppose the establishment of such a college in their town and passed a set of resolutions to block the plan. One New Haven man who supported the college published an account describing the sentiments he heard expressed around town: "We've got niggers enough in this place already. You get a gang of negroes here, and you would soon find the value of real estate would fall in this place at least twenty-five percent." Even worse, opponents of the college claimed that if blacks were educated, they would "cut the throats of our Southern brethren; or if [the black man] should stay among us, he will soon get to feel himself almost equal to whites. . . . Do you want to have your daughters marry *black husbands?* . . . Right or wrong, I want none of your Nigger Colleges about me. Tell about the blacks being born here—this being their native country—of having the same rights as whites, and all such contemptible nonsense! I want to hear none of it. Send them off to Africa, their native country, where they belong."[71] Although only a small minority (6 percent) of New Haven's residents were black, the breadth and nearly hysterical intensity of the prejudice they encountered in this "enlightened" northern community illustrate the forces arrayed against them. They would continue to speak publicly to defend their rights, but most of their organized activities were highly circumspect and directed inward toward self-improvement.

African American voluntary associations resembled those of whites. In New York City, the black Philomathean Society maintained a library of over 500 volumes and ran lecture series in the 1830s, including talks on the natural sciences, history, geography, oratory, logic, and Christianity. When the phrenology craze swept the United States in the late 1830s and 1840s, asserting a scientific basis for African American inferiority, the black graduate of the University of Heidelberg, James McCune Smith, delivered lectures exposing the fallacies of the phrenological analysis of skulls and mental attributes. In Philadelphia, African Americans established a similar organization and an even larger Library for Colored People in the 1830s. In smaller cities such as Pittsburgh, Buffalo, and Troy, New York, black residents formed "Mental and Moral Improvement" societies, which combined secular and religious reading, discussion, and debate. Even in smaller communities, blacks formed organizations, usually connected to their churches, to promote moral reform. Women sometimes participated with men in these groups or founded their own "Female" chapters.[72] The immediate personal objectives of those who participated in these activities varied, but according to African American leaders, the larger purpose of these groups was to develop informed, virtuous citizens who were clearly worthy of the rights they claimed. This program also carried an abolition message since, by their actions, free blacks would demonstrate the soundness of emancipation. They

Patrick Reason, said to be the first African American engraver, made this frontispiece for
The Liberty Bell *(Boston, 1839), an abolitionist annual gift book. The image conflates
American political liberty and the Christian message, "Truth shall make you free." At
the right, a white girl instructs black children in the alphabet. Courtesy American
Antiquarian Society.*

would prove that full citizenship was the proper alternative to slavery, not
colonization in Africa.

This viewpoint was often part of the larger political message of the movement for the education of free blacks, although some white clergymen, phil-
anthropists, educators, and public officials retained the old charity school
vision of blacks as a pious and literate race of servants, laborers, and craftsmen. The concern that blacks were "overreaching" had been one of the
justifications for opposition to the manual labor college in New Haven as
well as to Prudence Crandall's female academy for black girls in another part
of Connecticut. Many feared that educating African Americans above their
station would have dangerous logical consequences, namely, that they would

assert and perhaps achieve equality. Nevertheless, white-supported elementary education for black children, first under private auspices and later in northeastern public schools, was supplying the sort of literacy and numeracy that Thomas Jefferson had regarded as essential for citizens.

From a white perspective, the subject of African American education was encumbered with complexities. In the first decades of the nineteenth century, charity schools for urban blacks, both conventional and Lancasterian, were seen as desirable for the same reasons they were useful for poor whites: they would reduce crime and pauperism among blacks and increase their productivity. But in order to supply teachers, as well as to provide free blacks with their own clergymen, more than elementary education was required. The elite white quandary over higher education for blacks was epitomized by an 1816 program of the Presbyterian Synod of New York and New Jersey and by the African Education Society, a national, colonization-oriented group organized in 1829 in Washington, D.C.

The Presbyterians' African School proposal was aimed at "educating young men of colour, to be teachers and preachers to people of colour within these States and elsewhere," so that "the great negro-world" would enjoy "teachers of their own race." Furthermore, the Presbyterians believed that as Americans they bore a special responsibility to aid blacks since "no portion of the world is so deeply indebted to Africa" and "this land of freedom is the only enlightened land of slaves." By educating black missionaries, the synod would begin to pay back the "large arrears" the United States owed Africa, and in time, Africans would attain "a rank among the polished nations of Europe and America." This overseas mission, paradoxically, differed entirely from the school's domestic mission in the United States. Here, "only the most faithful and discreet" young blacks would be assigned to teach their fellow African Americans "subordination according to the apostolic example."[73] Although these northern Presbyterians believed that African Americans were capable of great achievements and deserved compensation for the historic wrongs they had endured, those achievements would have to occur on another continent. In the United States, the mission was to promote subjection.

The African Education Society, also inspired by "the wrongs and sufferings of Africa, inflicted by the hands of Americans," aimed as well to provide a kind of recompense "to those whom they have injured." But this group, which was an adjunct of the American Colonization Society and included slaveholders like the Marylander Francis Scott Key of "Star-Spangled Banner" fame and the Episcopal bishop of Virginia in addition to future abolitionists Gerrit Smith and Arthur Tappan, evaded the contradictions of the Presbyterian Synod by concentrating exclusively on preparing "persons of colour for usefulness in Africa." The projected African Education Society boarding school would provide training in "Letters, Agriculture, and the Mechanic Arts," not religion, so as to "qualify [graduates] for usefulness and influence in Africa."[74]

These teachers "destined to Africa" would be recruited chiefly by slave masters who wished to enroll particular slaves in this African project "on condition, after their education and liberation, of their emigrating to Africa." To assure that these newly educated, newly free blacks would actually leave the United States, they would all be required to make a formal pledge prior to their education and emancipation "that they will go to Africa when their education shall be completed."[75] Paradoxically, the objective of this novel scheme was to use African Americans to create an informed citizenry in Africa while simultaneously blocking the development of an informed African American citizenry in the United States.

This fantastic proposal never reached fruition, coming as it did on the eve of Nat Turner's slave rebellion and the publication of William Lloyd Garrison's immediate abolition newspaper, *The Liberator*. But the fact that such a project could have won the serious support of leading white men of goodwill is an indication of the confusion that confounded Americans when they attempted to reconcile their system of racial slavery with enlightened notions of an educated, progressive citizenry. As became evident in the generation culminating in the Supreme Court's 1857 Dred Scott decision, the operators of the slave system simply could not tolerate the idea that African Americans—former slaves and their descendants—could be fully enfranchised, engaged citizens. This kind of African American empowerment threatened slavery explicitly by making it possible for black reformers to agitate for abolition, while undermining it theoretically by giving black reformers the opportunity to demonstrate in their persons the faulty precepts on which the slave system rested.

In the 1840s and 1850s, when African Americans gained access to tax-supported public schools in states from Massachusetts to Michigan—partly as a result of demands by their state conventions—they proclaimed that they would be included in America's informed citizenry.[76] "Let us," the Michigan convention resolved in late 1843, "lay the corner stone with a mutual desire for the general diffusion of knowledge, based on the principles of Human Liberty and Equal Rights." Wedding the cause of equality to that of being informed, the convention proclaimed that "we will increase our individual happiness and prosperity, by improving the minds of our people, and elevating the standard of Liberty, raise ourselves up and take our stand with the well informed." Michigan African Americans would make themselves "the true Liberty and the Free-Knowledge-Dispensing Party."[77] This impassioned embrace of mainstream republican ideology made it difficult for northern whites to dismiss free black citizenship.

But the idea of slave citizenship, informed or not, was easy for whites to reject. It seemed self-contradictory on the surface, an oxymoron because historically being a free man was a defining characteristic of being a citizen. Moreover, for generations, historians have emphasized the proscriptions that southern states enacted to forbid slave literacy. Their research demonstrates that a policy based on law and custom linked denial of citizenship with denial of literacy in all of the slave states. But this reality, while dominant, was not as complete or as monolithic as some have supposed. No less a public figure than John Quincy Adams, one of the nation's most learned advocates, declared in the U.S. Congress that slaves possessed the right to petition: "No despot, of any age or clime, has ever denied this humble privilege to the poorest or meanest of human creatures. . . . It is a right that cannot be denied to the humblest, to the most wretched." True, the House of Representatives rejected Adams's view by voting to deny slaves the right to petition, but this was the same legislative body whose "gag rule" also denied this right to all other Americans, even though the First Amendment to the Constitution explicitly enjoined Congress from abridging "the right of the people . . . to petition the government."[78]

If, as Adams believed, slaves possessed the right to petition in common with citizens, and if, like citizens, they were also born in the United States, then arguably they had some claim, however frail, to American citizenship. Certainly no one contended that they were aliens, like immigrants and Native Americans. They were, it is true, always subject to the will of their masters and to corporal punishment at their hands, but so were citizens who were minors or wives. There was no need to address the issue of slave citizenship fully, given the ruling consensus prior to 1865, which relied on the legal fiction that slaves were chattels. But in a society where principles of natural equality mingled with the Christian belief in the equality of all people before God, and in a legal system where fathers normally passed along their citizenship to their offspring, the total exclusion of slaves from citizenship possessed some disquieting elements.

Yet because the security of their social and economic order rested on the slave system, southerners generally refused to acknowledge the contradictions it posed. Like William Harper, they preferred to think of their system as a superior form of classical republicanism. Still, in the minds of devout masters, the actual practices of some of their peers were worrisome. The problem was that sacrilegious, greedy masters, sometimes fearful of slave rebellion, were failing in their duty to provide their slaves with Christian instruction. To masters like the Reverend Charles Colcock Jones of Liberty County, Georgia, this omission constituted a grave southern problem.[79] Certainly those masters who shared Jones's views did not want slaves to become informed citizens, but privately and publicly they committed themselves to making enslaved African Americans informed Christians.

For Protestants, especially Presbyterians, who relied heavily on sermons and Bible study, it was hard to reconcile the needs of domestic security with the desire to promote Christian education. After David Walker published his 1829 appeal "to the coloured citizens of the world, . . . in particular, and very expressly, to those of the United States of America," which called for a revolution against slavery and was soon followed in 1831 by a rebellion led by the lay preacher Nat Turner, security concerns were paramount. In North Carolina, where a number of earlier attempts to prohibit slave literacy had failed, one as recently as 1827, the 1830 legislature reacted to Walker's appeal by passing a literacy ban permitting only "the use of figures." Their reasoning was clear: "Teaching slaves to read and write; thereby affording them facilities of intelligence and communication, [is] inconsistent with their condition, destructive of their contentment and happiness, and dangerous to the community."[80] In this legislation, the need for Christian education was brushed aside because the majority decided, even before the Turner uprising, that "the teaching of slaves to read and write has a tendency to excite dissatisfaction in their minds and to produce insurrection and rebellion."[81] The fact that after the repression of the Turner rebels some North Carolina slaves continued to challenge the system by "exercising the privilege of freemen" made the legislation imperative.[82]

But even under the threat of potential rebellion, some North Carolina delegates, about a third of the members of each house, saw the duties of Christian masters as sacred. Before the passage of the 1830 law, they worked to limit the ban to writing so that it would still be legal to teach slaves to read the Bible, and for several years afterward, some delegates mounted repeal efforts. The law stood in North Carolina, however, and the pattern was much the same elsewhere. Yet even in South Carolina, where fears of insurrection led to the passage of the most comprehensive antiliteracy legislation anywhere, substantial evidence exists that the laws were openly evaded by masters who believed that good Christians made good slaves.[83]

The legitimacy and practicality of African American literacy are suggested in this Arthur Anderson woodcut. Here a white clergyman or master hears a black child read lessons. From Publications of the American Tract Society, *vol. 1, ser. 2 (New York, [1827–33]). Courtesy American Antiquarian Society.*

In 1842 a group of Abbeville, South Carolina, Presbyterians went so far as to petition for the repeal of the antiliteracy laws on the grounds that they inhibited proper religious instruction and thereby violated South Carolina's provisions for religious freedom. "How," they demanded to know, "can an ignorant man, such as our servants are, be prepared for the Eternal state by hearing a sermon or a lecture once a week, much of which they do not understand?" Because oral instruction was inadequate, they claimed, the servants should be taught "to read with so much fluency and correctness, that they will be able to peruse the word of God and other religious books with pleasure and profit to their souls." Fulfilling this sacred duty to people "for whom Christ died" was a matter of conscience. "One of the chief privileges and enjoyments of our religious profession and worship," they testified, was "to search the scriptures for ourselves"; consequently, "that law which robs our servants of this enjoyment" was in open "violation of the Constitution."[84] According to this singular but futile argument, the constitutional rights of a citizen extended to his slave, so that an infringement on a slave's religious liberty was also an encroachment on that of the master. Such a direct religious challenge to the antiliteracy laws was exceptional, but the tension between such laws and religious instruction could never be wholly eased and inevitably led to lapses in their enforcement.[85]

The ongoing commitment to promoting informed Christian slaves was manifest in the proceedings of a multidenominational meeting held in Charleston in 1845 on "the Religious Instruction of the Negroes." The purpose of the gathering was to exchange information on methods of instruction and to publicize the "gratifying . . . effects of the religious instruction of negroes, upon *labour,* and upon *discipline.*"[86] Moreover, the meeting made clear that most religious training was being carried out entirely within the boundaries of the antiliteracy laws through oral instruction and memorization. But among the sixty-three letters from South Carolina, Georgia, and eight other slave states that were presented to the public, a number spoke favorably of slaves who could read. Several South Carolina masters seemed proud to announce that they used literate slaves to teach slave children the catechism, and one master reported that a slave read "the appointed service of our church" on Sundays during the summer.[87] A Presbyterian, John Blair of York, South Carolina, reported that in his district, some slaves had "received instruction in reading and religious training from their masters and mistresses" and were "so well qualified as to keep up family worship." These slaves, Blair wrote, displayed "surprising . . . fervency and intelligence."[88] This subversive theme of black intellectual capacity emerged in a number of reports. A Georgetown, South Carolina, master commented that "the degree of intelligence which, as a class, they are acquiring, is worthy of deep consideration."[89] Conceivably, they might become worthy of citizenship in time. Most remarkable of all was information on a black Alabama Presbyterian who could read Greek and Latin and was attempting to learn Hebrew. The synods of Alabama and Mississippi, it was reported, were proposing to purchase this man from his owner in order to send him to Africa as a missionary, a plan that recalled the stillborn scheme of the African Education Society.[90]

In all of these discussions, however, legislators and masters argued over means, not ends; they all agreed that slave subjection must be maintained. Therefore, whatever education slaves or free blacks who lived in slave states might be allowed, as in the old English charity schools, its function was to promote obedience. Being a good Christian was all very well, but political empowerment of any description was unthinkable. No matter what logical arguments Yankee fanatics might invent, slaves must not under any circumstances be citizens. Nevertheless, the steel barrier to their recognition as citizens showed tiny cracks. Already some northern states had created the precedent of emancipating slaves without compensation to owners, later admitting them to full enfranchisement as informed citizens. Generally, free blacks in the North were claiming citizenship based on principles embodied in the Declaration of Independence and the Constitution, while in the South, free blacks enjoyed some protections and some slave masters were actually empowering thousands of their slaves through literacy.[91] These African Americans were almost all born in the United States and thus, by recognized international standards as well as the nation's own law, enjoyed some claim to citizenship. The barrier against African American citizenship held firm in the 1850s, but the foundation for post-1865 citizenship and enfranchisement had been laid over preceding decades.

The role of women in the fulfillment of the idea of an informed citizenry contrasted starkly with that of African Americans in important respects, but there were also notable similarities. Although the inclusion of women in the mainstream notion of an informed citizenry was generally acknowledged and possessed a genealogy stretching back at least as far as Jefferson's Bill for a More General Diffusion of Knowledge, as with blacks, inclusion was problematic. Like African American men, women were seldom freeholders. When freehold barriers fell, women were more uniformly excluded from electoral politics than black men. Despite the fact that white women were generally more educated than black men, they were widely admonished to confine their knowledge primarily to domestic matters and to shun engagement in public affairs entirely. Consequently, even though no one questioned the reality of white women's citizenship, according to mainstream prescriptions, they should be informed only to promote morality, domestic economy, and their own and their families' personal fulfillment—not in order to preserve liberty or to ensure sound public policy directly.

Like African Americans, however, women challenged the restrictions that custom, law, and social prescription placed on their citizenship. Beginning with the politics of the temperance and abolition movements, and moving on to agitation for the recognition of married women's rights and the right of women to vote, women and some male allies subverted the concept of separate spheres in order to redefine women's place in the idea of an informed citizenry. The fact that some of the opponents of the full realization of women's citizenship professed to be women's truest friends, claiming that women were meant for higher, purer responsibilities than public affairs, gave the

ANTI-SLAVERY MEETING ON THE COMMON.

This image depicts an antislavery meeting held on the Boston Common in April 1851 to protect the capture of escaped slave Thomas Sims. The main speaker, Wendell Phillips, addresses an audience of both black and white men and women, notable for its inclusive representation of citizenship. From Gleason's Pictorial Drawing Room Companion, *May 3, 1851. Courtesy American Antiquarian Society.*

controversy a peculiar caste. Unable to rely on crass racism or old-fashioned elitism to justify their views—as was common among the enemies of African American citizenship—opponents of full citizenship rights for women tended to employ contorted, even fanciful arguments based on cultural preconceptions about sex and gender.

The conventional starting point for the consideration of women's citizenship was the legal and political position that women were, like children, dependent citizens who did not control property or possess independent voices. To the degree that they should be informed citizens, and the reformers of the early republic had proclaimed that goal, it was so that they could influence positively their sons and husbands—the *active* citizens. The idealized republican wife and mother would train men in virtue and civic consciousness while remaining aloof from the public realm.[92] The bizarre contradiction implicit in the idea that dependent women would teach men to be independent was overlaid with mantras to female virtue and self-sacrifice.

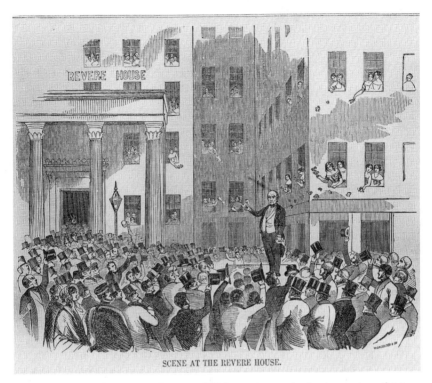

SCENE AT THE REVERE HOUSE.

This illustration of a reception for Daniel Webster portrays the dominant view of citizenship and political engagement. White men surround Webster, while white women look on from the windows above. Among the crowd of ground-level spectators, only three are women, and they are placed at the periphery. From Gleason's Pictorial Drawing Room Companion, *May 17, 1851. Courtesy American Antiquarian Society.*

Justifications for confining women to the status of subordinate citizenship rested on a doctrine of separate spheres that paralleled the old Mandevillean idea that it was necessary to keep the laboring classes ignorant. Because God and nature intended women for maternal and domestic duties, according to this view, the "fair sex" must not be ruined, just as laborers should not be spoiled, by an education that would make them discontented with their lot or encourage them to seek other roles in life. Unlike Mandeville's laborers, however, women's sphere was described in lofty rather than base terms. No praise, no flattery, seemed too extravagant. "Did Jesus Christ ever desire to be civil governor of Judea, or seek for any form of political preferment," the Yankee reformer Horace Mann asked. To women, he said, belonged "the empire of Home, that most important of empires, and the parent of all empires and emperors."[93] If they fulfilled their proper roles,

Mann implied, women could be at once like Jesus and Alexander the Great. On the other hand, "the idea of our wives and sisters mingling promiscuously with men in the varied affairs of life, industrial, social and political," was nothing short of revolting, and proposals advocating their suffrage, officeholding, and jury duty were "grotesque and unwomanly."[94] Women were extolled as "divinely-adapted" for "regenerating the world," but they must do it as wives, mothers, and schoolteachers. "Those who hold conventions, and shout from public rostrums, under the banner of 'Woman's Rights,'" Mann announced, "have unsexed themselves."[95] Beliefs like these, which presumed a kind of cultural and political specialized division of labor, were prevalent in all regions of the nation. Informing women in religious and domestic affairs, which were contrasted with the vanities of fashion, parties, and novel reading, was desirable, but no value was assigned to women's training in political economy and history, the fields that would have informed women as citizens.

The friends of women's full enfranchisement justified their position with three closely related arguments based on notions of self-realization, natural rights, and established principles of American law. As the national Women's Rights Convention of 1853 resolved: "Every human being, without distinction of sex, has an inviolable right to the full development and free exercise of all energies."[96] Like men, Frederick Douglass later asserted, women had their "own individuality, not only in form and features, but in thought and feeling." Women must have their own political voices, he said, so that their "citizenship would be full and complete."[97] Also, "if a minister can preach politics because he is a citizen" without risking his reputation for virtue and piety, Wendell Phillips pointed out, a woman "can meddle in politics and vote, because she is a citizen too."[98] Whatever rights and principles applied to men's citizenship must apply to women's citizenship as well.

Insofar as being virtuous and informed were criteria for enfranchisement, as republican theory had once demanded, some reformers argued that women were more qualified than masses of men. At Seneca Falls in 1848, Elizabeth Cady Stanton complained that "to have drunkards, idiots, horseracing, rumselling rowdies, ignorant foreigners and silly boys fully recognized, while we ourselves are thrust out from all the rights that belong to citizens, it is too grossly insulting to the dignity of woman."[99] Five years later, at the Women's Rights Convention held in Cleveland, William Lloyd Garrison presented a resolution that echoed Stanton's pronouncement: "So long as the most ignorant, degraded and worthless men are freely admitted to the ballot-box, . . . it is preposterous to pretend that women are not qualified to use the elective franchise."[100] Whereas social snobbery worked against African Americans, lending legitimacy to the denial of their rights, it worked to advance women's cause. Snobbery helped to undermine the legitimacy of male privilege. Nothing "can be more galling to an intelligent and highly educated American lady," a school reform journal noted, "than the fact that no qualification of birth, age, wealth or education can entitle her to the privilege, which her servant, without any of these claims, may freely enjoy."[101] Even if a woman was well informed and virtuous and owned extensive property that would have warranted a stake in representation, she was shut out.

What leaders in the women's movement sought to articulate was their recognition that egalitarian democracy had long since overwhelmed republican notions of a virtuous and informed citizenry. Like the emperor in the fable, the American citizen was not clothed in garments of virtue and information; he was naked after all. Education reformers continued to fight to give substance to the myth of an informed, virtuous citizenry, but in reality, the old standards of enfranchisement were obsolete. Consequently, the exclusion of women was based even more purely on notions of male supremacy than the exclusion of blacks was based on white supremacy. By the 1850s and 1860s, the barrier to male African American suffrage had been breached in more than half a dozen northern states, but the exclusion of women was complete. The events of the decade following the end of the Civil War would further undermine the legitimacy of racial discrimination, while public policy would leave intact, perhaps even fortify, gender-based discrimination.

During the third quarter of the nineteenth century, the idea of an informed citizenry, already a fixture in public rhetoric, shifted further away from its revolutionary era legacy. Now the belief that people should be informed for the sake of personal fulfillment and their own economic opportunity took precedence over the public's interest in an informed citizenry. Although advocates of public education continued to assert a combination of private and public benefits, the old idea that citizens must be virtuous and informed because they were voters had been undermined. Since politics had extended voting rights to nearly every white male citizen whether he was educated or not, it was only too evident that many voters, perhaps most, were neither virtuous nor informed.

This realization led some to oppose universal suffrage entirely in the post–Civil War era, for men as well as women. The idea of literacy tests, which was linked to the informed citizenry idea, acquired legitimacy, together with other voting restrictions that could be used to exclude the poor and uneducated of both races.[102] According to the Yankee evangelist Horace Bushnell, "our fathers of the American Revolution" themselves had erred in attaching their movement to what the jurist Rufus Choate disdainfully called "the glittering generalities" of "life, liberty, and the pursuit of happiness." The founding fathers had been led astray by none other than John Locke, who, although possessing a "really great mind," had himself been taken in by the "infection" of free thinking "without being duly aware of the sophistry and dangerous falsity covered up under these pretentious guises." Bushnell rejected the Declaration of Independence's general maxim that "governments . . . derive their just powers from the consent of the governed," just as he contested the doctrine that men and women possessed a natural right to the franchise. If this were true, Bushnell reasoned, then before 1776 no government in world history had ever been legitimate. This Connecticut clergyman was "shocked by the nonsense of our assumption" of the superior legitimacy of democratic government. The true tests for whether one should possess the full rights of citizenship were "considerations of benefit" and especially "the public good."[103] Although men like Bushnell had no real hope that they could roll back the tide of universal manhood suffrage in the United States, they did hope to arrest its progress at the boundary of sex. It was, they believed, bad enough that ignorant and irresponsible men voted; if they were joined by women, then all was lost in both the public and private domains.

Their boundary held in the 1860s and beyond. The majority of voters in states where the issue of women's suffrage was presented, Congress, and the Supreme Court defeated the movement toward women's enfranchisement. In the course of this struggle over women's and African Americans' voting rights, the idea of an informed citizenry was pushed out of the mainstream of electoral politics into the arena of cultural politics. The informed citizen as voter, an ideal that Congressman Henry Wise had sought to realize in the 1840s, now appeared to be not much more than a rhetorical ideal. Jacksonian Democrats had long since winked at the principle in building their majorities, and even earlier the old Federalist Abraham Van Vechten had recognized that it was impossible to "prescribe the moral and intellectual qualifications" of voters.[104] In the 1860s, the Republicans, hoping to establish their longevity as a national party by gaining black voters, followed suit. Frederick Douglass expressed his perceptions of the new reality in an 1863 speech in Brooklyn, New York:

I, myself, once had some high notions about this body politic and its high requirements, and of the kind of men fit to enter it and share its privileges. But a day's experience at the polls convinced me that the "body politic" . . . is a very mixed affair. I saw ignorance enter, unable to read the vote it cast. I saw the convicted swindler enter and deposit his vote. I saw the gambler, the horse jockey, the pugilist, the miserable drunkard just lifted from the gutter, covered with filth, enter and deposit his vote. I saw Pat, fresh from the Emerald Isle, requiring two sober men to keep him on his legs, enter and deposit his vote for the Democratic candidate amid the loud hurrahs of his fellow-citizens. The sight of these things went far to moderate my ideas about the exalted character of what is called the body politic, and convinced me that it could not suffer in its composition even if it should admit a few sober, industrious and intelligent colored voters.[105]

Douglass stated explicitly that the standard of informed citizenship no longer applied to voting. Who was included and who was kept out was a matter of politics more than principle.

As the struggle to enfranchise blacks and women came to a climax, the irrelevance of being informed was manifested repeatedly in the arguments of reformers and the actions of a wide range of organizations and officials. In New York in 1837, Judge Thomas Herttell had pointed to the state's constitutional guarantee that "no member of this state shall be disfranchised or deprived of any of the rights and privileges secured to any citizen thereof, unless by the law of the land, or the judgement of his peers."[106] Surely women were "members of this state," as were free, New-York-born African American taxpayers, yet they were arbitrarily denied the full "rights and privileges" of citizens. In 1838 John Quincy Adams, speaking in Congress, suggested that as citizens, women possessed not only the right to petition—a right shared by slaves—but also the right to vote.[107] The irrelevance of being informed was made explicit by the Connecticut senate in 1859 when it simultaneously rejected both an English literacy requirement for voters and the extension of suffrage to "colored men."[108] Ultimately, the requirements for representation were not residence or place of birth, not property or paying taxes, and not being virtuous or being informed; the fundamental requisite was to be white and male. Some reformers still clung to the old faith, such as the antislavery convention that resolved in 1860 "that the great want of our country . . . is a National Political Education Society, whose object shall be to educate the people, the rulers of the country, in a thorough knowledge of the fundamental principles of democratic government."[109] But by the era of the Civil War, such appeals had a quaint, even unworldly ring.

The advances toward full citizenship that African Americans made rested on partisan, if principled, political decisions. In 1861, for example, the new Republican secretary of state, William Seward, issued a passport to the reformer Henry Highland Garnet, thereby ruling that "a black man, of unadulterated negro blood, is declared before the civilized world to be entitled to the protection of the Government, as a citizen."[110] A year later, Lincoln's attorney general would carry the process of erasing the Dred Scott decision a step further with his decree that every free person born in the United States was, regardless of race, "at the moment of birth *prima facie* a citizen." At the same time, however, in a decision that affected blacks and women equally, the attorney general ruled that the possession of citizenship was not necessarily connected to "the legal capacity to hold office and the right of suffrage."[111] In the next several years, however, the paths to black and female enfranchisement—theoretically so similar and championed for years by many of the same reformers—would diverge. Not principle but politics, Republican electoral politics, supplied the explanation.[112]

As the Confederacy collapsed and the realization of emancipation became apparent in 1865, abolitionists calculated that if black suffrage could be achieved at all, it would only succeed through Republican support. Although many, such as Frederick Douglass, Abby Kelley Foster, Wendell Phillips, and Lucy Stone, would have liked to win full rights for women immediately, they agreed with Lincoln that one war at a time was enough. As Phillips put it when faced with the choice between fighting for both causes simultaneously or concentrating on African Americans, "this hour belongs to the negro."[113] Thus, although an American Equal Rights Association was formed in 1866 to advocate both black and women's suffrage, as events unfolded in the crucial year of 1867, it was clear that the two causes were weaker politically when joined than when they stood alone. Both causes were viewed as radical, but whereas granting blacks the right to vote touched only the public sphere and had been tested for decades in some states, to contemporaries the extension of the same rights to women suggested a revolution in gender relations that would reach into every family, every region, every class, and every occupation.

The differences between the two causes and their partisan implications were evident in the measures of the Radical Republican Congress, which voted in 1867 to enfranchise black men in the District of Columbia and the U.S. territories and to require the former Confederate states to include black suffrage in their Reconstruction constitutions. In this case, the Republican Congress, which overrode a presidential veto in order to create black voters in the old Confederacy, was much more reformist than the nation at large.[114] In the same year, Kansas voters turned down black suffrage in a referendum by an overwhelming majority, and in Ohio and Pennsylvania, the reform was also defeated. African Americans realized advances only in Iowa, where Republican voters led in ending discrimination at the polls in 1868, and in New York, where the Republican-dominated state constitutional convention voted (125 to 19) to abolish the discriminatory property requirement its predecessors had created in 1821.[115]

The cause of women's suffrage was even more controversial, and with only tepid support from some Republicans, the reform failed. When female en-franchisement was placed on the ballot alongside black men's suffrage in Kansas, it was defeated by an even wider margin than black voting.[116] In the New York constitutional convention, the women's "suffragist" and Republi-can reformer Horace Greeley had urged equal voting rights for blacks but re-fused to "recommend an extension of the elective franchise to women." Although Greeley said he favored women's right to vote "in theory, we are satisfied that public sentiment does not demand and would not sustain an innovation so revolutionary and sweeping, so openly at war with a distribu-tion of duties and functions between the sexes . . . and involving transfor-mations so radical in social and domestic life."[117] Greeley's assessment of public opinion in 1867 was sustained the following year by the Democratic Party, whose national convention, notwithstanding its egalitarian rhetoric, rejected the woman suffrage movement, as did the National Labor Congress, a union of skilled white workingmen.[118] The campaign for women's voting rights, now led primarily by Elizabeth Cady Stanton and Susan B. Anthony, was somewhat isolated politically and thus was being pushed toward the margin of public life.

The fact that after the break with their old abolitionist collaborators Stanton and Anthony allied themselves with George F. Train, a flamboyant racist demagogue, cast a retrograde shadow over the movement.[119] Indeed, by 1869 Stanton and Anthony were opposing passage of the Fifteenth Amendment because, though it would forbid racial discrimination in vot-ing, it would leave sex-based discrimination intact. Stanton was reported to have said that "she did not believe in allowing ignorant negroes and ignorant and debased Chinamen to make laws for her to obey."[120] This racist, xeno-phobic invocation of the idea of a virtuous and informed citizenry, however, lacked legislative muscle. When the Fifteenth Amendment was adopted in

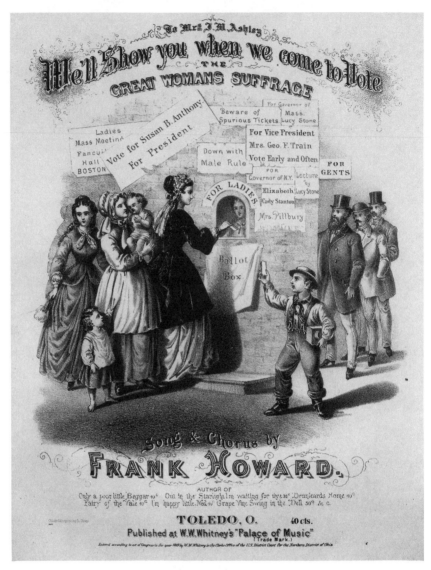

"*We'll Show You When We Come to Vote,*" *a popular song published in Toledo, Ohio, in 1869, was a manifestation of public interest in the suffrage issue. This cover illustration presents an imaginary scene of what would happen if women were enfranchised. Presumably women would cast their ballots separately from men. The posters suggest that respectable women wish to take control of government. The text of this song has not been located. Courtesy American Antiquarian Society.*

This depiction of the denial of Victoria Woodhull and her female associates' attempt to vote in New York City accompanied an amused news story in Harper's Weekly *of November 25, 1871: "When her right to vote was denied, she planted herself on the Constitution of the United States. . . . The Republican inspector was inclined to receive her vote, but his Democratic colleague . . . finally put an end to the scene by telling the persistent lady that she 'obstructed the polls, and must get out.'" The scene includes an African American voter at the left and voters who appear to be Irish and German (according to contemporary stereotypes) in the center. Courtesy American Antiquarian Society.*

1870, declaring that "the right of citizens . . . to vote shall not be denied or abridged by the United States or by any State on account of race, color, or previous condition of servitude," it seemed to complete the movement for universal suffrage—for men.[121]

A few years later, when, in separate cases, Susan B. Anthony and Virginia Minor both challenged the doctrine of female exclusion with the argument that voting was a right of citizenship and thus was protected constitutionally for women as well as men, they were defeated in court judgments. Virginia Minor's case went all the way to the Supreme Court, which ruled narrowly in 1875 "that the Constitution of the United States does not confer the right of suffrage upon any one"; rather, it specifically prohibited racial barriers only. By this judgment, the court left the way open for the use of other barriers—such as sex and class, as well as the surrogates for race used by post-Reconstruction southern states like literacy tests, grandfather clauses, poll

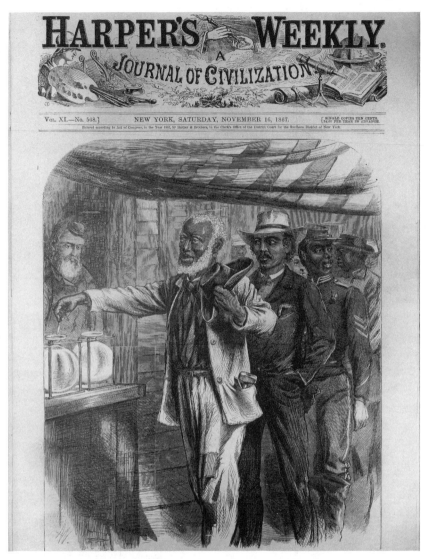

This illustration of African Americans voting in the South under the U.S. Reconstruction laws countered the numerous hostile and satirical images published by opponents of black enfranchisement. Appearing in Harper's Weekly *on November 16, 1867, it represents the Republican argument for the Fifteenth Amendment as expressed by the editors: "The good sense and discretion, and above all the modesty, which freedmen have displayed . . . have been most noticeable." Courtesy American Antiquarian Society.*

taxes, and white primaries.[122] As the years went on, it became evident that the abolitionists had been tactically correct to separate the two causes since neither one could command majority support among an almost exclusively white male electorate.

The defeat of women's suffrage in the 1870s made it clear that citizenship, which belonged to women, and suffrage, which did not, would remain separate and distinct—as the Supreme Court had ruled. The connection between being informed and being empowered, which workingmen, African Americans, and women had all invoked, was severed. Consequently, the old Radical Whig and republican idea of the informed citizen had become a political anomaly. The belief that voters should be expected to recognize the advancing steps of tyrants and demagogues and use their ballots to defend liberty seemed archaic. Orators and reformers continued to employ the rhetoric of an informed citizenry, but what they meant was an educated population—skilled, disciplined, productive, and cultivated. Universal education, which was good for individuals and for society as a whole, need not mean universal suffrage.

In time, of course, the idea that women should be totally excluded from the political sphere collapsed. When they were included in higher education, in the professions of law and medicine, and in a variety of workplaces, the doctrine of separate spheres faded. First, individual states extended full property rights to women, and then, as with African Americans earlier, particular states acted to enfranchise them.[123] As a result, by 1920, when the Nineteenth Amendment, which followed the language of the Fifteenth Amendment, declared that "the right of citizens . . . to vote shall not be denied or abridged . . . on account of sex," it rested on a broad base of national political support as well as widespread institutional practice.[124] Voting, after all, was not only among the great emblems of public standing, it was also, as one scholar explains, a symbolic "affirmation of belonging."[125] Henceforward, unlike the Fifteenth Amendment, no powerful constituencies would seek ways to circumvent women's suffrage at the state level. The question of whether women were informed would be pursued by such organizations as the League of Women Voters, but as far as public policy was concerned, as with other citizens, whether they were informed or not was their own private business.

Epilogue 🜹 Looking Backward 🜹 The Idea of an Informed Citizenry at the End of the Twentieth Century

If history has lessons to teach us today, what can we learn from studying the idea of an informed citizenry in the past? For an academic historian accustomed to drawing conclusions about the past from its documents, rather than reflecting upon contemporary society, this is a challenging question. To answer it demands a measure of speculation that is normally off-limits. The expression of opinion, after all, is not what historians regard as scholarship. But since the idea of an informed citizenry is a theme of considerable urgency in contemporary political, educational, and cultural debates, some historically informed commentary is appropriate. Journalists, critics, and reformers who assess today's schools and colleges within a matrix of cultural politics might even find a historian's perspective helpful. At the least, they will find precedents for their arguments in the historical record.

Few commentators in our own time express an optimistic view regarding the American citizenry's present level of information. Headlines cry out periodically that tens of millions of adults are functionally illiterate and cannot solve basic arithmetic problems.[1] If anything, youth are seen in an even more negative light, and schools are faulted for turning out a generation so ignorant as to make the United States "A Nation at Risk."[2] When many voters cannot name their U.S. senators and congressmen, let alone their state and local representatives, and cannot locate sites of international conflict and crisis on a map, it is hard to summon optimism.[3] One despairing *New York Times* commentator titled his column "A Nation of Nitwits."[4] Paradoxically, in spite of the vast array of educational institutions, public and private, that reach from preschool to postgraduate training, and notwithstanding the myriad information possibilities of electronic and printed media, today no voices are raised to proclaim the present era as the golden age of an informed citizenry in America.

Indeed, while some observers anticipate a future golden age of information, a time when computer networks will link everyone and everything, others look back to the 1950s or even to the nineteenth century as periods when Americans were comparatively well informed because they read newspapers and books and paid closer attention to political contests than they do today. At colleges and universities, it is said, grade inflation and the loss of the core curriculum in the history and culture of the Western world has led to dangerously low levels of knowledge of fundamental principles. In high schools, where aptitude and achievement scores have been declining in reading, geography, and history, the threat of "cultural illiteracy" among ignorant masses of American citizens seems especially critical.[5] Many public schools, particularly, have been assigned failing grades.

Most observers seeking a remedy for this apparent crisis of an informed citizenry agree that improved, publicly supported schooling is essential. But they disagree on how this schooling is to be improved. Many in the education establishment recommend that more teaching specialists and supporting personnel as well as more buildings and equipment be supplied. Taxpayer groups reject this approach and argue that private management and competition would make schools more efficient while enabling parents and children to weed out the weakest schools. Tuition vouchers, some argue, should be used to put public, private, and parochial schools into direct competition.

Significant conflict also exists over the diagnosis of the problems of public education and the ways that faulty schools will incapacitate the (uninformed) citizenry of the future. Almost everyone advocates better education, but they cannot agree on what that should be. Some believe that the most urgent crisis is the preservation of democratic political culture. If Americans, divided as they are by ethnicity, religion, and race, lack a common fund of values and experiences, their ability to live and work together to solve problems will be in jeopardy.[6] Others, however, see primarily a vocational and economic crisis, in which the expanding economy and rising standard of living that have sustained American democracy are threatened. According to this view, the world has entered an unprecedented era of competition in which "high performance work organizations" will dominate.[7] Only the best-trained societies, whether in Europe, Asia, Africa, or the Americas, will thrive. To a third group, who view the chief goals of education and citizenship as the full realization of personal development and individual aspiration, this vocational emphasis seems misguided. The only point on which all commentators agree is that American schools are falling short, causing the American citizenry to become at best inadequately informed and at worst dysfunctionally ignorant.

Broadly speaking, the polemical structure of debates on these issues has falsely imposed the appearance of a bipolar set of choices. Either more money should be invested exclusively in the public schools, or the public system should be broken up to encourage competing alternatives. Youth should be taught to live together in a common culture, or multicultural self-realization should be encouraged. The purpose of schools is to educate people for a life of personal fulfillment, or children should be trained to compete in the global economy. Framing the issues in this dichotomous manner has the advantage of drawing out key questions, but it is also misleading. Reformers and critics of all persuasions recognize that the development of an informed citizenry is more complicated and multidimensional than either/or prescriptions allow. Reality, they know, is not bipolar; it never has been.

The "lessons of history," moreover, give some comfort to all sides in our current debates, for the problems that are currently being addressed not only have long histories but also have never been resolved definitively. The question of inclusiveness, for example, which is today represented by the term "multiculturalism," has a long history in which social class, ethnicity, religion, and race have all figured. In eighteenth-century Pennsylvania, Benjamin Franklin and then Benjamin Rush led in attempts to use public education schemes to assimilate reluctant German settlers into British culture. Among those of British origin everywhere, the most vexed question of inclusion concerned property and whether the full rights of citizens should be confined to Christian gentlemen freeholders. Gradually, of course, this question was resolved in the generations following independence, so that all white men, whether propertied or impoverished, of any religion or none at all, came to be included in the privileged category. But no sooner was this new, more inclusive boundary established than it, too, came under challenge from African Americans and women, who, being born in the United States, laid claim to the full rights of citizens that were so readily granted to immigrant white men. African Americans', Asians', and women's struggles for full-fledged inclusion in the citizenry have taken longer, but the pattern set in the revolutionary era meant that neither race nor sex could stand permanently as an acceptable boundary for exclusion. Today, only children are denied the full rights and privileges of citizenship, but Americans have lowered the age of majority to eighteen years and invest substantially in preparing youth for the time they will reach it.

Debates over suitable curricula also stretch back across generations. In the early national era, reformers proposed the same basic public schooling in reading, writing, and arithmetic for all free inhabitants. Beyond that, children's training was the family's responsibility and should be appropriate to expectations of occupation and social rank. The instruction of citizens in a common culture was less the responsibility of schools than of families and society in general. Some citizenship training was implicit in textbooks for history and geography, but the largest share of such instruction was imparted by the vernacular institutions of community life. In New England, John Adams identified these communal sources of instruction as the church, the town meeting, and the militia, along with the local school.

Today's contests over how to transmit the culture of an informed citizenry across generations also have antecedents in the eighteenth and nineteenth centuries. Whether this task was a public responsibility to be carried out by legislative policy and financed publicly or whether it was chiefly the duty of parents was the major struggle of the two generations preceding the Civil War. Those who believed the function of education was primarily to prepare citizens generally favored public schools, whereas those who saw the training of youth as essentially vocational followed the old British tradition of requiring families, not the public, to pay for their children's start in life. Ultimately, the doctrine of public responsibility predominated, though not for many forms of vocational education and contrary views continued to be expressed. Parents who preferred a more elite education and could pay for it and those who insisted on a sectarian curriculum created and maintained private schools. The pathways to informed citizenship have never been unitary or uniform.

Judging from the constant division over programs and substance and contests over public policy, the history of the whole project of an informed citizenry may seem to be only one of conflict. But as persistent as conflict has been in this process—indeed, endemic to it—Americans have nevertheless shared a consensus on central elements of the means for ensuring an informed citizenry. Free speech and press have always been controversial in practice but have been honored as fundamental guiding principles for the American republic. A concomitant belief in the superiority and wisdom of competition among ideas and policies has, with a very few exceptions, ruled American public life in preference to the notion of monolithic, prescriptive monopoly. In the broadest terms, Americans and their institutions seem committed to the Miltonic notion, later restated by John Stuart Mill, that over the long run, truth, not falsehood, will prevail. Moreover, sufficient critics of "the truth" of any moment have always existed to assure that a monolithic policy cannot be put in place across the entire nation.

It is also a fact that the perception of a gap between expectations and reality has been chronic. As reformers today measure the achievements of American students against the performance of their Japanese and European counterparts, so too did Jefferson and Madison judge their Virginia compatriots in comparison to what they took to be the highly informed and educated citizenry of New England. In the 1830s, a New England–born reformer complained that American public schools were "a *failure;* and that not *one in twenty* of the boys and girls who attend upon it, is educated as the public good—nay, as the *public safety* and his own individual usefulness and happiness—require." Turning from the public and personal objectives of schooling to its vocational purposes, the same reformer announced that a master mechanic had complained to him that few apprentices were fully literate and that even among journeymen, it was rare "to find . . . such a common practical education as would enable him to take charge of any important branch of his business."[8]

Observations similar to those made over 150 years ago echo in contemporary reform rhetoric. In *Winning the Brain Race,* a high-tech executive and an educator declare that "we can't have a world-class economy without a world-class workforce. . . . And we cannot have a world-class workforce without world-class schools."[9] Expressing broader concerns, such leading education critics as Diane Ravitch and Chester E. Finn warn of "a generation at risk," noting that "neither our culture, our politics, our civic life, nor our principles of equal opportunity can satisfactorily be maintained if large numbers of youngsters enter adulthood with little knowledge."[10] Now, as in past generations, this gap between expectations and reality serves as an antidote to complacency and a spur to improvements.

Regrettably, however, accompanying the gap between expectations and reality is the chronic problem of "champagne tastes" and "beer budgets" that doomed Jefferson's program in Virginia. There has always been a much greater willingness to support the institutions that would create an informed citizenry with rhetoric than with cash.

Yet the history of early America teaches us that spending money is not, in itself, a panacea. Much of the activity that promoted an informed citizenry in the nineteenth century was inexpensive, do-it-yourself, and voluntary. This was the case because a large part of the population was convinced of the importance of being informed and believed that achieving this goal was largely an individual, family, and private-sector responsibility. Judging from the growth of the publishing industry alone, it is evident that Americans were willing to spend vast sums on becoming informed, but they did so according to their own preferences and as a matter of private volition rather than state coercion. Those who did not seek to become informed were seen as disempowering themselves politically, culturally, spiritually, and economically. Because they and their children were primarily the ones who suffered the consequences, public policies were indifferent, at least with respect to tax-supported programs. Although Christians spent heavily on spreading the Gospel at home and abroad, most informed citizens were not willing to tax themselves to coerce the ignorant to mend their ways. Since the United States was providing more opportunities for more people to become informed in the nineteenth century than any government in recent memory, such support did not seem necessary.

Today, both our perceptions and our calculations of social cost have changed. Compulsory education laws and truancy regulations indicate the belief that uninformed citizens are dangerous and expensive, and therefore, moral considerations aside, it is prudent to raise the general level of education. In an economy that needs fewer and fewer unskilled workers and supplies basic support to millions who are not at work, ignorance and incompetence put burdens on the public purse. In the words of a teachers' union bumper sticker, "If you think education is expensive, try ignorance." When associated costs of drug and alcohol addiction, medical care, and crime are factored in, few would regard the expenses of ignorance as acceptable.

Does the United States, then, face a crisis of an informed citizenry? Are the dire predictions of the revolutionary era imminent? These questions must be addressed regarding the interconnected spheres of politics, the economy, and social and cultural life. At one level, at least, history is reassuring. Even though the past 200-plus years have witnessed a generous allotment of demagoguery, which shows no signs of abating, the kinds and proportions of demagoguery that Americans have witnessed have not led to a generalized tyranny. Indeed, the tyranny of race under which the nation began has been ameliorated. No one could say that the danger of tyranny by a majority, an oligarchy, or a single dictator has vanished, but the historical record is encouraging. Using the institutions that the revolutionary generation launched—free speech and press; freedom of association; religious liberty; the division of governmental powers between the legislative, executive, and judicial branches; and the division of authority between the local, state, and national levels—the increasingly inclusive citizenry has been sufficiently informed to escape the characteristic tyrannies of the nineteenth and twentieth centuries.

The historical lesson is also heartening for the U.S. economy. Although the economy may not be all we wish it to be, no other national economy of comparable size or with an equally diverse population supplies such an extensive measure of well-being. Even the harshest critics of the training of

American citizens as producers recognize that American workers are in the world's upper echelon for productivity. As with the threat of tyranny against freedom, the nation cannot be assured of future economic success, but it approaches the future with more advantages and assets—material, social, and cultural—than most countries. Certainly public policy should be tailored to enhance the productivity of Americans in a global environment, but to say that in this respect the nation's current situation is perilous is to express fearful foreboding, not the current reality.

When one considers the social and cultural realities of the United States, it is impossible to offer an objective assessment of whether the American citizenry is adequately informed. Most people recognize that American society has profound fissures and flaws—of race, violence, injustice, family life, and the spirit. Some Americans seem complacent, whereas others are suffering, anxious, or angry. Certainly Americans and their institutions are not sufficiently well informed to cope with the vast array of personal and social problems they encounter, but even the suggestion that they could is absurdly utopian. Comparisons across time and among cultures are so subjective and impressionistic that they cannot be instructive. Reformers may be able to ameliorate but they cannot repeal the ills of the human condition.

Still, where there is smoke, there may well be fire, and the concern over the continuation of a unified public culture and discourse that has been expressed so widely in the past decade or two is undeniably real. The idea that such worries are merely an established elite's complaints over its loss of hegemony misses some deeper realities. Diversity and multiculturalism may enrich the substance of America's cultural consensus and enlarge its boundaries, but in a late twentieth-century environment that also encourages individualism, they may also promote ethnocultural sectarianism.[11] To those who reflect on the fragility of national unity, especially in multiethnic and multiracial states around the world, the political and cultural wholeness of the physically vast and ethnically diverse United States seems like a remarkable historical achievement, not an inevitable natural condition. Because American political and educational systems have been among the principal agencies for achieving national wholeness, it is no wonder that alarms sound when irreconcilable conflicts seem to multiply in politics and education. The inclusion and empowerment of more voices in politics has made issues of individual conscience and identity—such as abortion, school prayer, bilingual instruction, ethnic history and culture, gender and sexual orientation, affirmative action—disrupt unity and destabilize national consensus. Since divisions of conscience and identity led Americans into civil warfare in the nineteenth century, and considering that the twentieth century has not been more benign than earlier centuries, the concerns that critics raise must not be dismissed.

This is especially true because the agency that may be emerging as the most powerful educator and molder of an informed citizenry on a national scale is not the church or the state as in past centuries but the commercial sector. Two centuries ago, when New England clergymen warned against the vicious influence of novels on the minds and morals of youth, families and churches molded schools and communities and both limited and shaped the influence of commercial print culture. Now, however, the balance among these agencies of instruction has shifted dramatically toward the commercial sector. Commanding electronic and print technologies of extraordinary reach and power, the commercial sector not only fashions the products Americans consume but shapes their vocabulary and culture from infancy through old age.[12]

Spokesmen for the commercial media and the producers of the goods and services of the private marketplace claim that their activities merely reflect existing motives and preferences. They insist they are simply holding up a mirror to the social and cultural realities of the day, and they refuse to accept the role of scapegoat for all manner of social ills and cultural blemishes. After all, if people don't like what the commercial sector has to offer, they can reject it. Advertisers and producers, they argue, continually adapt to consumer tastes.

This is a clever argument, but it is one that so oversimplifies the nature of human behavior that it is misleading. The commercial sector does respond to existing needs and desires and cannot simply manufacture them. At the same time, however, it encourages some tendencies and values while discouraging others. Broadly speaking, the values of the commercial sector are material, secular, and selfish—oriented to personal pleasures, comforts, rewards, and advantages. Commercial advantage drives the process, so that common public goals, whether secular or spiritual, must be slighted. The growth of private luxury in the midst of public squalor is the logical consequence of the lessons that the commercial sector teaches.[13]

The commercial sector does not, of course, have the entire field to itself, but it has been approaching dominance in those parts of American culture that are common and general.[14] True, the private worlds of family and religion, as well as the communities and associations that like-minded people enter to satisfy personal or public goals and to defend against the relentless pressures of the commercial sector, are also powerful. Families, religions, and voluntary associations do provide a measure of countercultural force that sets limits on the hegemony of the commercial sector. But none of these countervoices speaks to all and for all. Only the commercial sector, with its grasp of communications media, informs the common culture of the American citizenry all day, every day, providing a lifelong curriculum of personal rewards that competes with, even as it influences, the curricula of families, churches, schools, and politics. This is one reason why concerns about school and college curricula are so urgently felt as well as why the introduction of commercial television into public schools meets opposition.

Some Americans are also worried about the state of the informed citizenry because the tabloid media and political talk radio seem to have proliferated to the point that they dominate public consciousness. As a result, they fear, the menu of public issues and the shape of public policy are unduly influenced by partially or wholly misinformed citizens.[15] With improved access to airwaves and audiences, a crude demagoguery seems to have expanded and intensified in recent years. This concern is heightened because, in contrast to the era when the United States was formed as a popular republic, the tendency of television journalism and talk radio is to encourage a quasi-plebiscitary democracy based on public opinion polls wherein a sample of uninformed people answer simple, multiple-choice questions on complex public policy issues. The fear is that public policy is being framed by elected officials who are too responsive to these influences.

Whether or not this is true, any movement approaching direct democracy at the state or national level—where citizens themselves make policy, whether by polls of their opinions based on the Progressive Era reforms of petition, referendum, and recall or by a futuristic national internet—requires a level of information and engagement quite different from that envisioned between the Revolution and the era of the Civil War. Then citizens were expected to be sufficiently informed to be able to identify the approach of tyranny and take action to block it. The preservation of liberty was thought to be safest in the hands of the people because they would not tyrannize themselves. Local affairs, too, since they lay within citizens' immediate purview and touched them directly, could be settled by citizens acting in local meetings. But general public issues of war and diplomacy, public finance and commerce, education, religion, justice, and law were to be considered only by deliberative, representative assemblies operating at the state and national levels. That private citizens would be sufficiently informed to make policy in all of these areas was never contemplated and would have seemed absurd. As one democratically oriented delegate remarked in the constitutional convention, "The people . . . should have as little to do as may be about the [national] Government. They want [i.e., lack] information and are constantly liable to be misled."[16]

Today, no public official or candidate for office would make such an unflattering, undemocratic statement. The first rule of political rhetoric is, after conducting appropriate public opinion research, to articulate voters' concerns and grievances while praising their judgment and common sense. Elected officials never advise their constituents that policies are too complex and voters too ignorant to make decisions anymore than they confess that they themselves cannot master the issues. Although no one believes it, in political rhetoric Americans pretend that they and their officials are sufficiently informed to be omnicompetent. Since the Jacksonian era, this has been one of the agreed-upon fictions of democracy.

But like many hypocrisies, this fiction encourages unrealistic expectations and disillusionment. Because Americans are so much less well informed about public affairs than their political rhetoric pretends, and because democratic culture encourages the vigorous expression of opinions with or without the benefit of knowledge, conscientious people are often distressed if not frightened by the ignorance on display. The dynamic and malleable ideal of a well-informed citizenry supplies a perennial text for American social criticism because it possesses a mythic power in the American imagination.

But the actual lesson of the historical record is that no precise meaning for an informed citizenry has ever been established. In the revolutionary era, being informed meant that citizens—particularly white freeholders—should acquire sufficient knowledge of history, law, and politics to be able to recognize and confront the approach of tyranny. Later, in the early republic of George Washington, John Adams, Thomas Jefferson, and James Madison, that meaning was augmented by the idea that voting citizens should be sufficiently informed and critically minded to be able to choose public officials wisely. Education and experience should enable them to see through the seductive rhetoric of demagogues and rise above parochial self-interest. Only then, it was agreed, would the people elect wise men of good character to carry out public policy. It was the task of rulers, men with some education and leisure, to inform themselves of the merits of political measures and to deliberate carefully before acting. Officials were set off from their constituents as rulers who should do what was best for the public good, not what was most popular. The ballot box would assure that rulers did not abuse their trust with impunity; elections would not serve as referenda.

But the competitive realities of electoral politics doomed this ideal of deference. By the 1830s, it was evident that flattering the voters was essential for the success of office seekers. At the same time, the way was opened for popular reform politics—the most successful of which were anti-Masonry, temperance, and abolition—activated by the democratic idea that citizens informed on the merits of a particular issue should organize to elect officials to do their bidding, not to serve as guides and guardians. This movement combined with the emergence of a cultural marketplace in which being informed came to include boundless occupational, cultural, and recreational possibilities to push the older ideas of an informed citizenry aside. Elements of revolutionary and early republican ideals were still pressed into rhetorical service but only as they were needed to help justify the agenda of the moment—nativist, suffragist, progressive, or conservative.

Today, the most powerful movements invoking the ideal of an informed citizenry point in several directions. Some business and education leaders assert that being informed is vital for economic competitiveness. But those who favor the diversity agenda for American institutions believe that the informed citizen is acquainted with and respectful of the cultures of the many peoples of the United States and thus is able to flourish in a multicultural society. Yet another movement promotes the vision of a grassroots plebiscitary democracy wherein citizens are adequately informed to make policy choices through techniques like the initiative and referendum and even an electronic national direct democracy.

To this observer, the most valuable elements of the idea of an informed citizenry—that people must be sufficiently informed in public affairs to safeguard liberty and act responsibly—need to be recognized within a framework that acknowledges that deference in public affairs can be legitimate. The wisest citizens responding to public opinion surveys may be the 10 percent who answer "don't know," not the 90 percent who are willing to voice a judgment. As members of a society in which we readily defer to experts every day in a multitude of occupations and professions—whether pilots, physicians, accountants, or electricians—we should also recognize that the complicated political judgments required to operate the machinery of American society with some efficiency, justice, and improvement also demand experience, learning, judgment, and character. The voice of the people, though it is only slightly informed, must be heard in the political process, but it must not be the only voice. Ultimately, people who are well informed should make policy, taking public opinion into account.

This is, admittedly, a utopian idea with elitist possibilities. The fact that politicians, like used car salesmen, are often ranked at the bottom of the public's hierarchy of trust and respect—even the word "politician" seems soiled—suggests that the restoration of any degree of deference may be fanciful. After all, public officials are lightning rods and scapegoats for our fears and difficulties, and in an environment of free speech, we attack them publicly without fear of retribution. Ordinarily we grant deference to those who seem to know more than we do about how to solve a particular problem, but when politicians take such a stance, we label them as arrogant and terminate their public careers. Moreover, whereas a physician or electrician can often solve a problem single-handedly by using knowledge and technology, political problems can rarely be solved single-handedly and often require so much compromise along the way that the outcome is tainted. The most effective officials are those who anticipate problems and resolve them before they explode, achievements that, however brilliant, go unrecognized because no explosion occurred.

We all know of public officials who—informed or not—are so mendacious or hateful in other ways that we would not dream of deferring to them, nor should we. But what the history of the idea of an informed citizenry suggests is that responsible citizens should exercise their judgment about worthy and unworthy public officials from a more detached perspective than is currently in vogue. We should evaluate the general competence and integrity of officials, not their specific position on a single issue. We should consider whether an official takes the time to be informed before making decisions and whether he or she encourages private citizens to be informed as well. Such a prescription will not restore confidence in public officials quickly— we have seen too much opportunism, fakery, and incompetence for that. But if this limited sort of deference is taught in schools and promoted by the media, then change is possible. The present citizenship model—which takes its cue from glib, superficially informed radio and television journalists and talk show hosts whose routine stance toward politicians is often cynical disrespect—generally presumes bad faith and doubtful honesty among all public officials.[17] This, I submit, is a self-fulfilling expectation that makes learning, judgment, and integrity handicaps more than assets in electoral politics. If Americans truly believe in these sterling qualities, they should look for them in candidates for public office and elevate these values above their own special interests or sensational issues when they cast their votes.

Notes

INTRODUCTION

1 A more problematic view of the connections between education and citizenship is expressed in Robert H. Wiebe, *Self-Rule: A Cultural History of American Democracy* (Chicago, 1995), 6–7, 157, 178.

CHAPTER ONE

1 Edmund S. Morgan, *Inventing the People: The Rise of Popular Sovereignty in England and America* (New York, 1988).
2 Steven Ozment, *When Fathers Ruled: Family Life in Reformation Europe* (Cambridge, Mass., 1983).
3 Aristotle, *Politics,* bk. 7, chap. 9, cited in Isaac Kramnick, *Republicanism and Bourgeois Radicalism: Political Ideology in Late Eighteenth-Century England and America* (Ithaca, N.Y., 1990), 1.
4 Keith Thomas, "The Meaning of Literacy in Early Modern England," in *The Written Word: Literacy in Transition,* ed. Gerd Baumann (Oxford, 1986), 121–22; Arthur B. Ferguson, *The Articulate Citizen and the English Renaissance* (Durham, N.C., 1965).
5 Ferguson, *The Articulate Citizen,* 139.
6 Clyde A. Duniway, *The Development of Freedom of the Press in Massachusetts* (Cambridge, Mass., 1906), 6n.
7 Quoted in Ferguson, *The Articulate Citizen,* 156, 157.
8 Ibid., 141.
9 Ibid., 146.
10 Ibid., 157.
11 Ibid., 142–43.
12 Ibid., 158–59, 406.
13 Jan. 17, 1604, Robert Ashton, ed., *James I by His Contemporaries* (London, 1969), 184. At the French court, James I was said to be "the wisest fool in Christendom," a remark attributed both to Henry IV (of Navarre) and to his minister Sully. John Bartlett, *Familiar Quotations,* ed. Emily Morison Beck, 15th ed., rev. and enl. (Boston, 1980), 175.
14 This doctrine was employed in the Treaty of Westphalia, which concluded the Thirty Years' War in 1648.

15 Jan. 17, 1604, Ashton, *James I by His Contemporaries,* 184.

16 Ibid., 183.

17 Duniway, *Development of Freedom of the Press in Massachusetts,* 11–13; Frederick S. Siebert, *Freedom of the Press in England, 1476–1776: The Rise and Decline of Government Controls* (Urbana, Ill., 1952).

18 John Milton, *Areopagitica,* ed. Richard C. Jebb (1918; reprint, New York, 1971).

19 Ibid., 50.

20 Ibid., 13–14.

21 Ibid., 51.

22 Ibid., 37.

23 Ibid., 47.

24 Ibid., 6.

25 Ibid., 26.

26 Ibid., 27. In Massachusetts Bay, the Puritan magistrates attempted for a time to supervise every tavern in every village, to regulate dress, and even to oversee conversation in family and social gatherings.

27 Ibid., 11, 31.

28 Ibid., 14, 40.

29 Ibid., 21.

30 Ibid., 43.

31 Ibid., 50.

32 Ibid., 59, 58.

33 Ibid., 52.

34 Ibid., 34.

35 Ibid., 38.

36 Ibid., xxix.

37 David Johnston, *The Rhetoric of Leviathan: Thomas Hobbes and the Politics of Cultural Transformation* (Princeton, N.J., 1986), 109.

38 Quoted in Arnold A. Rogow, *Thomas Hobbes: Radical in the Service of Reaction* (New York, 1986), 79.

39 Johnston, *Rhetoric of Leviathan,* 113.

40 Ibid., 125, 127–28.

41 Rogow, *Thomas Hobbes,* 42–43, 139.

42 J. G. A. Pocock, introduction to *The Political Works of James Harrington,* ed. J. G. A. Pocock (Cambridge, 1977), 1–152, esp. 54, 59, 63, 68–69, 99.

43 Lois G. Schwoerer, "Liberty of the Press and Public Opinion, 1660–1695," in *Liberty Secured?: Britain before and after 1688,* ed. J. R. Jones (Stanford, Calif., 1992), 202–3.

44 Ibid., 202–4.

45 Ibid., 206–7; George Kitchin, *Sir Roger L'Estrange* (London, 1913).

46 James Sutherland, *The Restoration Newspaper and Its Development* (Cambridge, 1986), 6–7.

47 L'Estrange, quoted in John Nichols, *Literary Anecdotes of the Eighteenth Century; comprizing Biographical Memoirs of William Bowyer, Printer, F.S.A., and many of his learned friends . . . with a very copious index,* 6 vols. (London, 1812–16), 4:56. Richard Atkyns, "Epistle to the Reader," in *The Origin and Growth of Printing: Collected Out of History, and the Records of this Kingdome* (London, 1664), Biv, cited in Schwoerer, "Liberty of the Press" (unpublished version), 15.

48 Schwoerer, "Liberty of the Press," 204.

49 Ibid., 211.

50 Ibid., 214.

51 Ibid., 214–15.

52 Ibid., 210–11, 215–16.

53 Jeremy Black, *The English Press in the Eighteenth Century* (Philadelphia, 1987), 5.

54 Ibid., 6.

55 Schwoerer, "Liberty of the Press," 215–18.

56 Ibid., 218; Schwoerer, "Liberty of the Press" (unpublished version), 37.

57 Schwoerer, "Liberty of the Press," 219–20.

58 Ibid., 221, 229.

59 Ibid., 222–23.

60 Ibid., 228–29.

61 Ibid., 214, 230.

62 Ibid., 229.

63 Gordon J. Schochet, "From Persecution to 'Toleration,'" in Jones, *Liberty Secured?,* 122–57.

64 Graham C. Gibbs, "Press and Public Opinion: Prospective," in Jones, *Liberty Secured?,* 235–37.

65 Ibid., 236–37; Black, *English Press,* 8.

66 Gibbs, "Press and Public Opinion," 238.

67 [Robert Molesworth, Viscount Molesworth], *An Account of Denmark as it was in 1692* (1693; 4th ed., London, 1738), x–xi.

68 Ibid., xi.

69 Ibid., xii.

70 Ibid., xiii.

71 [Jodocus Crull], *Denmark Vindicated: being an answer to a late treatise called An Account of Denmark, as it was in the year 1692* (London, 1694), 90.

72 John Locke, *Some Thoughts Concerning Education* (1693; 5th ed., London, 1705), in *The Educational Writings of John Locke: A Critical Edition with Introduction and Notes,* ed. James L. Axtell (Cambridge, 1968), 112.

73 Ibid.

74 Ibid.

75 Ibid., 112–13.

76 Ibid., 112n.

77 Ibid., 189, 190.

78 Ibid., 196.

79 Ibid., 192.

80 Ibid., 198.

81 Ibid., 289–314; *Some Thoughts Concerning Education by John Locke,* ed. John W. Yolton and Jean S. Yolton (Oxford, 1989), 253n.

82 Locke, *Some Thoughts Concerning Education,* in Axtell, *Educational Writings of John Locke,* 323.

83 G. A. Cranfield, *The Development of the Provincial Newspapers* (Oxford, 1962).

CHAPTER TWO

1 Bernard Bailyn, *The Ideological Origins of the American Revolution* (Cambridge, Mass., 1967), chaps. 2, 3; John Clive and Bernard Bailyn, "England's Cultural Provinces: Scotland and America," *William and Mary Quarterly,* 3d ser., 11 (1954): 200–213.

2 Clyde A. Duniway, *The Development of Freedom of the Press in Massachusetts* (Cambridge, Mass., 1906), 32, 54, 68–69, 79n.

3 Quoted in William Waller Hening, ed., *The Statutes at Large . . . of Virginia,* 13 vols. (New York, 1810–32), 2:511, 517.

4 Duniway, *Development of Freedom of the Press,* 64.

5 Graham C. Gibbs, "Press and Public Opinion: Prospective," in *Liberty Secured?: Britain before and after 1688,* ed. J. R. Jones (Stanford, Calif., 1992), 239.

6 Ibid., 240–41.

7 Ibid., 250.

8 Ibid., 250–54; John Brewer, "The Politics of Information: Public Knowledge and Private Interest," chap. 8 of *The Sinews of Power: War, Money, and the English State, 1688–1783* (New York, 1989), 221–49, esp. 230.

9 Daniel Defoe, *An essay on the regulation of the press* (1704), 10–12, quoted in Gibbs, "Press and Public Opinion" (unpublished version prepared for the Center for the History of Freedom, Washington University, St. Louis), 16.

10 Benjamin Franklin, "Silence Dogood," *New England Courant,* July 9, 1722, *Papers of Benjamin Franklin,* ed. Leonard W. Labaree (New Haven, Conn., 1959–), 1:27.

11 *The Letters and Papers of Cadwallader Colden,* vol. 68 of New-York Historical Society, *Collections* (New York, 1937), 267–68.

12 William Livingston et al., *The Independent Reflector; or, Weekly Essays on Sundry Important Subjects, More Particularly Adapted to the Province of New York,* ed. Milton M. Klein (Cambridge, Mass., 1963), 340. Authorship of this piece has not been established with certainty. Milton M. Klein explains that articles signed by "A," as this one was, were by William Smith. However, pieces by "A" were also examined by John Morin Scott and William Livingston. Klein notes

that much of the language of this essay is similar to language found in articles written by Livingston and that Livingston approved all of the material published in the *Independent Reflector*. Accordingly, he believes the essay on liberty of the press expresses "the sentiments of William Smith and William Livingston." Ibid., 343 (n. 3), 344 (n. 5); Klein, letter to author, Knoxville, Jan. 31, 1995. Leonard Levy attributes this essay to Livingston in his *Emergence of a Free Press* (New York, 1985) and in his edited *Freedom of the Press from Zenger to Jefferson* (Indianapolis, 1966).

13 Livingston et al., *Independent Reflector*, 340.

14 *Papers of Benjamin Franklin*, 1:84–85.

15 Jean Louis DeLolme, *The Constitution of England; or, an account of the English government; in which it is compared both with the republican form of government, and the other monarchies in Europe* (1775; rev. ed., London, 1800), 410, 297–98.

16 Ibid., 297, 414n.

17 Robert E. Brown, *Middle-Class Democracy and the Revolution in Massachusetts, 1691–1780* (Ithaca, N.Y., 1955); Robert E. Brown and B. Katherine Brown, *Virginia, 1705–1786: Democracy or Aristocracy?* (East Lansing, Mich., 1964).

18 Robert E. Brown, *Middle-Class Democracy;* John J. Waters, "Patrimony, Succession, and Social Stability: Guilford, Connecticut, in the Eighteenth Century," *Perspectives in American History* 10 (1976): 131–60.

19 David D. Hall, "The Uses of Literacy in New England, 1600–1850," in *Printing and Society in Early America,* ed. William L. Joyce et al. (Worcester, Mass., 1983), 26.

20 [James Burgh], *Crito, or Essays on Various Subjects* (London, 1766), 79, 80.

21 Isaac Kramnick, *Republicanism and Bourgeois Radicalism: Political Ideology in Late Eighteenth-Century England and America* (Ithaca, N.Y., 1990), 87; Caroline Robbins, *The Eighteenth-Century Commonwealthman: Studies in the Transmission, Development, and Circumstance of English Liberal Thought from the Restoration of Charles II until the War with the Thirteen Colonies* (1959; reprint, New York, 1968), 349.

22 James Burgh, *An Account of the First Settlement, Laws, Forms of Government and Police of the Cessares, A People of South America* (1764), 73, quoted in Kramnick, *Republicanism and Bourgeois Radicalism,* 226.

23 Kramnick, *Republicanism and Bourgeois Radicalism,* 224.

24 Burgh, *An Account of the First Settlement,* 73, quoted in Kramnick, *Republicanism and Bourgeois Radicalism,* 226.

25 Ibid.

26 Quoted in Jeremy Black, *The English Press in the Eighteenth Century* (Philadelphia, 1987), 298, 303.

27 Quoted in Richard D. Altick, *The English Common Reader: A Social History of the Mass Reading Public, 1800–1900* (Chicago, 1957), 31–32.

28 Robbins, *Eighteenth-Century Commonwealthman,* 14.

29 No. 294 (Feb. 6, 1712), in *The Spectator,* ed. Donald F. Bond, 5 vols. (Oxford, 1965), 3:48; Kramnick, *Republicanism and Bourgeois Radicalism,* 193.

30 No. 294 (Feb. 6, 1712), in Bond, *Spectator,* 3:49, 50.

31 Bernard de Mandeville, *The Fable of the Bees: or, Private Vices, Public Benefits,* ed. F. B. Kaye, 2 vols. (Oxford, 1924), 1:269n.

32 Ibid., 271.

33 Ibid., 275.

34 Ibid., 308.

35 Ibid., 311.

36 Ibid., 312–14.

37 Ibid., 287–88.

38 Ibid., 302.

39 Ibid., 289.

40 Ibid., 302.

41 Ibid., 276, 284.

42 Ibid., 269, 320.

43 Ibid., 320.

44 Ibid., 293–95, 337–38.

45 Benjamin Franklin, *Proposals Relating to the Education of Youth in Pennsylvania* (1749), in *Papers of Benjamin Franklin,* 3:399–400, 427.

46 In ibid., 3:397–421, Franklin quoted from John Milton; John Locke; David Fordyce, *Dialogues Concerning Education* (1745–48); Obadiah Walker, *Of Education, Especially of Young Gentlemen* (1687); Charles Rollin; and George Turnbull, *Observations upon Liberal Education, In all its Branches* (1742). The "Good Breeding" quotation is in *Papers of Benjamin Franklin,* 3:419.

47 *Papers of Benjamin Franklin,* 3:349, 4:108.

48 Benjamin Franklin to Samuel Johnson, Philadelphia, Aug. 23, 1750, ibid., 41.

49 Ibid., 3:427.

50 "Paper on the Academy," July 31, 1750, ibid., 4:36.

51 Ibid., 3:400n.

52 Robbins, *Eighteenth-Century Commonwealthman,* 249–52; Bailyn, *Ideological Origins,* 39, 40n, 42n, 50, 53, 57n.

53 Livingston et al., *Independent Reflector,* 419–20. See also Richard Buel, Jr., "Freedom of the Press in Revolutionary America: The Evolution of Libertarianism, 1760–1820," in *The Press and the American Revolution,* ed. Bernard Bailyn and John Hench (Worcester, Mass., 1980), 59–97.

54 Livingston et al., *Independent Reflector,* 420–21.

55 No. 66 (May 16, 1711), No. 314 (Feb. 29, 1712), and No. 534 (Nov. 12, 1712), in Bond, *Spectator,* 1:281–83, 3:139–40, 4:405–6.

56 Mandeville, *Fable of the Bees,* 2:172, 1:311.

57 "A Sea Captain's Letter," [1732], *Papers of Benjamin Franklin,* 1:254.

58 Gary B. Nash, *Forging Freedom: The Formation of Philadelphia's Black Commun-*

ity, 1720–1840 (Cambridge, Mass., 1988), 18–19, 22–23.

59 John Waring to Benjamin Franklin, London, Jan. 24, 1757, *Papers of Benjamin Franklin,* 7:100.

60 Benjamin Franklin to John Waring, London, Jan. 3, 1758, ibid., 356.

61 Benjamin Franklin to John Waring, Philadelphia, Dec. 17, 1763, ibid., 10:395–96.

62 Jean Fittz Hankins, "Bringing the Good News: Protestant Missionaries to the Indians of New England and New York, 1700–1775" (Ph.D. diss., University of Connecticut, 1993).

63 Henry Barclay to Cadwallader Colden, Dec. 7, 1741, *The Letters and Papers of Cadwallader Colden,* vol. 67 of New-York Historical Society, *Collections* (New York, 1937), 284–85.

64 John Sergeant, *A Letter from the Revd Mr. Sargent of Stockbridge, to Dr. Colman of Boston; Containing Mr. Sergeant's Proposal of a more effectual Method for the Education of Indian Children; to raise 'em if possible into a civil and industrious People; by introducing the English Language among them, and thereby instilling into their Minds and Hearts, with a more lasting Impression, the Principles of Virtue and Piety* (Boston, 1743), 3, 4, 5, 7; Joseph Sewall, *Christ Victorious over the Powers of Darkness, by the Light of his preached Gospel . . . Boston, December 12, 1733* (Boston, 1733).

65 Samson Occom (1723–92) was a Mohegan who was trained by the Reverend Eleazar Wheelock in 1743–47, was later ordained by the Long Island Presbytery, and accompanied the Reverend Nathaniel Whitaker to England on a fund-raising tour in 1765–68 to finance Wheelock's Native American college (later Dartmouth). In the 1770s, Occom fell into poverty and alcoholism. Later he formed the Native American community of Brothertown in western New York, where he lived after 1789. For a time, Occom was the Anglo-American missionaries' greatest success story. *Dictionary of American Biography,* 20 vols. (New York, 1928–36), 13:614–15.

66 Benjamin Franklin to Peter Collinson, [Philadelphia], May 9, 1753, *Papers of Benjamin Franklin,* 4:483.

67 Ibid., 483–85.

68 Ibid., 5:158.

69 William Smith to Richard Peters and Benjamin Franklin, Feb. 1754, ibid., 212, 216, 217.

70 Joseph Addison, No. 287 (Jan. 29, 1712), in Bond, *Spectator,* 3:22.

71 White Kennett, Lord Bishop of Peterborough, *A Sermon Preached before the Lords Spiritual and Temporal, in the Abbey-Church at Westminster, the 30th of January 1719* (London, 1720), 25.

72 Joseph Easterbrooke, 1705, quoted in Stephen Dworetz, *The Unvarnished Doctrine: Locke, Liberalism, and the American Revolution* (Durham, N.C., 1990), 179.

73 Kathleen Wilson, "A Dissident Legacy: Eighteenth-Century Popular Politics and the Glorious Revolution," in Jones, *Liberty Secured?*, 319.

74 Nathaniel Stone, 1720, quoted in Dworetz, *The Unvarnished Doctrine*, 179.

75 Nathaniel Appleton, 1742, quoted in ibid., 180.

76 No. 124 (July 23, 1711), in Bond, *Spectator*, 1:507.

77 Benjamin Franklin, "Address to Proprietors," July 1742, *Papers of Benjamin Franklin*, 2:348.

78 Wilson, "A Dissident Legacy: Eighteenth Century Popular Politics and the Glorious Revolution" (unpublished version prepared for the Center for the History of Freedom, Washington University, St. Louis), 37, cites *The Liveryman: or, Plain Thoughts on Publick Affairs* (1740), 13, to the effect that all men who "drink Beer, wear Shoes, or now and then smoak a Pipe of Tobacco" pay taxes and thus have the right to criticize the government.

79 Viscount Bolingbroke, quoted in Wilson, "A Dissident Legacy," 319; *The Craftsman*, May 23 and July 25, 1741, cited in Wilson, "A Dissident Legacy" (unpublished version), 37.

80 Cadwallader Colden to Benjamin Franklin, Coldenham, [N.Y.], Nov. 1749, *The Letters and Papers of Cadwallader Colden*, vol. 53 of New-York Historical Society, *Collections* (New York, 1921), 158.

81 *Diary and Autobiography of John Adams*, ed. L. H. Butterfield et al., 4 vols. (Cambridge, Mass., 1961), 1:219–20.

82 Aug. 19, 1760, quoted in ibid., 152–53.

83 Mandeville, *Fable of the Bees*, 1:290.

84 [Burgh], *Crito*, viii, 1–2. Kramnick, *Republicanism and Bourgeois Radicalism*, 228, interprets these passages slightly differently. Kramnick notes that the similarity between Adams's and Burgh's comments suggests either that Burgh had published substantially the same thoughts in an earlier essay that was accessible to Adams at the time he wrote his diary entry or, more likely, that both Adams and Burgh were drawing on a particular Radical Whig essay or the common fund of such writings available on both sides of the Atlantic.

85 [Burgh], *Crito*, 158, 2.

86 Society for Constitutional Information, *An Address to the Public from the Society for Constitutional Information* (London, 1780), 1–5, *Report of the Sub-Committee of Westminster, Appointed April 12, 1780 . . . relative to the Election of Members of Parliament* [London, 1780], 1–4, and *A Second Address to the Public from the Society for Public Information* (London, 1780), 16.

CHAPTER THREE

1 John Adams, "A Dissertation on the Canon and Feudal Law," *Boston Gazette*, Sept. 30, 1765, *Papers of John Adams*, ed. Robert J. Taylor et al. (Cambridge, Mass., 1977–), 1:120.

2 *New York Post-Boy,* Nov. 8, 1756, quoted in Jeffrey A. Smith, *Printers and Press Freedom: The Ideology of Early American Journalism* (New York, 1988), 130.

3 Jacob Duché, quoted in Lawrence A. Cremin, *American Education: The Colonial Experience, 1607–1783* (New York, 1970), 517.

4 Ibid., 531.

5 Ibid., 544–45.

6 Adams, "A Dissertation on the Canon and Feudal Law," *Papers of John Adams,* 1:120.

7 Measurement of literacy levels in the eighteenth century has necessarily been imprecise. The burden of scholarship, however, places New England at the top in colonial America and colonial America and Scotland above the rest of Britain and Europe. See Harvey J. Graff, *The Legacies of Literacy: Continuities and Contradictions in Western Culture and Society* (Bloomington, 1987), chap. 6, esp. 246–57; R. A. Houston, *Scottish Literacy and Scottish Identity: Illiteracy and Society in Scotland and Northern England, 1600–1800* (Cambridge, 1985), esp. 162–92; and Carl F. Kaestle et al., *Literacy in the United States: Readers and Reading since 1880* (New Haven, Conn., 1991), 3–32.

8 For newspapers, see Charles E. Clark, *The Public Prints: The Newspaper in Anglo-American Culture, 1665–1740* (New York, 1994), esp. chaps. 10, 11.

9 Boston town meeting, May 24, 1764, Boston Registry Department, *Records Relating to the Early History of Boston,* vol. 16, *Boston Town Records, 1758 to 1769* (Boston, 1886), 121–22.

10 The political mobilization of the people has been treated extensively in the scholarly literature, most recently in Gordon S. Wood, *The Radicalism of the American Revolution* (New York, 1992), part 3. See also Richard D. Brown, *Revolutionary Politics in Massachusetts: The Boston Committee of Correspondence and the Towns, 1772–1774* (Cambridge, Mass., 1970); Ronald P. Formisano, *The Transformation of Political Culture: Massachusetts Parties, 1790s–1840s* (New York, 1983); Edmund S. Morgan, *Inventing the People: The Rise of Popular Sovereignty in England and America* (New York, 1988); J. R. Pole, *The Gift of Government: Political Responsibility from the English Restoration to American Independence* (Athens, Ga., 1983), and *Political Representation in England and the Origins of the American Republic* (New York, 1966); Richard Alan Ryerson, *The Revolution Is Now Begun: The Radical Committees of Philadelphia, 1765–1776* (Philadelphia, 1978); and Chilton Williamson, *American Suffrage: From Property to Democracy, 1760–1860* (Princeton, N.J., 1960).

11 The publishing history of the work is described in *Papers of John Adams,* 1:103–5.

12 Ibid., 108.

13 Ibid.

14 Ibid., 108–10.

15 Ibid., 114.

16 Ibid.; *Diary and Autobiography of John Adams,* ed. L. H. Butterfield et al., 4 vols. (Cambridge, Mass., 1961), 1:257.

17 *Papers of John Adams,* 1:118.

18 Ibid.

19 Ibid., 120.

20 Ibid.

21 Ibid.

22 Ibid., 120–21.

23 Ibid., 121.

24 Ibid.

25 Ibid.

26 Ibid.

27 Ibid., 122.

28 Ibid., 126.

29 Ibid., 127.

30 Ibid., 128.

31 Pole, *Gift of Government,* 130, 171n; Boston town meeting, May 26, 1766, Boston Registry Department, *Boston Town Records, 1758 to 1769,* 183.

32 Quoted in Richard D. Brown, *Revolutionary Politics,* 43.

33 Carl F. Kaestle, "The Public Reaction to John Dickinson's *Farmer's Letters,*" *Proceedings of the American Antiquarian Society* 78, part 2 (1968): 325–26. Dickinson's *Letters* went through seven American pamphlet editions.

34 John Dickinson, *Letters from a Farmer in Pennsylvania to the Inhabitants of the British Colonies* (1767–68), in *Empire and Nation: Letters from a Farmer in Pennsylvania, John Dickinson/Letters from a Federal Farmer, Richard Henry Lee,* ed. Forrest McDonald (Englewood Cliffs, N.J., 1962), 3–85; Kaestle, "Public Reaction," 329–38.

35 [William Knox], *The Controversy Between Great Britain and Her Colonies Reviewed* (London, 1769).

36 Kaestle, "Public Reaction," 335–36; Lennard J. Davis, *Factual Fictions: The Origins of the English Novel* (New York, 1983).

37 Dickinson, *Letters from a Farmer,* in McDonald, *Empire and Nation,* esp. 3, 84.

38 Ibid., 3.

39 Benjamin Franklin, "Rules by Which a Great Empire May be Reduced to a Small One," Sept. 11, 1773, *The Papers of Benjamin Franklin,* ed. William B. Willcox (New Haven, Conn., 1959–), 20:392–93.

40 Bernard Bailyn, *The Ordeal of Thomas Hutchinson* (Cambridge, Mass., 1974), 199–201.

41 Richard D. Brown, *Revolutionary Politics,* 84–85.

42 Boston town meeting, Mar. 19, 1771, Boston Registry Department, *Records Relating to the Early History of Boston,* vol. 18, *Boston Town Records, 1770 through 1777* (Boston, 1887), 48.

43 Richard D. Brown, *Revolutionary Politics,* 44.

44 Quoted in ibid.

45 Ibid., chap. 4.

46 Ibid., 91.

47 Thomas Young to Hugh Hughes, Boston, Dec. 21, 1772, Miscellaneous Bound Manuscripts, Massachusetts Historical Society, Boston, Mass.

48 Richard D. Brown, *Revolutionary Politics,* 95, 167.

49 Quoted in ibid., 247.

50 Thomas R. Adams, *The American Controversy: A Bibliographical Study of the British Pamphlets about the American Dispute, 1764–1783,* 2 vols. (Providence, 1980), 1:422–24; Thomas Paine, *Common Sense,* ed. Isaac Kramnick (Harmondsworth, Eng., 1976), 8–9. Eleven other editions were printed that year, mostly in Britain.

51 Bernard Bailyn, "Common Sense," in *Fundamental Testaments of the American Revolution* (Washington, D.C., 1973), 7–22.

52 Bernard Bailyn, *The Ideological Origins of the American Revolution* (Cambridge, Mass., 1967), 288–91.

53 *The Works of John Adams,* ed. Charles Francis Adams, 10 vols. (Boston, 1850–56), 1:192, 195.

54 J. Paul Selsam, *The Pennsylvania Constitution of 1776: A Study in Revolutionary Democracy* (Philadelphia, 1936), 202–3; John L. Cheney, Jr., ed., *North Carolina Government, 1585–1979: A Narrative and Statistical History* (Raleigh, N.C., 1981), 815.

55 Samuel Adams to James Warren, Philadelphia, Nov. 4, 1775, *Warren-Adams Letters: Being chiefly a correspondence among John Adams, Samuel Adams, and James Warren,* vol. 72 of Massachusetts Historical Society, *Collections* (Boston, 1917), 171–72.

56 "Appeal to the Inhabitants of Quebec," Oct. 26, 1774, in *American Political Writing during the Founding Era, 1760–1805,* ed. Charles S. Hyneman and Donald S. Lutz (Indianapolis, 1983), 233–34; Richard Buel, Jr., "Freedom of the Press in Revolutionary America: The Evolution of Libertarianism, 1760–1820," in *The Press and the American Revolution,* ed. Bernard Bailyn and John B. Hench (Worcester, Mass., 1980), 59–97.

57 Thomas Paine, "The Magazine in America," *Pennsylvania Magazine,* Jan. 2, 1775, *Complete Writings of Thomas Paine,* ed. Philip S. Foner, 2 vols. (New York, 1945), 2:1112.

58 *The Papers of George Mason, 1725–1792,* ed. Robert A. Rutland, 3 vols. (Chapel Hill, N.C., 1970), 1:288; *The Papers of Thomas Jefferson,* ed. Julian P. Boyd et al. (Princeton, N.J., 1950–), 1:344–45, 353, 363, 6:288, 304.

59 Phillips Payson, Massachusetts election sermon, 1778, in Hyneman and Lutz, *American Political Writing,* 1:530.

60 Thomas Jefferson to John Adams, n.p., May 16, 1777, *Papers of Thomas Jefferson,*

2:19. During the war an armed insurrection by citizens of backcountry Virginia was afterward explained by some of the insurgents and their opponents as having been caused by the insurgents' lack of adequate information regarding state government policies. See David J. Kiracofe, "Treason and the Development of National Identity in Revolutionary America, 1775–1815" (Ph.D. diss., University of Connecticut, 1995), esp. 119, 123.

61 John S. Whitehead, *The Separation of College and State: Columbia, Dartmouth, Harvard, and Yale, 1776–1876* (New Haven, Conn., 1973); Howard Miller, *The Revolutionary College: American Presbyterian Higher Education, 1707–1837* (New York, 1976), 155–56.

62 Payson, Massachusetts election sermon, in Hyneman and Lutz, *American Political Writing*, 1:530.

63 John Adams to Abbé de Mably, Paris, Oct. 1782, *Works of John Adams*, 5:494–96.

64 Miller, *Revolutionary College*, 155–56.

65 "A Dissertation on Education in the Form of a Letter from James Maury to Robert Jackson, July 17, 1762," ed. Helen Duprey Bullock, *Papers of the Albemarle County Historical Society* 2 (1942): 40, 41, 43, 46, 47, 49, 58.

66 *Diary of Landon Carter*, ed. Jack P. Greene, 2 vols. (Charlottesville, Va., 1965), 1:372–73.

67 Henry Laurens to William Fisher, Charles Town, S.C., Mar. 28, 1763, *Papers of Henry Laurens*, ed. Philip M. Hamer et al. (Columbia, S.C., 1968–), 3:383.

68 Henry Laurens to James Grant, Charleston, S.C., Nov. 24, 1770, ibid., ed. George C. Rogers, Jr., et al., 7:407.

69 Henry Laurens to James Habersham, Charleston, S.C., Jan. 11, 1770, ibid., 212.

70 Henry Laurens to Benjamin Elliott, New York, Sept. 9, 1771, ibid., 586–87.

71 Henry Laurens to Benjamin Elliott, Chelsea, Eng., Nov. 4, 1771, ibid., ed. George C. Rogers, Jr., et al., 8:31; Henry Laurens to Thomas Savage, Westminster, Eng., Dec. 5, 1771, ibid., 75.

72 Henry Laurens to Richard Clarke, Charles Town, S.C., Apr. 6, 1771, ibid., 7:481. Laurens was writing about his second son, Henry.

73 Robert Morris to Matthew Ridley, Philadelphia, Oct. 14, 1781, *The Papers of Robert Morris*, ed. E. James Ferguson et al. (Pittsburgh, 1975–), 3:56–57.

74 Ibid., 57; Robert Morris to Benjamin Franklin, Philadelphia, Oct. 14, 1781, ibid., 53.

75 John Adams to John Quincy Adams, Amsterdam, Dec. 23, 1780, *Adams Family Correspondence*, ed. L. H. Butterfield and Marc Friedlaender (Cambridge, Mass., 1963–), 4:49.

76 John Adams to Abigail Adams, The Hague, June 16, 1782, ibid., 325.

77 John Jay to Robert Morris, Paris, Oct. 13, 1782, *Papers of Robert Morris*, ed. John Catanzariti et al., 6:577.

78 Henry Laurens to Thomas Savage, Westminster, Eng., Dec. 5, 1771, *Papers of Henry Laurens*, 8:75.

79 Henry Laurens to James Laurens, Westminster, Eng., Dec. 12, 1771, ibid., 91.

80 *Royal American Magazine* (Boston), Jan. 1774, Isaiah Thomas, publisher, 10, quoted in part in Linda K. Kerber, *Women of the Republic: Intellect and Ideology in Revolutionary America* (Chapel Hill, N.C., 1980), 191.

81 Kerber, *Women of the Republic,* chap. 7; Jan Lewis, "The Republican Wife: Virtue and Seduction in the Early Republic," *William and Mary Quarterly,* 3d ser., 44 (1987): 689–721.

82 Thomas Jefferson, "A Bill for Amending the Constitution of the College of William and Mary, and Substituting More Certain Revenues for Its Support," as reported by the Committee of Revisions, June 18, 1779, *Papers of Thomas Jefferson,* 2:538. See also Lawrence A. Cremin, *American Education: The Colonial Experience, 1607–1783* (New York, 1970), 347–56.

83 Jon Teaford, "The Transformation of Massachusetts Education, 1670–1780," *History of Education Quarterly* 10 (1970): 287–307, esp. 295; Robert Middle-kauff, *Ancients and Axioms: Secondary Education in Eighteenth-Century New England* (New Haven, Conn., 1963), 40.

84 Quoted in Merrill D. Peterson, *Thomas Jefferson and the New Nation* (New York, 1970), 151.

85 Thomas Jefferson, "A Bill for the More General Diffusion of Knowledge," as reported by the Committee of Revisions, Jan. 6, 1779, *Papers of Thomas Jefferson,* 2:526–27.

86 Ibid.

87 Ibid., 530–31.

88 Ibid., 531. It is ironic that in some particulars Jefferson's plan echoed one presented by Mandeville in his "Essay on Charity and Charity Schools" of 1714. Referring to gentlemen, Mandeville had argued that "all the Liberal Arts and every Branch of Literature should be encouraged throughout the Kingdom. . . . In every County there should be one or more large Schools erected at the Publick Charge for *Latin* and *Greek.*" These schools were to have six or more grades. Bernard de Mandeville, *The Fable of the Bees; or, Private Vices, Public Benefits,* ed. F. B. Kaye, 2 vols. (Oxford, 1924), 1:295. James Burgh advocated government construction of schools in all parishes wherein "one half of the day [was to be] spent learning useful trades and employments, the other half reading, writing and understanding accounts" (*An Account of the First Settlement, Laws, Forms of Government and Police of the Cessares, A People of South America* [1764], quoted in Isaac Kramnick, *Republicanism and Bourgeois Radicalism: Political Ideology in Late Eighteenth-Century England and America* (Ithaca, N.Y., 1990), 226).

89 Jefferson, "Bill for the More General Diffusion of Knowledge," *Papers of Thomas Jefferson,* 2:532.

90 Ibid., 533.

91 Jefferson, "Bill for Amending the Constitution of the College of William and Mary," ibid., 540–42.

92 Thomas Jefferson, *Notes on the State of Virginia, The Writings of Thomas Jefferson,* ed. Paul Leicester Ford, 12 vols. (New York, 1904–5), 4:61, 64.

93 John Adams to Jonathan Dickinson Sergeant, Philadelphia, July 21, 1776, *Papers of John Adams,* 4:397.

94 John Adams to Joseph Hawley, Philadelphia, Aug. 25, 1776, ibid., 495–97.

95 Gordon S. Wood, *The Creation of the American Republic, 1776–1787* (Chapel Hill, N.C., 1969), chap. 12.

96 John Adams to Joseph Hawley, Philadelphia, Aug. 25, 1776, *Papers of John Adams,* 4:495–97.

97 Payson, Massachusetts election sermon, in Hyneman and Lutz, *American Political Writing,* 1:526–27.

98 Ibid., 527.

99 Massachusetts constitution of 1780, in *The Popular Sources of Political Authority: Documents on the Massachusetts Constitution of 1780,* ed. Oscar Handlin and Mary F. Handlin (Cambridge, Mass., 1966), 442–43.

100 Ibid., 446.

101 Ibid.

102 Ibid., 465.

103 Ibid., 467.

104 Nathan O. Hatch, *The Sacred Cause of Liberty: Republican Thought and the Millennium in Revolutionary New England* (New Haven, Conn., 1977), chap. 4.

105 Quoted in Miller, *Revolutionary College,* 119, 118.

106 Ezra Stiles, *The United States Elevated to Glory and Honor* (New Haven, Conn., 1783), 34; Benjamin Rush to John Armstrong, Philadelphia, Mar. 19, 1783, *Letters of Benjamin Rush,* ed. L. H. Butterfield, 2 vols. (Princeton, N.J., 1951), 1:294.

107 Samuel Eliot Morison, ed., *Sources and Documents Illustrating the American Revolution, 1764–1788, and the Formation of the Federal Constitution,* 2d ed. (New York, 1972), 207.

CHAPTER FOUR

1 Gordon S. Wood, *The Radicalism of the American Revolution* (New York, 1992).

2 Joan R. Gundersen, "Independence, Citizenship, and the American Revolution," *Signs* 13 (1987): 59–77; Linda K. Kerber, "The Revolutionary Generation: Ideology, Politics, and Culture in the Early Republic," in *The New American History,* ed. Eric Foner (Philadelphia, 1990); Paul Kleppner, "Defining Citizenship: Immigration and the Struggle for Voting Rights in America," in *Voting and the Spirit of Democracy: Essays on the History of Voting and Voting Rights in America,* ed. Donald W. Rogers (Urbana, Ill., 1992), 43–52; Barbara Clark Smith, "Food Rioters and the American Revolution," *William and Mary Quarterly,* 3d ser., 51 (1994): 3–38.

3 *London Public Ledger,* quoted in *Connecticut Courant* (Hartford), Jan. 20, 1766, 1.

4 Thomas Paine, "The Magazine in America," *Pennsylvania Magazine,* Jan. 2, 1775, *Complete Writings of Thomas Paine,* ed. Philip S. Foner, 2 vols. (New York, 1945), 2:1110.

5 "Draft of Virginia Declaration of Rights," May 1776, *The Papers of George Mason, 1725–1792,* ed. Robert A. Rutland, 3 vols. (Chapel Hill, N.C., 1970), 1:288; June 8, 1789, *The Papers of James Madison,* ed. Charles F. Hobson and Robert A. Rutland, 17 vols. (Chicago, 1962–91), 12:201; Henry Steele Commager and Milton Cantor, eds., *Documents of American History,* vol. 1, 10th ed. (Englewood Cliffs, N.J., 1988), 146.

6 *General Advertiser, and Political, Commercial, Agricultural and Literary Journal,* 1790, edited by Benjamin Franklin Bache, quoted in Jeffrey A. Smith, *Printers and Press Freedom: The Ideology of Early American Journalism* (New York, 1988), 158. Bache was raised under the supervision of his grandfather, Benjamin Franklin.

7 Thomas Jefferson to George Washington, Sept. 9, 1792, quoted in Jeffrey A. Smith, *Printers and Press Freedom,* 40.

8 Thomas Jefferson, "Notes for a Constitution," [1794], quoted in ibid., 89.

9 Thomas Jefferson to Elbridge Gerry, Philadelphia, Jan. 26, 1799, *The Writings of Thomas Jefferson,* ed. Andrew A. Lipscomb and Albert Ellery Bergh, 20 vols. (Washington, D.C., 1903–4), 10:78; Thomas Jefferson to Mr. Pictet, Washington, D.C., Feb. 5, 1803, ibid., 357; Thomas Jefferson, "Second Inaugural Address," Mar. 5, 1805, ibid., 3:381.

10 Jefferson, "Second Inaugural Address," ibid., 3:380; Thomas Jefferson to John Norvell, Washington, D.C., June 11, 1807, ibid., 11:224–25; Thomas Jefferson to President James Madison, Monticello, Mar. 17, 1809, ibid., 12:267; Thomas Jefferson to Walter Jones, Monticello, Jan. 2, 1814, ibid., 14:46.

11 Thomas Paine, "Liberty of the Press," *American Citizen,* Oct. 20, 1806, *Complete Writings of Thomas Paine,* 2:1010.

12 Thomas Jefferson to Col. Charles Yancey, Monticello, Jan. 6, 1816, *Writings of Thomas Jefferson,* 14:384; Thomas Jefferson to Monsieur A. Coray, Monticello, Oct. 31, 1823, ibid., 15:489; Thomas Jefferson to James Monroe, Monticello, Feb. 4, 1816, ibid., 14:430; Thomas Jefferson to Albert Gallatin, Monticello, Feb. 15, 1818, ibid., 19:258; Thomas Jefferson to Charles Pinckney, Monticello, Sept. 30, 1820, ibid., 15:279.

13 John Adams to Samuel Adams, New York, Oct. 18, 1790, *The Works of John Adams,* ed. Charles Francis Adams, 10 vols. (Boston, 1850–56), 6:414–16.

14 Samuel Adams to John Adams, Boston, Nov. 25, 1790, *The Writings of Samuel Adams,* ed. Harry A. Cushing, 4 vols. (1904–8; reprint, New York, 1968), 4:347, 349.

15 Ibid., 349.

16 *Papers of James Madison,* ed. Robert A. Rutland et al., 17 vols. (Charlottesville, Va., 1962–91), 14:170.

17 George Washington, Farewell Address, Sept. 19, 1796, *The Writings of George Washington,* ed. John C. Fitzpatrick, 39 vols. (Washington, D.C., 1931–44), 35:230.

18 The law is reprinted in James Morton Smith, *Freedom's Fetters: The Alien and Sedition Laws and American Civil Liberties* (Ithaca, N.Y., 1966), 442.

19 Zephaniah S. Moore, *An Oration on the Anniversary of the Independence of the United States of America . . . July 5, 1802* (Worcester, Mass., 1802), 16.

20 Richard R. John, *Spreading the Word: The American Postal System from Franklin to Morse* (Cambridge, Mass., 1995), chap. 2; Richard B. Kielbowicz, *News in the Mail: The Press, Post Office, and Public Information, 1700–1860s* (New York, 1989).

21 *National Gazette,* [Dec. 19, 1791], *Papers of James Madison,* ed. Robert A. Rutland and Thomas A. Mason, 14:170.

22 John Russell petition, Boston, Feb. 3, 1786, in John B. Hench, "Massachusetts Printers and the Commonwealth's Newspaper Advertisement Tax of 1786," *Proceedings of the American Antiquarian Society* 87, part 1 (Apr. 1977): 203.

23 Thomas Jefferson to Edward Carrington, Paris, Jan. 16, 1787, *The Papers of Thomas Jefferson,* ed. Julian P. Boyd et al. (Princeton, N.J., 1950–), 11:49; Roger Sherman, quoted by James Madison, Philadelphia, May 31, 1787, in *The Records of the Federal Convention of 1787,* rev. ed., ed. Max Farrand, 4 vols. (New Haven, Conn., 1937), 1:48.

24 Jan. 9, 1792, in Congress, *Papers of James Madison,* ed. Rutland and Mason, 14:186; John Steele to constituents, Jan. 15, 1792, in *Circular Letters of Congressmen to Their Constituents, 1789–1829,* ed. Noble E. Cunningham, Jr., 3 vols. (Chapel Hill, N.C., 1978), 1:9.

25 James Madison to Edmund Randolph, [Philadelphia], Jan. 28, 1783, *Papers of James Madison,* ed. William T. Hutchinson and William M. E. Rachal, 6:156.

26 Commager and Cantor, *Documents of American History,* 1:125–26.

27 James Madison to Thomas Jefferson, New York, Feb. 15, 1787, *Papers of Thomas Jefferson,* 11:152. Ibid., 2:535n, includes editor Julian P. Boyd's discussion of the education bill.

28 Rhys Isaac, *The Transformation of Virginia, 1740–1790* (Chapel Hill, N.C., 1982), 294–95; Merrill D. Peterson, *Thomas Jefferson and the New Nation* (New York, 1970), 150.

29 Commager and Cantor, *Documents of American History,* 1:124, 131.

30 Quoted in Frederick Rudolph, ed., *Essays on Education in the Early Republic* (Cambridge, Mass., 1965), xv.

31 Benjamin Rush, *A Plan for the Establishment of Public Schools and the Diffusion of Knowledge in Pennsylvania; to Which Are Added, Thoughts upon the Mode of*

Education, Proper in a Republic, Addressed to the Legislature and Citizens of the State (Philadelphia, 1786), in ibid., 13; Benjamin Rush to James Hamilton, Philadelphia, June 27, 1810, *Letters of Benjamin Rush,* ed. L. H. Butterfield, 2 vols. (Princeton, N.J., 1951), 2:1053.

32 Thomas Jefferson to Dupont de Nemours, Poplar Forest, Apr. 24, 1816, *Writings of Thomas Jefferson,* 14:491. A year and a half later, Jefferson suggested that a sanction against families in which parents did not educate their sons be enacted whereby the uneducated would be disfranchised. A law was proposed to deny citizenship to future inhabitants who could not "read readily in some tongue, native or acquired." Thomas Jefferson to Joseph C. Cabell, Poplar Forest, Sept. 9, 1817, ibid., 17:423n, 424.

33 John Adams to Benjamin Rush, Quincy, Aug. 28, 1811, *Works of John Adams,* 9:639.

34 Ibid., xv; Samuel Harrison Smith, *Remarks on Education* (1798), in *Essays on Education in the Early Republic,* ed. Frederick Rudolph (Cambridge, Mass., 1965), 190n, 210; Samuel Knox, *An Essay on the Best System of Liberal Education* (1799), in ibid., 311.

35 Benjamin Rush to Richard Price, Philadelphia, May 25, 1786, *Letters of Benjamin Rush,* 1:388; Benjamin Rush, "Address to the people of the United States," *American Museum, or Repository* 1 (Jan. 1787): 11. For a discussion of the use of the Spartan educational model in conjunction with contradictory practical and commercial goals, see Lorraine Smith Pangle and Thomas L. Pangle, *The Learning of Liberty: The Educational Ideas of the American Founders* (Lawrence, Kans., 1993), chap. 2.

36 James McLachlan, "Classical Names, American Identities: Some Notes on College Students and the Classical Tradition in the 1770s," in *Classical Traditions in Early America,* ed. John W. Eadie (Ann Arbor, 1976), 81–98; Stephen Botein, "Cicero as a Role Model for Early American Lawyers: A Case Study in Classical Influence," *Classical Journal* 73 (1977–78): 313–21; James M. Farrell, "*Pro Militibus Oratio:* John Adams's Imitation of Cicero in the Boston Massacre Trial," *Rhetorica* 9 (Summer 1991): 233–49.

37 David Hume, "Of the Study of History" (1741), in *Essays: Moral, Political, and Literary,* ed. Eugene F. Miller, rev. ed. (Indianapolis, 1987), 565.

38 James Wilson, "Of the Study of the Law of the United States" (1790–91), *Works of James Wilson,* ed. Robert Green McCloskey, 2 vols. (Cambridge, Mass., 1967), 1:88–89; John Adams to Abigail Adams II, Paris, Aug. 13, 1783, *The Book of Abigail and John: Selected Letters of the Adams Family, 1762–1784,* ed. L. H. Butterfield, Marc Friedlaender, and Mary-Jo Kline (Cambridge, Mass., 1975), 360.

39 May 1785, *The Diaries of George Washington,* ed. Donald Jackson and Dorothy Twohig, 6 vols. (Charlottesville, Va., 1976–79), 4:140n. Washington also proposed the establishment of national military academies in a letter to Alexander

Hamilton, Newburgh, N.Y., May 2, 1783, *Writings of George Washington,* 26:375, 396–97.

40 George Washington to Alexander Hamilton, Philadelphia, Sept. 1, 1796, *Writings of George Washington,* 35:199.

41 Benjamin Rush to Richard Price, Philadelphia, May 25, 1786, *Letters of Benjamin Rush,* 1:388; Benjamin Rush, "To Friends of the Federal Government: A Plan for a Federal University," *Federal Gazette,* Oct. 29, 1788, ibid., 492–94.

42 *Writings of George Washington,* 30:494, 31:279–80; David Madsen, *The National University: Enduring Dream of the USA* (Detroit, 1966), 24–37.

43 George Washington to Vice President John Adams, Nov. 15, 1794, *Writings of George Washington,* 34:23; George Washington to Thomas Jefferson, Mar. 15, 1795, ibid., 148.

44 James Madison, "Seventh Annual Message," Dec. 5, 1815, *The Writings of James Madison,* ed. Gaillard Hunt, 9 vols. (New York, 1900–1910), 8:343.

45 George Washington to Thomas Jefferson, Philadelphia, Mar. 15, 1795, *Writings of George Washington,* 34:147.

46 Thomas Jefferson to Gen. James Breckinridge, Monticello, Feb. 15, 1821, *Writings of Thomas Jefferson,* 15:315; Thomas Jefferson to John Taylor, Monticello, Feb. 14, 1821, ibid., 18:313; Thomas Jefferson to Gen. James Breckinridge, Monticello, Apr. 9, 1822, ibid., 15:364–65; Thomas Jefferson to Joseph C. Cabell, Monticello, Jan. 31, 1821, ibid., 311.

47 Thomas Jefferson to [?], Monticello, Feb. 3, 1825, ibid., 16:104.

48 Commager and Cantor, *Documents of American History,* 1:126.

49 Samuel Austin, *The Diffusion of Correct Knowledge of the True God, A Leading Object of the Christian Ministry: A Sermon delivered at the Tabernacle in Salem, April 20, 1803* (Salem, Mass., 1803), 22.

50 Zephaniah S. Moore, *Oration on the Anniversary of the Independence of the United States,* 24.

51 Carl F. Kaestle, *Pillars of the Republic: Common Schools and American Society, 1780–1860* (New York, 1983), chaps. 1–3.

52 Benjamin Rush, "To the Citizens of Philadelphia: A Plan for Free Schools," *Independent Gazetteer* (Philadelphia), Mar. 28, 1787, *Letters of Benjamin Rush,* 1:413.

53 Ibid.

54 Ibid., 414–15.

55 Samuel Adams to James Warren, Philadelphia, Nov. 4, 1775, *Warren-Adams Letters: Being chiefly a correspondence among John Adams, Samuel Adams, and James Warren,* vol. 72 of Massachusetts Historical Society, *Collections* (Boston, 1917), 171–73.

56 In *American Political Writing during the Founding Era, 1760–1805,* ed. Charles S. Hyneman and Donald S. Lutz, 2 vols. (Indianapolis, 1983), 1:555.

57 John Adams to John Jebb, London, Sept. 10, 1785, *Works of John Adams,* 9:540.

58 John Adams, *A Defense of the Constitutions of Government of the United States of America* (1788), ibid., 6:168.

59 Ibid., 198–99.

60 John Adams to Benjamin Waterhouse, Quincy, Aug. 7, 1805, *Statesman and Friend: Correspondence of John Adams with Benjamin Waterhouse, 1784–1822,* ed. Worthington Chauncey Ford (Boston, 1927), 25.

61 Thomas Jefferson to George Wythe, Paris, Aug. 13, 1786, *Papers of Thomas Jefferson,* 10:245; Thomas Jefferson, "Sixth Annual Message," Dec. 2, 1806, *Writings of Thomas Jefferson,* 3:423.

62 Thomas Jefferson to John Adams, Monticello, July 5, 1814, *Writings of Thomas Jefferson,* 14:150–51; Thomas Jefferson to John Adams, Monticello, Oct. 28, 1813, *The Adams-Jefferson Letters: The Complete Correspondence between Thomas Jefferson and Abigail and John Adams,* ed. Lester J. Cappon, 2 vols. (Chapel Hill, N.C., 1959), 2:290.

63 Thomas Jefferson, "Autobiography," Jan. 6, 1821, *Writings of Thomas Jefferson,* 1:71–72; William Wirt, *Letters of a British Spy,* 10th ed. (1803; reprint, New York, 1832), in *Papers of Thomas Jefferson,* 2:534–35n.

64 James Madison to W[illiam] T. Barry, Aug. 4, 1822, *Writings of James Madison,* 9:104–7.

65 Kaestle, *Pillars of the Republic,* chaps. 1–3.

66 Peter Onuf, "State Politics and Republican Virtue: Religion, Education, and Morality in Early American Federalism," in *Toward a Usable Past: An Examination of the Origins and Duplications of State Protections of Liberty,* ed. Paul Finkelman and Stephen E. Gottlieb (Athens, Ga., 1991), 91–116.

67 Lawrence A. Cremin, *American Education: The National Experience, 1783–1876* (New York, 1982), 9–10, 401.

68 See James Willard Hurst, "The Release of Energy," in *Law and the Conditions of Freedom* (Madison, Wis., 1956), 3–32.

69 Quoted in Sherman Williams, "Jedidiah Peck: The Father of the Public School System of the State of New York," *Quarterly Journal of the New York State Historical Association* 1 (1920): 221, 222.

70 Ibid., 226, 236–39.

71 Ibid., 236.

72 Richard D. Brown, *Knowledge Is Power: The Diffusion of Information in Early America, 1700–1865* (New York, 1989), 286–96.

73 John Adams to Abigail Adams, Philadelphia, Aug. 13, 1776, *Adams Family Correspondence,* ed. L. H. Butterfield and Marc Friedlaender (Cambridge, Mass., 1963–), 2:90.

74 James Madison to W[illiam] T. Barry, Aug. 4, 1822, *Writings of James Madison,* 9:108–9.

75 Printers' petition, Feb. 2, 1785, in Hench, "Massachusetts Printers," 208; Noah Webster, *On the Education of Youth in America* (1790), in Rudolph, *Essays on Education,* 65.

76 Benjamin Rush to John Armstrong, Philadelphia, Mar. 19, 1783, *Letters of Benjamin Rush,* 1:294.

77 *Diary and Autobiography of John Adams,* ed. L. H. Butterfield et al., 4 vols. (Cambridge, Mass., 1961), 3:240–41.

78 Benjamin Rush to Jeremy Belknap, Philadelphia, June 13, 1789, *Letters of Benjamin Rush,* 1:521; Pangle and Pangle, *The Learning of Liberty,* 30–31.

79 Webster, *On the Education of Youth,* in Rudolph, *Essays on Education,* 50–51.

80 Ibid., 66.

81 Robert Coram, *Political Inquiries: to Which is Added, a Plan for the General Establishment of Schools throughout the United States* (1791), in Rudolph, *Essays on Education,* 113, 138, 141.

82 Benjamin Rush to John Adams, Philadelphia, Feb. 4, 1811, Oct. 2, 1810, July 2, 1789, *Letters of Benjamin Rush,* 2:1080–81, 1067, 1:518; John Adams to Benjamin Rush, June 19, 1789, ibid., 1:518n. Rush even urged that the training of Presbyterian clergy be restricted to the study of religious texts and the history and culture of the biblical era. He sought to preserve "a pious ignorance . . . of the crimes of heathen gods" and mythology. Benjamin Rush to [Ashbel Green], Philadelphia, May 22, 1807, ibid., 2:946–48.

83 Samuel Harrison Smith, *Remarks on Education: Illustrating the Close Connection Between Virtue and Wisdom, To Which Is Annexed a System of Liberal Education, Which, Having Received the Premium Awarded by the American Philosophical Society, December 15th, 1797, Is Now Published by Their Order* (1798), in Rudolph, *Essays on Education,* 188, 189, 195, 196.

84 Richard D. Brown, *Knowledge Is Power,* 282, 286.

85 Marian Barber Stowell, *Early American Almanacs: The Colonial Weekday Bible* (New York, 1977); James A. Bear, Jr., and Mary Caperton Bear, *A Checklist of Virginia Almanacs, 1732–1850* (Charlottesville, Va., 1962). See also George L. Kittredge, *The Old Farmer and His Almanac* (Boston, 1904).

86 James D. Watkinson, "Useful Knowledge?: Concepts, Values, and Access in American Education, 1776–1840," *History of Education Quarterly* 30 (1990): 351–70. Information on the *Christian Herald and Seaman's Magazine* was provided by Professor Paul A. Gilje.

87 Gordon S. Wood, "The Democratization of Mind in the American Revolution," in *Leadership in the American Revolution* (Washington, D.C., 1974), and *The Radicalism of the American Revolution* (New York, 1992); Neil McKendrick, "Commercialization and the Economy," in Neil McKendrick, John Brewer, and J. H. Plumb, *The Birth of a Consumer Society: The Commercialization of Eighteenth-Century England* (Bloomington, Ind., 1982),

9–194; Richard L. Bushman, *The Refinement of America: Persons, Houses, Cities* (New York, 1992), part 2.

88 Watkinson, "Useful Knowledge?," 355.

89 Ibid., 352.

90 Richard D. Brown, *Knowledge Is Power,* chap. 8; Louise Chipley, "William Bentley, Journalist of the Early Republic," *Essex Institute Historical Collections* 123 (1987): 331–47.

91 Watkinson, "Useful Knowledge?," 359–62, 366, 370.

92 *Papers of Benjamin Franklin,* ed. Leonard W. Labaree et al. (New Haven, Conn., 1959–), 2:380–83. This proposal would soon lead to the formation of the American Philosophical Society.

93 Nathan O. Hatch, "Elias Smith and the Rise of Religious Journalism in the Early Republic," in *Printing and Society in Early America,* ed. William L. Joyce et al. (Worcester, Mass., 1983), 250–77, and *The Democratization of American Christianity* (New Haven, Conn., 1989), chaps. 2, 3, 5, 6.

94 David Paul Nord, "The Evangelical Origins of Mass Media in America, 1815–1835," *Journalism Monographs,* no. 88 (May 1984); R. Laurence Moore, "Religion, Secularization, and the Shaping of the Culture Industry in Antebellum America," *American Quarterly* 41 (June 1989): 216–42; Karl Eric Valois, "To Revolutionize the World: The American Tract Society and the Regeneration of the Republic, 1825–1877" (Ph.D. diss., University of Connecticut, 1994).

95 William J. Gilmore, *Reading Becomes a Necessity of Life: Material and Cultural Life in Rural New England, 1780–1835* (Knoxville, 1989); Richard D. Brown, *Knowledge Is Power,* 12–15, 290.

96 Richard D. Brown, "The Emergence of Urban Society in Rural Massachusetts, 1760–1820," *Journal of American History* 61 (1974): 29–51; Alexis de Tocqueville, *Democracy in America,* ed. Phillips Bradley, 2 vols. (New York, 1945). Bacon's general influence, and his impact on Thomas Jefferson and the idea of "useful knowledge," is discussed in Joseph F. Kett, "Education," in *Thomas Jefferson: A Reference Biography,* ed. Merrill D. Peterson (New York, 1986), 244.

97 Joseph F. Kett and Patricia A. McClung, "Book Culture in Post-Revolutionary Virginia," *Proceedings of the American Antiquarian Society* 94, part 1 (1984): 97–147.

98 American Bible Society, *Resolutions of the American Bible Society, and an Address to the Christian Public, on the subject of supplying the Whole World with the Sacred Scripture; within a Definite Period* (New York, 1833), 1, 5; Peter J. Wosh, *Spreading the Word: The Bible Business in Nineteenth-Century America* (Ithaca, N.Y., 1994).

99 Aaron Bancroft, *The Importance of Education, Illustrated in an Oration, Delivered before the Trustees, Preceptors, and Students of Leicester Academy, on the 4th of July, 1806* (Worcester, Mass., 1806), 11.

100 Zephaniah S. Moore, *Oration on the Anniversary of the Independence of the United States,* 24.

101 Ibid., 14, 16–17.

102 John Adams to John Taylor of Caroline, Va., [1814], *Works of John Adams,* 6:518, 519.

103 Ibid., 521.

104 Daniel Webster, in *American Oratory, or Selections from the Speeches of Eminent Americans,* compiled by a Member of the Philadelphia Bar (Philadelphia, 1836). See also Harlow Sheidley, "Sectional Nationalism: The Culture and Politics of the Massachusetts Conservative Elite, 1815–1836" (Ph.D. diss., University of Connecticut, 1990).

105 Webster, in *American Oratory,* 449.

106 Ibid., 447.

107 Ibid., 444–45.

108 Joseph Story, *A Discourse, Pronounced at Cambridge, before the Phi Beta Kappa Society . . . on the thirty-first day of August, 1826,* in ibid., 507–8.

109 The Reverend Samuel Stillman, Feb. 6, 1788, quoted in *Connecticut Courant* (Hartford), Mar. 31, 1788, 2; O[rsamus] C[ook] Merrill, *The Happiness of America: An Oration Delivered at Shaftesbury, Vermont* (Bennington, Vt., 1804), 13. The latter reference was provided by Professor Peter Onuf.

110 Story, *A Discourse, Pronounced at Cambridge,* in *American Oratory,* 509.

CHAPTER FIVE

1 Donald W. Rogers, ed., *Voting and the Spirit of American Democracy: Essays on the History of Voting and Voting Rights in America* (Urbana, Ill., 1992); Judith N. Shklar, *American Citizenship: The Quest for Inclusion* (Cambridge, Mass., 1991).

2 On the American Tract Society, see David Paul Nord, "The Evangelical Origins of Mass Media in America, 1815–1835," *Journalism Monographs,* no. 88 (May 1984), "Systematic Benevolence: Religious Publishing and the Marketplace in Early Nineteenth-Century America," in *Communications and Change in American Religious History,* ed. Leonard I. Sweet (Grand Rapids, Mich., 1994), and "Religious Reading and Readers in Antebellum America," paper presented at the meeting of the Society for Historians of the Early American Republic, Chapel Hill, N.C., July 1993; Lawrence Thompson, "The Printing and Publishing Activities of the American Tract Society from 1825 to 1850," *Papers of the Bibliographical Society of America* 35 (1941): 81–114; and Karl Eric Valois, "To Revolutionize the World: The American Tract Society and the Regeneration of the Republic, 1825–1877" (Ph.D. diss., University of Connecticut, 1994).

3 James D. Watkinson, "Useful Knowledge?: Concepts, Values, and Access in American Education, 1776–1840," *History of Education Quarterly* 30 (1990): 351–70.

4 American Society for the Diffusion of Useful Knowledge, *Prospectus of the American Library for Schools and Families* (New York, 1837), 27. The society was established on October 17, 1836, and incorporated on May 16, 1837.

5 Ibid., title page.

6 *The Pursuit of Knowledge Under Difficulties; Illustrated by Anecdotes,* vol. 8 of the Library of Entertaining Knowledge (Boston, 1831), title page; American Society for the Diffusion of Useful Knowledge, *Prospectus,* 22.

7 Thomas Dick, *On the Improvement of Society by the Diffusion of Knowledge: . . . The advantages which would result from a more general diffusion of rational and scientific information among all ranks* (Glasgow, 1833). This work was reprinted eighteen times in New York, Philadelphia, and Hartford between 1834 and 1854.

8 Ibid., v–x.

9 No. 93 (June 16, 1711), in *The Spectator,* ed. Donald F. Bond, 5 vols. (Oxford, 1965), 1:397.

10 *Pursuit of Knowledge,* 2.

11 William Watkins, *An Address Delivered Before the Moral Reform Society in Philadelphia, August 6, 1836* (Philadelphia, 1836), 13. Watkins was an African American. See Dorothy Porter, ed., *Early Negro Writing, 1760–1837* (Boston, 1971), 155–66.

12 *Pursuit of Knowledge,* 2.

13 Ibid.

14 Ibid., 2–3.

15 [Frederick A. Packard], *Thoughts on the Condition and Prospects of Popular Education in the United States* (Philadelphia, 1836), 2.

16 Daniel Walker Howe, *The Political Culture of the American Whigs* (Chicago, 1979), 21, 23–42, 150–80.

17 American Society for the Diffusion of Useful Knowledge, *Prospectus,* appendix, 12–13.

18 Watkins, *Address Delivered Before the Moral Reform Society,* 14.

19 American Society for the Diffusion of Useful Knowledge, *Prospectus,* 6 (actually p. 3).

20 Quoted in Rush Welter, *The Mind of America, 1820–1860* (New York, 1974), 284.

21 Noah Webster, *Elements of Useful Knowledge,* vol. 1 (Hartford, Conn., 1806), iii.

22 William Mavor, *Catechism of Universal History* (Boston, 1814), and *Catechism of General Knowledge* (Boston, 1815), title pages.

23 *Address, delivered by Charles W. Peale, to the Corporation and Citizens of Philadelphia, on the 18th day of July, in Academy Hall, Fourth Street* (Philadelphia, 1816), 9–11, 14.

24 Joel J. Orosz, *Curators and Culture: The Museum Movement in America, 1740–1870* (Tuscaloosa, Ala., 1990), 130, 132, 119, 175.

25 Ibid., 155, 157; David Madsen, *The National University: Enduring Dream of the USA* (Detroit, 1966), 58–63. Madsen explains that Congress accepted the Smithson bequest precisely because it promoted a broad diffusion of information instead of a centralized, elite national university.

26 Donald M. Scott, "Print and the Public Lecture System, 1840–1860," in *Printing and Society in Early America,* ed. William L. Joyce, David D. Hall, Richard D. Brown, and John B. Hench (Worcester, Mass., 1983), 278–99. See also Christopher Yong-Min Chi, "Diffusing Useful Knowledge in Worcester and Concord: The Early Lyceum Movement in Two Massachusetts Towns," honors thesis, Harvard University, 1993; Katherine M. Grant, "The Lyceum Movement in America, 1826–1860" (Ph.D. diss. in progress, Yale University).

27 Scott, "Print and the Public Lecture System." Mary Kupiec Cayton notes that these were the kinds of audiences Emerson particularly sought (*Emerson's Emergence: Self and Society in the Transformation of New England, 1800–1845* [Chapel Hill, N.C., 1989], 150–51).

28 Horace Mann, 1848 report, *Life and Works of Horace Mann,* ed. Mary Mann, vol. 3, *Annual Reports on Education* (Boston, 1868), 687.

29 [Samuel Kettell], "Proceedings of the Society for the Diffusion of Useless Knowledge," in Timothy Titterwell, *Yankee Notions: A Medley* (Boston, 1838), 183, 186.

30 "Popular Lectures," in *Pills for the People* (Boston, 1844), 34. Professor Ronald J. Zboray generously called my attention to this work.

31 Ibid., 28, 29, 32.

32 Ibid., 30–32.

33 "Popular Lectures," 32, 35, 36, 38, 39.

34 See Stuart M. Blumin, *The Emergence of the Middle Class: Social Experience in the American City, 1760–1900* (Cambridge, 1989); Gordon S. Wood, *The Radicalism of the American Revolution* (New York, 1992); and Ronald J. Zboray, *A Fictive People: American Economic Development and the American Reading Public* (New York, 1993).

35 Robert A. Gross, "Much Instruction from Little Reading: Books and Libraries in Thoreau's Concord," *Proceedings of the American Antiquarian Society* 97, part 1 (1987): 129–88; Jesse H. Shera, *Foundations of the Public Library: The Origins of the Public Library Movement in New England, 1629–1855* (Chicago, 1949).

36 David Kaser, *A Book for a Sixpence: The Circulating Library in America* (Pittsburgh, 1980), 44–45; Shera, *Foundations of the Public Library.*

37 Quoted in Mary [Peabody] Mann, *Life of Horace Mann,* 2d ed. (Boston, 1865), 13.

38 *Works of Horace Mann,* 3:44, 45.

39 American Society for the Diffusion of Useful Knowledge, *Prospectus,* 11.

40 Kaser, *A Book for a Sixpence,* 64–81, 92–102; Zboray, *A Fictive People,* 74.

41 John M. Bernhisel, broadside circular letter to "Authors, Editors and Publishers of the United States," Nov. 12, 1850, Broadside Collection, American Antiquarian Society, Worcester, Mass. As early as 1816, the constitution of the state of Indiana included provision for public county libraries.

42 *Works of Horace Mann,* 3:568–69, 562.

43 Quoted in Frederick Rudolph, ed., *Essays on Education in the Early Republic* (Cambridge, Mass., 1965), xv.

44 DeWitt Clinton, "Address," 1809, in *Joseph Lancaster and the Monitorial School Movement,* ed. Carl F. Kaestle (New York, 1973), 156–57.

45 *Address of the Committee for Promoting the Royal Lancasterian System for the Education of the Poor* (n.p., [1810]), 2, box 15, folder 10, Joseph Lancaster Papers, American Antiquarian Society, Worcester, Mass.

46 *Education on the Plan of Mr. Lancaster* (Nottingham, 1810), broadside, box 15, folder 10, ibid.

47 *Proposal for the Establishment of Schools in the City of Glasgow on the Plan of Mr. Joseph Lancaster* (Glasgow, 1810), broadside, box 15, folder 10, ibid. As late as 1826, Sir John Sinclair wrote that in Scotland even though popular moral and religious education was proper, literacy could be subversive because "the great mass of people may thus be infected with principles destructive to the church and state." Quoted in R. A. Houston, *Scottish Literacy and Scottish Identity: Illiteracy and Society in Scotland and Northern England, 1600–1800* (Cambridge, 1985), 231.

48 *Address of the Committee for Promoting the Royal Lancasterian System,* 1.

49 Clinton, "Address," in Kaestle, *Joseph Lancaster,* 157–59.

50 "Constitutional Provisions Respecting Education," *American Journal of Education* 17 (Sept. 1867): 81–124, supplies a compilation of constitutional provisions involving education in all of the states through 1866. It was produced under the supervision of U.S. Commissioner of Education Henry Barnard.

51 Ibid., 105.

52 Anonymous letter reported in *Common School Advocate* 1, no. 7 (July 1837); "Common Education Should be the Best Education," *Connecticut Common School Journal* 2, no. 10 (Mar. 1, 1840): 152.

53 John L. Cheney, Jr., ed., *North Carolina Government, 1585–1979: A Narrative and Statistical History* (Raleigh, N.C., 1981), 815.

54 Charles L. Coon, *The Beginnings of Public Education in North Carolina: A Documentary History, 1790–1840,* 2 vols. (Raleigh, N.C., 1908), 1:xxxix.

55 In ibid., 54.

56 Gov. David Stone, annual message, 1810, in ibid., 63.

57 Gov. Benjamin Smith, annual message, 1811, in ibid., 80.

58 Jeremiah Battle, "Education in Edgecombe County," [1812], *North Carolina University Magazine,* Apr. 1861, in ibid., 70.

59 A. D. Murphey et al., report on "Public Instruction," Dec. 19, 1816, in ibid., 108, 143–45.

60 Ibid., 171–72, 175.

61 Ibid., 188–89.

62 Charles L. Coon, *North Carolina Schools and Academies, 1790–1840: A Documentary History* (Raleigh, N.C., 1915), xl–xlv, xlvii–lii.

63 John M. Walker, report on education, Dec. 8, 1817, in Coon, *Beginnings of Public Education,* 1:151–52.

64 N.C. Senate Committee Report on Education, Dec. 1824, in ibid., 227–28.

65 Gov. Gabriel Holmes, message to the legislature, 1824, in ibid., 217; action of N.C. House of Commons, in ibid., 223.

66 Edgecombe County appeal for free schools, *Raleigh Register,* Dec. 3, 1824, in ibid., 244–45.

67 N.C. House of Commons, report on a system of general education, Nov. 23, 1825, and actions of the state pursuant thereto, in ibid., 268–82.

68 Robert Potter, regarding proposed "Political College of North Carolina," Jan. 22, 1827, in ibid., 313; "Upton," *Fayetteville Observer,* n.d., and *Raleigh Register,* Oct. 26, 1827, in ibid., 357–59.

69 N.C. House of Commons, Committee on Education, report on bill to abolish the literary fund, Dec. 31, 1827, in ibid., 377.

70 North Carolina Literary Board Report, Feb. 1, 1827, in ibid., 348–49.

71 Nathan O. Hatch, *The Democratization of American Christianity* (New Haven, Conn., 1989), 45–46, and *The Sacred Cause of Liberty: Republican Thought and the Millennium in Revolutionary New England* (New Haven, Conn., 1977), 146–56.

72 Letter in *Raleigh Register,* Nov. 9, 1829, in Coon, *Beginnings of Public Education,* 1:432.

73 Ibid., 432–33.

74 Quoted in [Thomas Cooper], "Agrarian and Education Systems," *Southern Review* (Charleston, S.C.) 6, no. 11 (Aug. 1830): 11.

75 Thomas Cooper, *Lectures on the Elements of Political Economy* (Columbia, S.C., 1826), 267–68.

76 [Cooper], "Agrarian and Education Systems," 16, 17.

77 On Georgia, see Keith Whitescarver, "Creating Citizens for the Republic: Education in Georgia, 1776–1810," *Journal of the Early Republic* 13 (Winter 1993): 455–79.

78 Articles in *Raleigh Register,* Jan. 14 and Apr. 6, 1839, in Coon, *Beginnings of Public Education,* 2:897–99.

79 Carl F. Kaestle, *Pillars of the Republic: Common Schools and American Society, 1780–1860* (New York, 1983), 210–11.

80 Henry B. Stanton, *Ultraists—Conservatives—Reformers: An Address delivered be-*

fore the Adelphic Union Society of Williams College, August 20, 1850 (New York, 1850), 33–34.

81 [Packard], *Thoughts on the Condition and Prospects of Popular Education,* 5, 6, 10, 14.

82 Ibid., 23, 24, 26–29.

83 Wise address, Mar. 9, 1844, in *Niles National Register, containing Political, Historical, Geographical, Scientifical, Statistical, Economical, and Biographical Documents, Essays and Facts: together with Notices of the Arts and Manufactures, Record of the Events of the Times* 26 (Mar.–Sept. 1844): 25–26.

84 Theodore Parker, "The Public Education of the People," address delivered to the Onandoga Teachers' Institute, Syracuse, N.Y., Oct. 4, 1849, in *Speeches, Addresses, and Occasional Sermons,* 3 vols. (New York, 1864), 2:139.

85 Horace Mann, 1847 report, *Works of Horace Mann,* 3:626–27.

86 Horace Mann, 1839 report, ibid., 6.

87 *Niles National Register,* 26 (Mar.–Sept. 1844): 25.

88 Horace Mann, 1848 report, *Works of Horace Mann,* 3:668.

89 *Niles National Register,* 26 (Mar.–Sept. 1844): 25.

90 Horace Mann, 1839 report, *Works of Horace Mann,* 3:10.

CHAPTER SIX

1 Chilton Williamson, *American Suffrage: From Property to Democracy, 1760–1860* (Princeton, N.J., 1960). Marc Kruman shows that although landowning requirements were dropped, twelve states preserved requirements for some form of property ownership or the payment of some form of taxes prior to 1860 ("The Second American Party System and the Transformation of Revolutionary Republicanism," *Journal of the Early Republic* 12 [Winter 1992]: 517–18).

2 *Noah Webster's First Edition of An American Dictionary of the English Language,* 2 vols. (New York, 1828; reprint, San Francisco, 1967), 1:38.

3 Quoted in Susan Strane, *A Whole-Souled Woman: Prudence Crandall and the Education of Black Women* (New York, 1990), 110.

4 Ibid.; *Webster's First Edition of An American Dictionary,* 1:38.

5 William Harper, *Anniversary Oration; Delivered . . . in the Representative Hall, on the 9th of December, 1835* (Washington, D.C., 1836), 9, 10.

6 Ibid., 11, 12. Harper claimed that classical Greek and Roman experience demonstrated that slavery fostered energy and character within the master class. Ibid., pp. 14–15.

7 William Goodell, *Our National Charters: For the Millions* (New York, 1857), 15n. According to the naturalization law of March 26, 1790, any "free white person" could qualify for citizenship. *Annals of the Congress of the United States: The*

Debates and Proceedings in the Congress of the United States; with an Appendix, containing Important State Papers and Public Documents, and all the Laws of a Public Nature; with a Copious Index, comp. Joseph Gales, 42 vols. (Washington, D.C., 1834–56), 2:2205–6.

8 Judith Apter Klinghoffer and Lois Elkis, "'The Petticoat Electors': Women's Suffrage in New Jersey, 1776–1807," *Journal of the Early Republic* 12 (Summer 1992): 159–93.

9 *Proceedings of the Woman's Rights Convention, held at the Broadway Tabernacle, in the City of New York, on Tuesday and Wednesday, Sept. 6th and 7th, 1853* (New York, 1853), 64; Judge [Thomas] Herttell, *Remarks comprising in substance Judge Herttell's Argument in the House of Assembly of the State of New-York, in the session of 1837, in support of the bill to restore to married women "The Right of Property," as guarantied by the constitution of this state* (New York, 1839), 52–53.

10 Dumas Malone, *The Public Life of Thomas Cooper, 1783–1839* (New Haven, Conn., 1926); [Thomas Cooper], "Agrarian and Education Systems," *Southern Review* (Charleston, S.C.) 6, no. 11 (Aug. 1830): 21, 29.

11 Thomas Cooper, *Lectures on the Elements of Political Economy* (Columbia, S.C., 1826), 267.

12 Ibid., 268.

13 George Fredrickson, quoted in Rogers M. Smith, "'One United People': Second-Class Female Citizenship and the American Quest for Community," *Yale Journal of Law and the Humanities* 1 (1989): 250–51.

14 *New England Artisan and Laboring Man's Repository* (Pawtucket, R.I.), Mar. 15, 1832, 2–3.

15 Ibid.

16 Ibid., 3.

17 *To the Citizens and Legislators of the United States of America* (n.p., Feb. 22, 1833), 3–4.

18 Edward Everett, "The Advantage of Useful Knowledge to Workingmen," introductory lecture in the Franklin lecture series, Boston, Nov. 14, 1831, in *Importance of Practical Education and Useful Knowledge* (New York, 1859), 160–61.

19 Edward Everett, "On the Importance of Scientific Knowledge, to Practical Men, and on the Encouragements to its Pursuit," first delivered to a mechanics' institute in 1827, in ibid., 99.

20 Proceedings of meeting of the New England Association of Farmers, Mechanics, and Other Workingmen, Boston, Feb. 16, 1832, in *New England Artisan and Laboring Men's Repository* (Pawtucket, R.I.), Feb. 23, 1832, 2.

21 *New England Artisan and Laboring Man's Repository* (Boston), Jan. 3, 1833, 1.

22 John B. Eldredge, address to the convention of the New England Association of Farmers, Mechanics, and Other Workingmen, Boston, Sept. 6, 1832, in *New England Artisan and Workingmen's Repository* (Providence, R.I.), Oct. 18, 1832, 2.

23 "Essays on Public Education," nos. 5 and 6, in *New England Artisan and Laboring Man's Repository* (Boston), May 30, 1833, 1. [William Heighton], *An Address to the Members of the Trade Societies, and to the Working Classes Generally: . . . By a Fellow-Labourer* (Philadelphia, 1827), argued that positive change could only be achieved by "THE DEVELOPEMENT OF INTELLECT AND THE DIFFUSION OF KNOWLEDGE" (42–43) (reference courtesy of Professor Bruce M. Laurie).

24 In *New England Artisan and Workingmen's Repository* (Providence, R.I.), Oct. 18, 1832, 2. Eldredge's arguments and rhetoric anticipate Seth Luther's *Address on the Origin and Progress of Avarice, and its deleterious effects on human happiness, with a proposed remedy for the countless evils resulting from an inordinate desire for wealth* (Boston, 1834).

25 *New England Artisan and Laboring Men's Repository* (Pawtucket, R.I.), Feb. 2, 1832, 2.

26 *New England Artisan and Laboring Man's Repository* (Boston), Apr. 4, 1833, 2. Certainly this had been William Heighton's message in Philadelphia a few years earlier.

27 "Education," *Workingmen's Press* (New Bedford, Mass.), reprinted in *New England Artisan and Workingmen's Repository* (Providence, R.I.), Sept. 6, 1832, 4.

28 Jacob Frieze, editorial, *New England Artisan and Laboring Men's Repository* (Pawtucket, R.I.), Mar. 22, 1832, 3.

29 For example, see Theodore Parker, "The Education of the Laboring Classes," address to American Institute for Instruction, Aug. 1841, reprinted in 1843, in *Social Classes in a Republic,* ed. Samuel A. Eliot (Boston, [1911]), 101.

30 *New England Artisan and Laboring Men's Repository* (Pawtucket, R.I.), Apr. 19, 1832, 2.

31 Letter, *New England Artisan and Laboring Man's Repository* (Boston), Dec. 20, 1832, 2.

32 Resolutions of New England Association of Farmers, Mechanics, and Other Workingmen, Boston, Sept. 7, 1832, *New England Artisan and Workingmen's Repository* (Providence, R.I.), Oct. 11, 1832, 3.

33 Ibid.

34 *New England Artisan and Laboring Man's Repository* (Boston), Nov. 8, 1832, 2.

35 Ibid., Apr. 4, 1833, 2.

36 Quoted in ibid., Nov. 15, 1832, 4.

37 George W. Light account, in ibid., Nov. 8, 1832, 2.

38 Ibid., Nov. 15, 1832, 4.

39 Luther, *Address on the Origin and Progress of Avarice,* 13; New England Association of Farmers, Mechanics, and Other Workingmen, *Proceedings of the Working-Men's Convention,* Oct. 2, 1833 (n.p., n.d.), 2. The same kind of views were expressed in *New England Artisan and Laboring Man's Repository* (Boston), Apr. 4, 1833, 2.

40 Luther, *Address on the Origin and Progress of Avarice,* 35.

41 Ibid., 35–36.

42 Parker, "Education of the Laboring Classes," 91.

43 Ibid., 94.

44 Williamson, *American Suffrage*, 257, 268; Marvin E. Gettleman, *The Dorr Rebellion: A Study in American Radicalism, 1833–1849* (New York, 1973), chaps. 6, 7; David Montgomery, *Citizen Worker: The Experience of Workers in the United States with Democracy and the Free Market during the Nineteenth Century* (Cambridge, 1993), chap. 1, esp. 14–25.

45 U.S. Constitution, art. 1, sec. 2, 8.

46 *Cherokee Phoenix* (New Echota), Apr. 17, 1828, 1.

47 Cherokee constitution, art. 6, no. 10, in ibid., Mar. 6, 1828, 1.

48 *American Society for Promoting the Civilization and General Improvement of the Indian Tribes in the United States, First Annual Report* (New Haven, Conn., 1824), 3, 4, 5, 10, 16.

49 William Jenks to Jedidiah Morse, Boston, Nov. 17, 1823, in ibid., 39.

50 *Cherokee Phoenix* (New Echota), July 23, 1828, 1.

51 Ibid., Feb. 18, 1829, 2.

52 Ibid., Feb. 8, 1834, 1.

53 Joseph Lancaster, *Letters on National Subjects, auxiliary to Universal Education, and Scientific Knowledge* (Washington, D.C., 1820), 39; *Cherokee Phoenix* (New Echota), Aug. 13, 1828, 3.

54 *Cherokee Phoenix* (New Echota), Jan. 7, 1829, 2.

55 Peter A. Jay expressed the view that as aliens, "Indian tribes" were "no more entitled to vote in our elections, than Englishmen, Frenchmen, or other foreigners." In William Yates, *Rights of Colored Men to Suffrage, Citizenship and Trial by Jury: being a book of facts, arguments and authorities, historical notices and sketches of debates—with notes* (Philadelphia, 1838), 21.

56 Ibid., 10.

57 Mr. Briggs, quoted in ibid., 32.

58 Ibid., 13, 14, 16.

59 Ibid., 17, 18.

60 Ibid., 20.

61 Ibid., 25–26.

62 Ibid., 12.

63 Ibid., 17.

64 Ibid., 34. See also Harry J. Carman, ed., *Jesse Buel, Agricultural Reformer* (New York, 1951).

65 Yates, *Rights of Colored Men to Suffrage*, 23.

66 Ibid., 29.

67 *Colored American* (New York), Apr. 1, 1837, 2.

68 Philip S. Foner and George E. Walker, eds., *Proceedings of the Black State Conventions, 1840–1865*, 2 vols. (Philadelphia, 1979), 1:130.

69 *Minutes and Proceedings of the First Annual Convention of the People of Colour, . . . in . . . Philadelphia, June 6–11, 1831* (Philadelphia, 1831), 4–5.

70 See Foner and Walker, introduction to *Proceedings of the Black State Conventions.*

71 *An Account of the New-Haven City Meeting and Resolution, with Recommendations of the College, and Strictures upon the Doings of New Haven* (n.p., 1831), 23. The author of this work may have been Simeon S. Jocelyn, a white clergyman who ministered to a local black congregation.

72 *Colored American* (New York), May 27, 1837, 4, July 8, 1837, 4, Mar. 29, 1838, 4, Sept. 16, 1837, 3, Dec. 2, 1837, 3, Sept. 2, 1837, 1, Feb. 3, 1838, 2, Oct. 14, 1837, 3, Aug. 12, 1837, 4, June 3, 1837, 4. The activities of African American voluntary associations were reported routinely in the *Colored American.*

73 *An Address to the Public on the subject of the African School, lately established under the care of the Synod of New-York and New-Jersey, By the Directors of the Institution* (New York, 1816), 3, 4, 6–8. Ironically, it was this synod that ordained the Reverend Samuel T. Cornish, who became a pioneer in African American journalism and a leader in the movement for equal rights.

74 *Report of the Proceeding of the Formation of the African Education Society, Washington, Dec. 28, 1829* (Washington, D.C., 1830), 12, 3.

75 Ibid., 3, 12.

76 Foner and Walker, *Proceedings of the Black State Conventions,* 1:190, 281, 2:65. After the Fugitive Slave Act of 1850 put free blacks at risk, their interest in emigration to Haiti and Canada increased.

77 Ibid., 1:190.

78 John Quincy Adams, quoted in Leonard L. Richards, *The Life and Times of Congressman John Quincy Adams* (New York, 1986), 130; U.S. Constitution, amend. 1.

79 Mitchell Snay, *Gospel of Disunion: Religion and Separatism in the Antebellum South* (Cambridge, 1993), chap. 3, esp. 88–96. See also Robert Manson Myers, ed., *The Children of Pride: A True Story of Georgia and the Civil War* (New Haven, Conn., 1972), 11–17. Charles Colcock Jones was the author of two major works aimed at slave instruction: *A Catechism of Scripture Doctrine and Practice, for Families and Sabbath Schools designed also for the oral instruction of Colored Persons* (Savannah, Ga., [1837]) and *The Religious Instruction of the Negroes in the United States* (Savannah, Ga., 1842).

80 Charles L. Coon, *The Beginnings of Public Education in North Carolina: A Documentary History, 1790–1840,* 2 vols. (Raleigh, N.C., 1908), 1:175, 287, 344, 479.

81 Ibid., 484.

82 Report from the Committee on Slaves, etc., in Senate, Dec. 24, 1831, in ibid., 505.

83 Janet Duitsman Cornelius, *When I Can Read My Title Clear: Literacy, Slavery, and Religion in the Antebellum South* (Columbia, S.C., 1991), 37, 54–55.

84 Quoted in ibid., 56.

85 Ibid., 56–63.

86 *Proceedings of the Meeting in Charleston, S.C., May 13–15, 1845, on the Religious Instruction of the Negroes* (Charleston, S.C., 1845), 9.

87 Ibid., 35–36, 49.

88 Ibid., 23–24.

89 Ibid., 35.

90 Ibid., 65.

91 Cornelius, *When I Can Read,* 9, estimates that slave literacy reached 10 percent of the slave population, although she does not define "literacy" precisely. Reading was probably much more widespread than writing.

92 Jan Lewis, "The Republican Wife: Virtue and Seduction in the Early Republic," *William and Mary Quarterly,* 3d ser., 44 (1987): 689–721; Linda K. Kerber, *Women of the Republic: Intellect and Ideology in Revolutionary America* (Chapel Hill, N.C., 1980), chap. 7.

93 Horace Mann, *A Few Thoughts on the Powers and Duties of Women: Two Lectures* (Syracuse, N.Y., 1853), 131, 125.

94 Ibid., 105–6, iv, 91.

95 Ibid., 51.

96 *Proceedings of the Woman's Rights Convention,* 6.

97 Douglass speech, May 24, 1886, *The Frederick Douglass Papers,* ed. John W. Blassingame and John R. McKivigan, ser. 1 (New Haven, Conn., 1979–), 5:255, 262.

98 *Proceedings of the Seventh National Woman's Rights Convention, held in New York City, at the Broadway Tabernacle, on Tuesday and Wednesday, Nov. 25th and 26th, 1856* (New York, 1856), 25.

99 *Address of Mrs. Elizabeth Cady Stanton, delivered at Seneca Falls & Rochester, N.Y., July 19th & August 2d, 1848* (New York, 1870), 10–11.

100 *Proceedings of the National Women's Rights Convention, held at Cleveland, Ohio, on . . . October 5th, 6th, and 7th, 1853* (Cleveland, 1854), 56.

101 "Immigration and Education," *Common School Journal* 14, no. 17 (Sept. 1852): 267. Ralph Waldo Emerson expressed similar views in "Woman," in *Miscellanies* (Boston, 1884), 353.

102 Susan B. Anthony anticipated that this might happen. See Ellen Carol DuBois, "Outgrowing the Compact of the Fathers: Equal Rights, Woman Suffrage, and the United States Constitution, 1820–1878," *Journal of American History* 74, no. 3 (Dec. 1987): 860.

103 Horace Bushnell, *Women's Suffrage; The Reform Against Nature* (New York, 1869; 2d ed., New York, 1870), 34, 35, 38, 42, 44, 70.

104 Quoted in Yates, *Rights of Colored Men to Suffrage,* 16.

105 "Present & Future of the Colored Race in America," May 15, 1863, *Frederick Douglass Papers,* ser. 1, 3:578–79.

106 Herttell, *Remarks comprising in substance Judge Herttell's Argument,* 9, 16, 20, 23.

107 *Speech of John Quincy Adams, of Massachusetts, Upon the Right of the People, Men and Women, to Petition; on the Freedom of Speech and of Debate . . . relating to the Annexation of Texas to this Union* (Washington, D.C., 1838), June 16–July 7, 1838, 76–77.

108 *Douglass' Monthly* (Rochester, N.Y.) 2 (July 1859): 112.

109 Ibid. 3 (Nov. 1860): 361.

110 Ibid. 4 (Nov. 1861): 557.

111 *Frederick Douglass Papers,* ser. 1, 3:550n.

112 Joan Hoff, *Law, Gender, and Injustice: A Legal History of U.S. Women* (New York, 1991), 149–50.

113 Quoted in Ellen Carol DuBois, *Feminism and Suffrage: The Emergence of an Independent Women's Movement in America, 1848–1869* (Ithaca, N.Y., 1978), 59. Much of the following discussion relies on DuBois's study.

114 Ibid., 67.

115 Ibid., 88, 96; Robert R. Dykstra, *Bright Radical Star: Black Freedom and White Supremacy on the Hawkeye Frontier* (Cambridge, Mass., 1993), 216–37.

116 Ibid., 96.

117 Ibid., 87–88.

118 Ibid., 110, 111, 124.

119 Ibid., 97, 98.

120 Frederick Douglass, quoting or paraphrasing Elizabeth Cady Stanton, in "We Welcome the Fifteenth Amendment," address delivered to American Equal Rights Association meeting, presided over by Stanton and Susan B. Anthony, New York City, May 27, 1869, *Frederick Douglass Papers,* ser. 1, 4:219.

121 U.S. Constitution, amend. 15.

122 DuBois, "Outgrowing the Compact of the Fathers," 860; Norma Basch, "Reconstructing Female Citizenship: Minor v. Happersett," in *The Constitution, Law, and American Life: Critical Aspects of the Nineteenth-Century Experience,* ed. Donald G. Nieman (Athens, Ga., 1992), 52–66.

123 Basch, "Reconstructing Female Citizenship," 57, notes that by 1870 women were already allowed to vote in the Wyoming and Utah territories, and DuBois, *Feminism and Suffrage,* 84, points out that beginning in 1859, women were allowed to vote in Kansas school district elections.

124 U.S. Constitution, amend. 19.

125 Kim Ezra Schienbaum, quoted in Judith N. Shklar, *American Citizenship: The Quest for Inclusion* (Cambridge, Mass., 1991), 26.

EPILOGUE

1 For example, see William Celis III, "Study Says Half in U.S. Can't Read or Handle Arithmetic," *New York Times,* Sept. 9, 1993, 1.

2 National Commission on Excellence in Education, *A Nation at Risk: The Imperative for Educational Reform,* report to the secretary of education (Washington, D.C., 1983).

3 Among the works that support these observations are R. C. Anderson et al., *Becoming a Nation of Readers: The Report of the Commission on Reading* (Washington, D.C., 1985); James Atlas, *Battle of the Books* (New York, 1990), and *The Book Wars* (Knoxville, 1990); Benjamin R. Barber, *An Aristocracy of Everyone: The Politics of Education and the Future of America* (New York, 1992); Paul Berman, *Debating P. C.: The Controversy over Political Correctness on College Campuses* (New York, 1992); Allan Bloom, *The Closing of the American Mind* (New York, 1987); J. S. Chall, C. Snow, et al., *Families and Literacy,* report to the National Institute of Education (Washington, D.C., 1982); *Changes in Political Knowledge and Attitudes, 1969–1976: Selected Results from the Second National Assessments of Citizenship and Social Studies* (Denver, 1978); Dinesh d'Souza, *Illiberal Education: The Politics of Race and Sex on Campus* (New York, 1991); Jean Bethke Elshtain, *Democracy on Trial* (New York, 1995); Paul Gagnon and the Bradley Commission on History in the Schools, eds., *Historical Literacy: The Case for History in American Education* (Boston, 1989); Darryl J. Gless and Barbara Herrnstein, eds., *The Politics of Liberal Education* (Durham, N.C., 1992); Gerald Graff, *Beyond the Culture Wars: How Teaching the Conflicts Can Revitalize American Education* (New York, 1992); E. D. Hirsch, Jr., *Cultural Literacy: What Every American Needs to Know* (Boston, 1987); Christopher Jencks et al., *Inequality: A Reassessment of the Effects of Family and Schooling in America* (New York, 1972); Michael B. Katz, *Reconstructing American Education* (Cambridge, Mass., 1987); David T. Kearns and Denis P. Doyle, *Winning the Brain Race: A Bold Plan to Make Our Schools Competitive* (San Francisco, 1988); Jonathan Kozol, *Illiterate America* (New York, 1985); National Center on Education and the Economy, *America's Choice: High Skills or Low Wages,* report of the Commission on the Skills of the American Workforce (Rochester, N.Y., 1990); National Education Goals Panel, *National Education Goals Report: Building a Nation of Learners* (Washington, D.C., 1993); Francis Oakley, *Community of Learning: The American College and the Liberal Arts Tradition* (New York, 1992); Diane Ravitch, *The Schools We Deserve: Reflections on the Educational Crises of Our Times* (New York, 1985); Diane Ravitch and Chester E. Finn, Jr., *What Do Our Seventeen-Year-Olds Know?: A Report of the First National Assessment of History and Literature* (New York, 1987); Arthur M. Schlesinger, Jr., *The Disuniting of America: Reflections on a Multicultural Society* (New York, 1992); Page Smith, *Killing the Spirit: Higher Education in America* (New York, 1990); Thomas Sowell, *Inside Education: The Decline, the Deception, and the Dogmas* (New York, 1993); and Joel Spring, *Educating the Worker-Citizen: The Social, Economic, and Political Foundations of Education* (New York, 1980).

4 Bob Herbert, "A Nation of Nitwits," *New York Times,* Mar. 1, 1995, A19.

5 Ravitch and Finn, *What Do Our Seventeen-Year-Olds Know?;* Hirsch, *Cultural Literacy.*

6 Barber, *An Aristocracy of Everyone;* Schlesinger, *Disuniting of America.* John Dewey's *Democracy and Education* (1916) was a seminal work whose influence is traced in Robert B. Westbrook, *John Dewey and American Democracy* (Ithaca, N.Y., 1991).

7 National Center on Education and the Economy, *America's Choice;* Kearns and Doyle, *Winning the Brain Race.*

8 [Frederick A. Packard], *Thoughts on the Condition and Prospects of Popular Education in the United States* (Philadelphia, 1836), 5, 10.

9 Kearns and Doyle, *Winning the Brain Race,* 4.

10 Ravitch and Finn, *What Do Our Seventeen-Year-Olds Know?,* 200, 252.

11 Jean Bethke Elshtain discusses the civic consequences of one form of multicultural education in *Democracy on Trial,* chap. 3, esp. 77–84.

12 A generation ago, Vance Packard called attention to these issues in widely read popular works. See Daniel Horowitz, *Vance Packard and American Social Criticism* (Chapel Hill, N.C., 1994).

13 Both Vance Packard and John Kenneth Galbraith (*The Affluent Society* [1958]) spoke of private opulence and public poverty. Horowitz, *Vance Packard,* 124, 128. Here Bernard de Mandeville's eighteenth-century observation that private vice promoted public virtue seems to be inverted.

14 In *The Waste Makers* (1960), Packard said that commercialization was "becoming so all pervasive that at times it seems to be getting into the air." Horowitz, *Vance Packard,* 126. Insofar as the commercial sector fills the airwaves with electronic signals, Packard's observation is literally true.

15 For example, see "Boom Vox," *New Yorker,* Feb. 22, 1993, 6–8. See also Daniel Yankelovich, *Coming to Public Judgment: Making Democracy Work in a Complex World* (Syracuse, N.Y., 1991).

16 Roger Sherman, quoted by James Madison, Philadelphia, May 31, 1787, in *The Records of the Federal Convention of 1787,* rev. ed., ed. Max Farrand, 4 vols. (New Haven, Conn., 1937), 1:48.

17 The journalist-as-citizen role model was suggested by Professor Kenneth Moynihan of Assumption College, Worcester, Massachusetts, at the American Antiquarian Society, 1992–93.

Index

Abbeville, S.C., 181

Academy of Natural Sciences (Philadelphia), 127

Adams, John, 45–48, 51, 52, 54–58, 61, 64–66, 75, 77–82, 89, 90, 105–8, 114, 199; on popular citizenship, 46, 47, 66, 216 (n. 84); "A Dissertation on the Canon and Feudal Law," 54–58; on education, 55, 56, 71, 72, 78, 80, 81, 85, 96, 100, 101, 113; on free speech, 56, 57, 86; on religious establishment, 68, 79, 82, 106; and Massachusetts constitution, 79

Adams, John Quincy, 72, 179, 189

Adams, Samuel, 62, 63, 67, 89, 90, 100

Adams, Reverend Zabdiel, 100

Addison, Joseph, 44–45

African Americans, xv, 41, 155–57, 159, 167, 170–83, 190, 198, 239 (n. 79); African American reformers, 154, 173–75; voting rights, 170–73, 188–90, 194; state conventions, 173, 174; African American women, 175; voluntary associations, 175. See also Citizenship; Education

African Education Society, 177, 178

African slaves, 50

Alabama, 182

Alexander, Governor Nathaniel, 142

Almanacs, 108, 109

American Bible Society, 112, 113, 117

American Colonization Society, 177

American Equal Rights Association, 190

American Philosophical Society, 93, 94, 117, 134

American Society for Promoting the Civilization and General Improvement of the Indian Tribes in the United States, 168

American Society for the Diffusion of Useful Knowledge, 121, 124–26

American Sunday School Union, 124

American Tract Society, 111, 121

Anglican Church. See Church of England

Anthony, Susan B., 191, 193

Anti-intellectualism, 77–78, 166

Aristotle, 2, 4

Arkansas, 139, 141

Arkwright, Richard, 121

Asians, 157, 198

Baltimore, 139

Baptists, 5, 17, 27, 82, 92. See also Dissenters; Religion

Barclay, Reverend Henry, 41

Barnum, Phineas T., 127

Bentley, Reverend William, 110

Berkeley, Governor William, 27

Bible, 6, 46; reading of, 3, 6, 104, 106, 112, 135, 149, 169, 180–82. See also Education; Religion

Bill of Rights (British), 16, 28

Bill of Rights, U.S., 87, 90. See also Constitution, U.S.: First Amendment

Blair, John, 182

Blasphemy, 13, 17

Blount, Charles, 13, 18

Bolingbroke, Henry St. John, Viscount, 45